My Mother's *Voice*

My Mother's Voice

◆

CHILDREN, LITERATURE,
AND THE HOLOCAUST

◆

Adrienne Kertzer

broadview press

NATIONAL LIBRARY OF CANADA CATALOGUING IN PUBLICATION DATA

Kertzer, Adrienne, 1949–
    My mother's voice : children, literature, and the Holocaust

Includes bibliographical references and index.
ISBN 1-55111-340-6

    1. Children's literature — History and criticism.
    2. Holocaust, Jewish (1939-1945), in literature.   I. Title.

PN1009.5.W35K47 2001   809'.93358   C2001-903237-4

Broadview Press, Ltd.

is an independent, international publishing house, incorporated in 1985.

North America	United Kingdom
Post Office Box 1243,	Thomas Lyster, Ltd.
Peterborough, Ontario,	Unit 9, Ormskirk Industrial Park
Canada K9J 7H5	Old Boundary Way, Burscough Rd.
Tel: (705) 743-8990	Ormskirk, Lancashire L39 2YW
Fax: (705) 743-8353	Tel: (01695) 575112
	Fax: (01695) 570120
3576 California Road,	books@tlyster.co.uk
Orchard Park, New York	
USA 14127	Australia
	St. Clair Press
customerservice@broadviewpress.com	P.O. Box 287, Rozelle, NSW 2039
www.broadviewpress.com	Tel: (612) 818-1942
	Fax: (612) 418-1923

Broadview Press gratefully acknowledges the financial support of the Book Publishing Industry Development Program, Ministry of Canadian Heritage, Government of Canada.

Cover design by Lisa Brawn. Typeset by Zack Taylor.

Printed in Canada

For my mother, Olga Haas.

Olga bude pucovať.

Contents

List of Illustrations

Plate 1: 220. Illustration copyright © 1967 by Anita Lobel, from *Potatoes, Potatoes* (New York: Harper and Row Publishers). Used by permission of the author/illustrator.

Plate 2: 222. Illustration copyright © 1994 by Anita Lobel, from *Away from Home* (New York: Greenwillow 1994). Used by permission of HarperCollins.

Plate 3: 241. Illustration copyright © 1993 by Karen Ritz, from *A Picture Book of Anne Frank* by David A. Adler. Used by permission of Holiday House, Inc.

Plate 4: 242. Illustration copyright © 1993 by Karen Ritz, from *A Picture Book of Anne Frank* by David A. Adler. Used by permission of Holiday House, Inc.

Plate 5: 243. Illustration copyright © 1993 by Karen Ritz, from *A Picture Book of Anne Frank* by David A. Adler. Used by permission of Holiday House, Inc.

Plate 6: 248. Illustration copyright © 1994 by Karen Ritz, from *Hilde and Eli: Children of the Holocaust* by David A. Adler. Used by permission of Holiday House, Inc.

Preface

In Art Spiegelman's *Maus: A Survivor's Tale, II: And Here My Troubles Began*, Art visits Pavel, his psychiatrist, who, like Art's parents, is a survivor of the camps. Art, who wears a mouse mask in this scene, and functions throughout the work as an ambiguous mask for Spiegelman, is upset.[1] The first volume of Spiegelman's Holocaust memoir in comic book form, *Maus: A Survivor's Tale, I: My Father Bleeds History*, is a success, but knowledge of history—"Between May 16, 1944, and May 24, 1944 over 100,000 Hungarian Jews were gassed in Auschwitz" (Spiegelman 41)—and of specific family history —his troubled relationship with his father, his mother's suicide—overwhelms him.[2] When Pavel observes that all the books written on the Holocaust have made no difference, that maybe "it's better not to have any more stories" (45), Art is reminded of Samuel Beckett's statement that silence might be the best response. But like Theodor Adorno's oft-quoted statement that to write poetry after Auschwitz is barbaric, Art's reference to Beckett generates more talk, as Spiegelman draws first a panel depicting silence and then a second panel in which Art points out that even injunctions to silence are a form of talk. But what really bothers Art is his inability "to imagine what [Auschwitz] felt like" (46). Pavel, wondering

11

how best to explain, leans over and screams "BOO!" (46). The terrified Art, already shrunk by his depression and his visit to his "shrink" (43) into a very tiny figure, bounces off the chair in terror. Pavel admits that even this does not quite express the experience of Auschwitz: "It felt a little like **that**" (46).

The subject of My Mother's Voice is Holocaust representation in children's books. Pavel's words signal the difficulty of communicating what it felt like; Art's reaction shows the danger of turning the Holocaust into just another horror story. Spiegelman is aware of this danger. Although he depicts both Pavel and Art as human figures wearing mouse masks, in the panel when Pavel shouts, the drawing's perspective obscures the fact that Art, too, is wearing a mask. What the viewer sees is a man in a mask terrifying a childlike figure. How do we tell children about the Holocaust without terrifying them, and what kind of knowledge do we convey when we are determined not to frighten? If to write poetry after Auschwitz is barbaric, what can we say about telling children stories about genocide? How do we respond to Geoffrey H. Hartman's call for an "impossible" sefer hashoah, which "allow[s] the limits of representation to be healing limits, yet [does] not allow them to conceal an event we are obligated to recall and interpret" (131)?

My mother, one of the few Hungarian Jews who survived Auschwitz, never told me what Auschwitz felt like. She told limited facts, but, determined not to frighten her three children, she told her story so that I grew up knowing what Auschwitz was, but only in a way that kept me safe. In writing this book, I have examined North American assumptions about the kind of Holocaust knowledge appropriate for children, not just in comparison to my mother's story, but also constantly attentive to the very different kinds of knowledge produced by works not intended for children. The process has made me sensitive to the multiple challenges of Holocaust representation and to the particular representational challenges of children's books. The knowledge I have gained extends far beyond what I have learned about the genre to an appreciation of my mother's ability to turn the Holocaust into a kind of children's story that did not terrify. At least, that is the way that I heard it.

This book began in 1996 when Marie Davis talked to me about a special issue of *Canadian Children's Literature* on Holocaust children's literature. In the essay that appears here as Chapter One, I contrast my memory of my mother's story with the coherent narratives found in children's books. Despite how little I know of her story, that knowledge affects how I read these books and how I have come to appreciate that their implied reader is constructed as "the one who needs to know." Because the child reader is presumed to be ignorant of the Holocaust and the pedagogical purpose is to produce some clear knowledge, children's books about the Holocaust have little interest in traumatized voices. By the end of the story, the child knows more, and what she knows, because it works within the representational limits of children's books, still allows her to hope. The linking of knowledge and hope is less evident in adult works where we are far more likely to accept a perspective such as that offered by the narrative voice in "Henryk's Sister": "They made me understand, destroyed my hope" (Fink 140). Ida Fink's work challenges the pedagogy of knowledge in children's books; the adolescent able and willing to read Fink is moving beyond the hopeful and coherent narratives of children's literature.

Part One: Maternal Voices examines how children represent the voices of mothers and grandmothers in Holocaust narratives and how aesthetic choices and pedagogical beliefs intersect to make the stories that we give children very different from the stories given to adults. In the fictionalized memoirs of Aranka Siegal, the Holocaust fairy tale of Jane Yolen, and the multiple versions of Isabella Leitner's memoirs, the conventions of children's literature define what can and cannot be said to young readers. Part Two: The Voices of Children examines the debate over Anne Frank's *Diary of a Young Girl* in terms of how adults imagine the voice of the Holocaust child and how that debate clarifies the public reaction to Binjamin Wilkomirski's *Fragments: Memories of a Wartime Childhood.* It then turns to a similar debate over Carol Matas's *Daniel's Story.* Part Three: The Child in the Picture focuses on visual depictions, asking how we look at children in film, illustrations, and photographs, and how the child's looking determines what we see and know. In Roberto Benigni's *Life Is Beautiful,* the child's voice functions very differently than the voice in Anita Lobel's *No Pretty Pictures: A Child of War.* The Holocaust rightly terrifies adults as well as children, and this often means that works intended for adults can be equally, if not more, protective of adult sensibilities than the works given to children. Lobel's picture books provide a different kind of knowledge, as do the photograph-inspired illustrations found in other such works. Part Four: History and Pedagogy studies the representational implications of two different subgenres of children's literature—historical fiction and contemporary young adult fiction—and examines how the latter often calls into question the confident narratives of the former.

Five of the chapters first appeared as articles and are reprinted with permission. Except for Chapter One, they have all been significantly revised and expanded. "My Mother's Voice: Telling Children About the Holocaust" appeared in *Children of the Shoah: Holocaust Literature and Education*, a special issue of *Canadian Children's Literature 95*, 25:3 (Fall 1999): 13-28. A version of Chapter Two appeared as "'Do You Know What *Auschwitz* Means?': Children's Literature and the Holocaust" in *The Lion and the Unicorn* 23 (1999): 238-56. A version of Chapter Three appeared as "'What happened?': The Holocaust Memoirs of Isabella Leitner" in *Transcending Boundaries: Writing for a Dual Audience of Children and Adults*, edited by Sandra L. Beckett (Garland Publishing, 1999), 167-82. A version of Chapter Six, "Like a Fable, Not a Pretty Picture: Holocaust Representation in Roberto Benigni and Anita Lobel" appeared in *Secret Spaces of Childhood*, a special issue of *Michigan Quarterly Review* 39:2 (Spring 2000): 279-300. A version of Chapter Seven, "Saving the Picture: Holocaust Photographs in Children's Books" appeared in *The Lion and the Unicorn* 24 (2000): 402-31.

My thinking on this subject has benefited from the opportunity to present conference papers at the Biennial Congresses of the International Research Society for Children's Literature, University of York, 1997, and University of Calgary, 1999; the International Society for the Study of European Ideas, Haifa University, 1998; The Twentieth-Century Literature Conference, University of Louisville, 1999; Border Subjects IV: Growing Up Postmodern, Illinois State University, 1999; Children's Literature Association Conference, Roanoke, Virginia, 2000; International Symposium on

Reading Pictures: Art, Narrative, and Childhood, Homerton College, Cambridge, 2000; and Fourth Biennial Conference on Modern Critical Approaches to Children's Literature, Middle Tennessee State University, 2001. I have also benefited from the financial support of the Faculty of Humanities and the Vice-President (Research), University of Calgary. I am grateful to the University of Manitoba for a T. Glendenning Hamilton Research Grant, which enabled me to work on the Carol Matas papers, and to Carol Matas for permission to quote from them. I thank Isabella Leitner for giving me permission to quote from *Fragments of Isabella: A Memoir of Auschwitz* © Isabella Leitner 1978; *Saving the Fragments: From Auschwitz to New York* © Isabella Leitner 1985; *Isabella: From Auschwitz to Freedom* © Isabella Leitner 1994; and *The Big Lie: A True Story* © Isabella Leitner 1992. I am also thankful for the assistance of Michael Moosberger, Archivist, University of Manitoba Archives and Special Collections; Jeffrey E. Carter, Records Management Officer and Institutional Records Archivist; and Chris Sims, Photo Research Coordinator, United States Holocaust Memorial Museum. Jon Kertzer read every chapter (but never quite cured me of my fondness for parenthetical statements). Joshua and Nicholas Kertzer remind me every day why the subject of this book matters. But the book that began in 1996 with an essay for *Canadian Children's Literature* really began with my mother's voice a long time ago.

NOTES

1. The ambiguity lies in the method of representation. Although the narrative encourages us to see the character, Art, as a figure for the author/illustrator, it also discourages this because Spiegelman draws Art

either as a human with a mouse head, or as a human wearing a mouse mask. The representational practice undercuts any transparent relationship between the author/illustrator and the character who has the same name.

2. No single label seems adequate to describe *Maus*. To call it a comic book ignores the way that it is also documentary, father-son story, animal fable, and more. See LaCapra (139-79) for his analysis of the work's complex representational practices. LaCapra quotes Spiegelman's letter to *The New York Times Book Review* after *Maus II* appeared on their fiction list: "I know that by delineating people with animal heads I've raised problems of taxonomy for you. Could you consider adding a special 'nonfiction/ mice' category to your list?" (145). The paper moved *Maus* to the nonfiction list.

PART ONE

◆

Maternal Voices

1

My Mother's Voice: Telling Children About the Holocaust

This is an essay about memory and voice, about how a child makes meaning out of the story her mother tells; this is a story about my mother's voice.[1] It is not her voice that tells the story, for my mother will not speak publicly. More than 50 years in Canada, a woman whose ability to speak more than one language may have helped save her life (this reason is as good as any other—I am looking for a reason—there is no reason), my mother remains embarrassed by her English. When I tell her that I wish to write this essay and need her permission, she agrees so long as I am careful to correct her grammar. She does not want to sound "stupid." I know objectively that I am old enough to make my own decisions, yet I also know that I will never be old enough to write this essay without her permission. I promise my mother that she will not sound stupid.

My need to write her words, to write as a daughter, sets up an internal dialogue as I address my various anxieties. The word, "Holocaust," is itself so intimidating.[2] Not a survivor myself, how dare I write about what I have not witnessed? Even though as a literary critic, a reader of texts, I recognize that the tendency to value "objective" eyewitness accounts of the Holocaust (Young, *Writing* 6) betrays a naïve faith that the eyewitness makes no choices in what she sees and what she is willing and able to put into language, this knowledge is an adult knowledge alien to my child self; the memories I want to explore are those of a child, myself but not myself, one who answers to a different name and listens in another language. The impossibility of restoring speech to that child. Even if I could empower that child to speak again, my scholarly work on the difficulty of hearing mothers' voices in children's literature makes me suspicious of daughters who tell/mask/revise their mothers' stories. Having written on the careful way we control maternal voices in children's literature, what do I think will happen if I tell my own mother's story?

If that question doesn't stop me, then should I consider whether I am too close to my subject? Helen Epstein, in *Children of the Holocaust: Conversations with Sons and Daughters of Survivors*, reports studies that suggest the survivor's pathology is passed on to her children. Perhaps my instinctive rejection of this idea only confirms its existence. My mother pathological? I can hear her voice in Slovak telling me exactly what she thinks of this idea. And yet Epstein also describes how survivors' children tend to idealize and protect their parents. While I do not recognize myself or my mother in many of the Epstein interviews, I know that this proves nothing. Then I consider how my relationship with my mother does not fit the classical Freudian story in which daughters inevitably move away from mothers (and even feminists have tended to write as daughters, not as mothers). Perhaps my resistance to the Freudian story about mothers and daughters is itself a product of my mother's voice and the story she told.

In the end, however, what outweighs my doubts is the recognition that my ambivalence is itself the good daughter's extension of my mother's own reluctance to speak and that, if I give in to this reluctance, I will not be able to put to rest a frustrating conversation I began years ago. When I first heard news reports about the antisemitic teachings of Jim Keegstra, I began to hold lengthy imaginary and absurd conversations with him—"What do you mean the Holocaust never happened? Let me tell you about my mother."[3] Aware of the dangers of a daughter's narrative, knowing that in the end the essay I write will be more my story than hers, I resist my mother's own incredulity that anyone is interested in her experience, and start to write what I remember. What I offer here is not so much the testimony of a Holocaust survivor, as it is the memory of a child who witnessed her survivor/ mother speak.

The eldest of three children, I was named Adrienne both after a friend of my mother and in recognition of her father murdered five years before in Auschwitz. In my case, the Jewish custom of naming children in honour of dead relatives had to be altered slightly. Had I been a boy, this still would have been the case, for her father's name was Adolf, a name for obvious reasons no longer available for Jewish children. The A was a gesture, a partial recognition of a life that had itself been abbreviated, a life whose story I would only very partially and indirectly know (even now I still think of him as my mother's father, not my grandfather). Adrienne in turn was supposedly a safe name in that it was not recognizably a Jewish name. In choosing it, my mother was following in the tradition of her own parents, Adolf and Josephine Fodor, who had given their three daughters names that were considered non-Jewish: Marta, Olga (my mother), and Magda. Names made no difference to Hitler, but the persistence of this naming strategy is inevitably part of the story I know. Indeed the name, Adrienne, was not a name I used until university; I was Ada, a name that fit better with the Slovak that was my first language. To my parents and siblings, I am still the person who answers to that name.

When I puzzle over my knowledge of her story, my inability to remember a time when I did not know that her father had been murdered, as opposed to my mother's insistence today that she did not want to tell me very much until I was around 12, I focus on this lost language. When I was three, my parents, realizing that I could not speak English, abruptly switched languages, and I lost the ability to speak Slovak. What I never lost was my passive understanding, and I wonder now how much of what I remember of my mother's story was being spoken around me, not to me, for, while my parents now spoke English to me, they continued to speak Slovak to each other. This story of a lost language in which I spied is admittedly my version, not hers; when my father agrees that this might have happened, my mother dismisses the idea.[4] Her memory is that she did not tell me, or anyone else, very much. No one was interested, she says. They didn't want to hear. Nobody believed the stories, so why talk? Why frighten children? Fear was part of the Nazi legacy, the sick jokes like herding my mother and other women into one of the gas chambers at Auschwitz-Birkenau, turning out the lights, and then (for some reason, there is no reason) not gassing them. To tell a story like that would have been too frightening.[5]

Her question about the motivation for frightening children resonates and remains with me, for much as I insist that I always knew, I cannot remember being scared. My first memory is of winter; my mother and I are walking on the stone and gravel driveway that circles our Southern Ontario farmhouse. Inside, my baby sister is sleeping. Although I can convince myself that I can still hear my mother's voice, I can no longer hear what she is saying. I know that I feel safe. This feeling astonishes me when I now read memoirs by survivors' children or catch myself crying as I read memoirs by survivors themselves. Why do I have no recollection of nightmares provoked by the Holocaust? The childhood nightmares I recall were nearly all provoked by visual images: the face of the Wicked Witch in *The Wizard of Oz*; the recurring nightmare about a nuclear bomb after I watched a TV drama whose title, *Alas Babylon*, I can still recall. Such nightmares may have been substitutes for the really horrific, but what is more apparent is that visual images frightened, my mother's voice protected.[6] In my child's memory, anything she said was tolerable, because the voice demonstrated her magic power; she was a survivor.

Was my feeling of safety the result of the way she as mother and survivor censored her story or my childish, cruel indifference to the deaths of others? Think about the distancing revealed when I write "my mother's father" rather than "grandfather." Had I in my child's necessary egotism decided that since my mother had survived Auschwitz, therefore I was safe? Had I absorbed her need to feel that emigration in 1947 and marriage to my father in 1948 meant that now she too was safe? If today, I read Holocaust fiction with great tension, in particular fiction that focuses on mothers and children, is this because I am now aware of what I refused to imagine when young? Am I afraid that I will find the details my mother's story omits? The more I remember, the more questions I have, and I think that these questions may reveal something about the strategies children themselves set up as a way of making and controlling meaning when they are told stories about the Holocaust. I have no doubt that children, and not just survivors' children, can handle stories about the Holocaust; my question is directed rather to the meaning children construct. What happens to Holocaust stories when children listen to them? It is not simply a matter of the choices survivors make as they tell their stories; their children too make choices in what they are able and willing to hear.

It is impossible for me to disentangle my mother's voice and my childhood interpretation of that voice. Clearly in a different narrative situation—for example, being videotaped and encouraged to speak in the psychoanalytic context Dori Laub outlines in "Bearing Witness or the Vicissitudes of Listening"—my mother would speak differently. Witnesses, Laub reminds us, are always "talking *to somebody*" (71). But my mother refuses to speak publicly, and I refuse, am unable, to psychoanalyze her narrative. Like many of the survivors' children interviewed by Epstein, my memories are in fragments that cluster around certain key stories. Convinced that I have repressed details, in late June 1996 I phone my mother repeatedly and do not so much interview her as review what I remember. I tell her that I am puzzled by that sense of safety, and think that she must have deliberately decided not to tell me about the really horrific events she witnessed. Horror is comparative, right? I cannot believe I am saying this; she lost her father and nearly all her relatives. I know this, and yet I have decided she censored her own voice? Yes, why else do I only recall her moments of defiance and resistance, moments when she talked back to the Kapos and got away with it, moments when she stole an extra few minutes from work?

ADRIENNE: What I mean is that you never talked to me about dead people.

OLGA: I never saw a dead person.

ADRIENNE: What? I don't believe this. You were in Auschwitz. How could you not see a dead person?

OLGA: I didn't look, just like I would never look the soldiers in the eye. We were in horrible barracks but the chimneys were elsewhere. The Polish girls in charge, the Kapos, would threaten us by saying, "See those chimneys. That's where you'll go." We didn't believe it. We didn't believe it even there.

In 1938, when Hitler annexed the Sudetenland and proceeded to dismember Czechoslovakia, Nové Zámky, the Slovak town where my mother lived, became part of Hungary. Overnight the family switched to speaking Hungarian, a language she already knew to a certain extent. The three daughters became Christian, but when continuing in school meant having to go to confession, my mother refused. Crying that she could not go, she rebelled, and her father let her stay home. Her two sisters finished that year at school, but my mother was 16 and never returned to *gymnasium*.

ADRIENNE: What did you do to become Christian?

OLGA: We became Catholic. We had to go to a priest and say the Lord's Prayer in Latin [here she starts to recite *Pater Noster*].

ADRIENNE: If you could go through that ceremony, why
   did saying confession bother you? You weren't religious.
OLGA: I know, but I was Jewish inside. It was a feeling that
   I had. I just couldn't do it.

Trying to find some work still permissible under anti-
Jewish legislation, she eventually became an apprentice seam-
stress, and it was from the other seamstresses that she first
heard Yiddish. In her family, Yiddish was regarded as a language that modern people did not need. The daughters
already knew many other languages; in addition to the Slovak
and Hungarian they spoke at home, at school they had
studied Latin, French, and German. During the war, there
were private English lessons: "The woman who gave us the
lessons, she died too."

The fact that her Jewish father had become a lawyer, a
civil servant employed by the state, was a sign of the liberal
possibilities that existed in Czechoslovakia between the wars.
In my memory, my mother recalls walks with her father when
he drilled her on the Latin she had trouble with; she swam,
exercised, and spent time in the sun. The emphasis on physical strength and exposure to the sun is important, for part of
my mother's narrative is surviving the endless Auschwitz
zählappell (roll calls) through her ability to tolerate the sun
(she is looking for a reason; I am looking for a reason; there
is no reason): "Other people passed out from the sun. They
were covered with sores."

In mid-May 1944, my mother, her sisters Marta and
Magda, and her parents were ordered to move first to a ghetto and then two weeks later to a brick factory. What appeared
to be the luck of sitting out the war in the relative safety of

Hungary was rapidly falling apart. Even as signs were apparent that Germany was losing the war, the "final solution" was imposed on Hungarian Jews with a rapidity and efficiency only years of experience can give. The Russian army was approaching from the East, and in the ghetto, listening to an illegal radio, her father heard about the Allied invasion on D-Day. My mother never tells me that in May and June 1944, 437,000 Hungarian Jews were deported to Auschwitz where the vast majority were murdered immediately (Hilberg, *The Destruction* 547).[7] Why frighten a child, and who, child or adult, can imagine the deaths of so many? Instead she tells me that when any of the family complained about conditions in the ghetto (where they slept in one room) or the brick factory (where they slept outside), her father would say, "I wouldn't mind staying here until the end of the war." On June 14, 1944, her twenty-second birthday, the family was sent to Auschwitz.

One of the many gaps in my memory of her story is what she did between the first Auschwitz selection and the one two months later. Knowing that Elie Wiesel and other Jews deported in 1944 talk in their memoirs about the contemptuous reception they received from the few Auschwitz inmates who had managed to survive years of imprisonment, I ask her now whether this accords with her memory:

OLGA: The Polish girls, the Kapos, they were so mean, especially to old people [Is she thinking of my grandmother, who at 46 was regarded as old and had lied about her age during the first selection?]. The Polish girls had survived for three years; their parents were dead. They were angry and they blamed us: "While you were dancing, we were here."

ADRIENNE: What did you say to them?

OLGA: Nothing. What could we say? When they learned we could speak Slovak and so could understand them, they weren't so mean. And we were young so that made a difference. Sometimes when they wanted everyone to be quiet in the barracks, they would ask Marta to sing. She could sing opera so beautifully. But she said she was too hungry, so they gave her food, and then she sang.

In my mother's story, the arrival at Auschwitz is the worst moment, for that is when she last saw her father:

OLGA: We arrived at the station around 4 a.m. There was screaming, rushing, the SS with their rifles and their dogs, the *Arbeit Macht Frei* sign. I saw hanging people.

ADRIENNE: What do you mean? You just told me ten minutes ago that you never saw a dead person at Auschwitz.

OLGA: Oh, I must have forgotten. [She pauses.] Yes, there were dead bodies, hanging people. The bodies were there to scare us.

Has she forgotten to mention this because a mother does not scare a child, even a child now older than the grandmother who lied about her age? Has she forgotten because forgetting was her way to survive? "I didn't look." Or has she forgotten the dead bodies because the real trauma was what happened next?

ADRIENNE: So this was where you were separated from your father?

OLGA: Yes, the men and women were separated. He kissed us all, and looked at us with such sadness. He knew what was going to happen. He had always said he did not want to grow old. He got his wish. He turned to Magda [my mother's younger sister] and said, "Watch over them." He knew she was the most capable. He was right.

In my mother's story, her father survived the initial selection, working first at Auschwitz and then in Dachau, but he lost the will to live when a neighbour from Nové Zámky told him that his wife and daughters had been taken away from Auschwitz. Concluding that they were dead, not knowing that they were now working in a factory in the Sudetenland, he no longer cared to live. After the war, a man who had been with him at this time told the family that in full knowledge of what would happen if he said he was sick and was sent back to Auschwitz, he chose to do this. He was gassed October 25, 1944. My mother even now insists that there was a day that October when she could not stop crying. She is convinced that it was around October 28, a Czech national holiday that the family used to celebrate. When she spoke to her mother later (it was one of the many days my grandmother was in the infirmary), she learned that my grandmother too had cried all day.[8]

ADRIENNE: Did you not think about him the rest of the time? I know you say you only cried that one time.

OLGA: I was always hopeful. I was always an optimist. After the war, I would look out the window waiting for him to return. People did not all come back at once. When I realized that he was not coming back, that is when I got upset because I was so disappointed. That one day I remember crying in the *Lager*, it was a nice day. That made it somehow worse. I was thinking that he was all alone. Not too many were together, three daughters and a mother.[9] It still scares me even now when I get feelings about what will happen to people. I remember crying once on the farm when it was his birthday.

ADRIENNE: I remember seeing you cry one other time; it was in the summer.

I do not tell her that as a child I also fantasized that my grandfather would suddenly show up, that I too recall obsessively looking out windows. I do not mention that my father jokes that my mother is a *bosorka* (a witch) because she always knows who is about to phone her.

Lawrence L. Langer would call my mother's memory of her father's death a perfect example of "retrospective sentiment" (*Versions of Survival* 56), of the way memory constructs an order, shape, and meaning to an experience whose first achievement was the disruption of the prisoner's ability to make meaning. How can she remember what she thought on a certain day when she admits that the arrival at Auschwitz shocked her? The process of selection, followed by the stripping and shaving, the putting on of clothes that had been disinfected but that she still recalls as stained with the blood of former prisoners, seems intended to humiliate and disorder memory and identity. She tells me: "They shaved us all over." How can that statement exist beside the narrative of her father's choice?

Langer further reminds us in *Versions of Survival: the Holocaust and the Human Spirit* that Auschwitz meant "the death of choice" (67); that the will to live "made no difference to [the] murderers" (55); that all Jews were intended for extermination; that had the Nazis won, no Jews would have survived; that the language of moral choice, of cause and effect, is inappropriate when writing about Auschwitz. Langer insists that "The literature of the Holocaust is not a literature of hope" (157). Nevertheless, these are the words of my mother's story. If they are not accurate to what she thought in 1944 (how can we ever reconstruct what we actually thought at a certain time?), they are the words that she needed to help her survive afterwards. If the positive attitude she dwells on did not help her survive then, it remains a main component of the story I remember. When my grandmother in Auschwitz would say, "We'll never get out of here," my mother tells me that she would try to get out of the filthy barracks and look at the sky: "I'd think how nice the sky was. It was the same sky everybody saw. The Nazis could not take that sky away."

Because Langer argues in *Versions of Survival* that the inhumanity of Auschwitz requires a new vocabulary, a "vocabulary of annihilation" (68), he is quick to point out how the language of tragic heroism consoles and deceives (92). In the same mode, he contemptuously dismisses Victor Frankl's account of the way he responded to the beauty of the Salzburg mountains during a forced march as "maudlin rhetoric" (236). Langer speaks of the difficulty of "learning to live with a double vision and to speak with two voices—the voice of Auschwitz and the voice of civilization" (28). The story my mother tells me, like children's literature in general about the Holocaust, clearly chooses the voice of civilization, yet the more I as adult talk to my mother, the more I suspect that it was my role as child witness that ensured that the story I heard was the simple, hopeful version. The minimal details of her account, her memory that she did not tell me very much, surely reveals that there are parts of her story that I will never know. One possible reason that she did not like to dwell on her experience is that non-survivors wanted to hear a different, more heroic story:

> I remember people talking in Canada that X had saved so many Jews, that X was a hero. What kind of hero? If he got one person off the trains, that meant another had to be sent. When people talked like that, I didn't say anything.

In place of Langer's double vision, I substitute the decision that guided my mother's narrative. Why scare children? The hope that figures so largely in her story may indicate a naïve faith in 1944 that hope would protect her, but it may also reflect a later narrative decision that fear would not damage her children. At the heart of her story is an ambiguity that we never talk about: the hope that kept her going, the hope that her father would return, was not fulfilled; the Nazi decision to send the four women away from Auschwitz she herself constructs as contributing to her father's despair. This is not to say that there is any ambiguity about who is guilty of her father's murder; theories about survivor guilt do not apply to her.

So in the way I remember my mother's story, my grandfather remains forever a tragic noble figure and my aunt Magda is still the fairy-tale heroine, the youngest child, who ensures that the sisters and mother survive. She is the one who, assigned to the kitchens, steals food for my grandmother. She is the one who, when they are liberated, is so good-looking (how can anyone be good-looking who has been in Auschwitz?) that she is offered first a motorcycle by Russian soldiers and then a ride on a truck by partisans (as in a comic fairy tale, she accepts the latter, but only on condition that the partisans also take her mother and two sisters; then she mentions that there are 20 other prisoners to whom they have to give rides also). She is the one who, in August 1944 during a selection organized by Mengele, sneaks along with her sister, Marta, from one line to another, so that the three sisters and their mother can remain together.

It is essential to the story I remember that Magda and Marta do this, for it gives my mother another reason for explaining her survival. That moment during the selection when her sisters changed lines is a moment she incessantly returns to. She can no longer recall how many times she saw Mengele, and, because she did not know at the time which line was the best line, she is no longer even certain whether she went to the left or the right. In any case, in her story there are three lines: she now knows the line she and her mother were placed in was for work; she thinks the line Magda and Marta were initially sent to was for harder work; the other she concludes must have been the line for those who were to be killed. She mentions, but does not dwell on the trauma, of walking naked, hands up, in front of Mengele, each of the daughters in turn asking to remain with their mother. She adds that, during the selection, Mengele was himself struck by Magda's strong appearance and said, "*Das schon ja.*"[10]

Spooked by this statement, even though I have heard this story before, I write down her words and ask more questions:

ADRIENNE: How exactly did Magda and Marta sneak over?
OLGA: Remember that we could speak Slovak and this helped us with the Polish Kapos. Slovak was close enough to Polish that the Kapos could talk to us and order us. They gave us jobs distributing food. Magda and Marta pretended to be cleaning dishes and changed lines. When Magda looked to see if she had been observed, the SS girl slapped her for looking around.

It was following this selection that my mother was marched to Birkenau, shut up in the room, and not gassed. Was the room a shower, was it a gas chamber? The intentional deception of Nazi language confuses me here. This fact makes as much sense as the fact that the four women were now transported to the Sudetenland to work in a factory in Trutnov. Unable to recall any longer what exactly she did in the factory other than the speed with which she did it, she still remembers that they gave her cabbage and potato for the first meal. There was always the threat that if the women disobeyed or got sick, they would be sent back to Auschwitz, so when my grandmother was sick and in the infirmary, the French prisoner doctor would substitute for hers the names of the three daughters. Through such tricks and with hope—for liberation and that the Trutnov train station be bombed since they slept in another town and had to take the train twice a day (she recalls waving at airplanes)—the women worked in Trutnov for nine months. Eating everything in order to survive (here too she praises

Magda as a leader), imagining the meals they would have when they were free, they woke up one day and the Nazis were gone. It was May 9, 1945.

In my memory, as in her telling, my mother's story of liberation exists as a series of fragments, a world of delirium and an obsession with food. Slowly sneaking out of the barracks, they see defeated German soldiers retreating, soldiers who refuse to share their chicken; then the Russian soldiers arrive, open a local warehouse, and encourage the survivors to eat and rob. Getting sick from overeating. At night, their first night sleeping outside the *Lager*, they hear drunken Russian soldiers banging on the doors; my grandmother, fearing the rape of her daughters, lies on top of one daughter to hide her; another older woman lies on top of another. My mother, left on her own, feeling sick from eating raw eggs, no longer certain whether she is pretending or is really going to vomit, mutters to the Russian soldier looming over her, "*zle, zle*" (I feel sick, sick). The soldier disappears.

If this episode, like much of my mother's story, were in a children's book, I would dismiss it as incredible, unrealistic, too full of contrived lucky escapes—clearly, a book trying too hard to be a children's version of the Holocaust. What differentiates it from a children's book, however, are the gaps, the narrative disorder, the refusal of an overriding explanatory myth or possible moral vision. Unlike the protagonist in Carol Matas's *Daniel's Story*, for example, my mother does not review her past in any coherent way. She sticks mainly to details, creating what Shoshana Felman sees as the different power of description versus explanation ("The Return of the Voice" 218). Her focus on concrete detail "resists [...] any

possible canonization of the experience of the Holocaust"
("The Return of the Voice" 219).

However, if we treat my mother's story as a children's
book, our narrative expectations for children's literature and
the problem of meaning that results become apparent.
Immediately we ask, What does this story prove? What lesson does it teach about the Holocaust? Here is where I hesitate and admit my impatience with the simplistic Holocaust
lessons that often appear in children's books. The very fact
that we want to tell children stories about the Holocaust suggests that we think there is a lesson to be taught. But what is
the lesson we think that they will learn? I have no doubt,
based on my own experience, which was reinforced when I
watched my eight-year-old son interview his grandmother in
1992, that we can indeed tell children stories about the
Holocaust, but I remain ambivalent about the result. My
memories caution me that children's need to protect themselves, a need reinforced by the adult storyteller's desire not to
recreate in the child listener the fear that the Nazis created in
her, may mean that the only way children can and will hear
these stories is through strategies that inevitably diminish,
distance, and distort. The very need to put a shape, to find a
lesson in my mother's survival (I am looking for a reason;
there is no reason) distracts me from its random and absurd
aspects. The frightening lesson, that there is no logical explanation for her survival, is something that challenges the
narrative expectations of most children's fiction.

Yet if children need to hear stories that emphasize hope
and luck—and I am not sure if this is natural or the way children are constructed by our adult desire to protect them—
are adults any different? And if no language is appropriate to

"the experience of annihilation" (Langer, *Versions of Survival* 10), then is children's literature any different from any literature that writes about these events? For if all language is inadequate, as many Holocaust writers say, then ultimately all literature about the Holocaust may be a form of children's literature, trying to describe events with a very limited vocabulary.

Sometimes I think that it is enough that we tell these stories so that they will not be forgotten. When stories are the only way we can know the past, when survivors are now elderly and our ability to hear their voices diminishes even as their memories grow uncertain, when the alternative is Holocaust denial, why am I quibbling over children finding hopeful lessons? I know that Keegstra will not be interested in my mother's story, even as I know that telling it will make no difference to the genocide that I read about every day in the newspaper. I write her story because if the Holocaust was designed to be *"an event without a witness"* (Felman, "The Return of the Voice" 211), I challenge that definition by listening, by becoming witness to her story.

Elie Wiesel is justified in saying that "if the choice is between a trivialization of the event and nothing, I prefer nothing" ("Interview" 158), for his are the unbearable memories of "processions of children walking, walking" (166). But my memories are of my mother's voice as we walk in a circle, and this makes all the difference. Perhaps that is why, during a Christmas vacation in 1992, I hear myself say to my son, "Why don't you interview your grandmother?" No longer the child who listens, I become witness to the way my mother tells another child a story about the Holocaust. Despite the differences in our written versions—my son's greater optimism about the lesson to be learned, his omission of any reference to my grandfather's death, differences that only confirm the extent to which he as child controls the meaning of her story—in our endings we agree. The three of us know that a children's story, even this kind of story, demands a happy ending. Like Claude Lanzmann, I do not have the right to give this story a happy ending (Felman, "The Return of the Voice" 241); my mother is the only one who can speak it. So once again, for a moment, I am safe, protected by her voice as she tells me/him a story. It is dawn on a sunny day in mid-May 1945. My mother is riding in an open wagon, listening to French and Italian prisoners of war singing, "O Solo Mio": "That was when I felt free. It was beautiful. I can never forget it."

"Six Years of Terror," by Joshua Kertzer

As I sat with my grandmother in her house, I said, "Olga. Tell me what it was like to be in World War II." I took out my notebook and pencil and my grandmother started her story.

OLGA'S STORY

All the Jews had to go to a certain ghetto of their town. They were required to bring their belongings with them, and so they carried what they could on their backs. From here they were taken somewhere else where they worked in a brick factory. They were required to work in the brick factory during the day. At night time they slept on the ground by a railroad. This continued for two weeks.

On June 14, everyone was squished into a cattle train. There were two buckets. One bucket was for drinking, and one bucket was for the toilet. No one could ever use these two buckets, though, because there were just too many people crowded into the cattle car. People were squashed in—there was no room to even sit down. We travelled for three days and three nights like this.

On the fourth morning our train arrived at Auschwitz. The doors opened and we saw daylight for the first time in three days. There were huge dogs—German Shepherds—standing guard, ready to attack, beside the German soldiers who greeted us. The soldiers were carrying whips and shouting at us. "Wiet! Wiet! Schnell! Jetz!" (Out! Out! Quick! Now!)

The soldiers separated the men from the women. They asked us our age. If you were between 20 and 45 years old and you were strong, you went to the left to work. If you were a mother or father and were carrying a child, you were sent to a gas chamber where you and your child would be killed. Old people were killed as were young children. What the Germans had left were people who could work. I was one of the people who was strong and would work.

We were gathered together and more German soldiers arrived. They ordered us to take all our clothes off while they watched with their whips in their hands and their dogs at their sides. Next they shaved all our hair from our heads until we were bald. Some more German soldiers then came and gave us lice-bitten, infested clothes. We knew that these clothes had been on our people who had been held captive by these same German soldiers and who were now dead. We were then put into a big barrack. We had to sleep on the floor, but we never got much sleep because we didn't have enough room to stretch our feet out. At 4:30 a.m. each morning, we were rudely awakened and it was another day of hard work.

Auschwitz was very cold. Each morning the Germans made us stand in a line of five people so they could count us. It took hours. They deliberately counted very slowly just to see if we could endure all the waiting. When this was finished we went to work for the day. At times the sun got so hot at Auschwitz that some people got terrible sores. When the German soldiers discovered that the people had sores, they sent the people with the sores to the gas chamber to be killed.

*Six weeks after we arrived at Auschwitz the German soldiers started selecting people for transport. We didn't know where we were going. The selecting was done by Dr. Mengele. We didn't know at that time, but the people who were selected by Dr. Mengele, to be used by him, were used for experimental purposes. The other people were divided into other groups. You could be sent to do hard work, not so hard work, and the gas chambers. The way we were selected was very awful. Each of us had to remove all our clothes and walk completely naked in a line watched by Dr. Mengele. We were selected for a group depending upon how we walked. After this ordeal everyone was ordered into a room which said, "*GAS*" on it. People were so afraid. People started screaming, they were so afraid. It was all a stupid trick, though. The Germans had tried to kill us by shock. After this we had to dress. Our clothes were different from those we had before. We were transported to Sudetenland to a work camp called Trutnov.*

At Trutnov we slept on bunk beds. We got up at 5:00 a.m. and worked in a factory all day. All we ate was stale bread with some horrible soup called Eintopf. *The Germans never fed the older people properly, so once I went and stole bread for a week so I could feed my mother. It was fairly dangerous to do this, but my mother was starving. We worked at Trutnov for a year.*

On May 9, 1945 there was no wake-up call by the Germans. We slept in late. Then someone said, "The Germans are all gone." We didn't know why. The next day the Russians came and freed all of us. They gave my sister a motorcycle, but she didn't know how to ride it so she left it behind. We travelled home on an open wagon. We couldn't believe it, "We were going home!" We were going home with the prisoners of the war who were singing an Italian song "O Solo Mio." The sun was rising and we were free. We had lived and survived Auschwitz and Trutnov and Dr. Mengele.

This is my grandmother's story. This is a story I want to—no, I need to—remember. Six million Jews were killed in six years during World War II. This was done because one person did not like, or understand Jewish people. It is a story that should never be repeated. No people should ever be subject to such hatred, persecution, and death. It is a story that all people must remember so that this never happens again. It is now my responsibility to keep my grandmother's story alive. But now that you have heard this story, it becomes your responsibility, too. Keep it well and tell it well.[11]

NOTES

1. I thank my mother, Olga Haas, for telling me her story. I thank my son, Joshua Kertzer, for teaching me how to write it down.

2. When I first wrote this chapter as an essay for *Canadian Children's Literature*, my timidity about writing on the subject of Nazi genocide did not make me hesitate about referring to "the Holocaust" as the label for that genocide. Part of the coming to knowledge produced by the writing of this book has been a greater awareness of the problems of using the term, Holocaust. In this book, I continue to refer to the Holocaust since other terms seem equally unsatisfactory and since Holocaust is the term most often used in North America, evidence for which lies in my naïve use of it in 1996, ignorant that three years before, 1993 had been dubbed The Year of the Holocaust, or that in writing the essay I was participating in what many call the Americanization of the Holocaust. In the story

that my mother told in my childhood, I have no recollection of any reference to "the Holocaust," but neither was there any reference to Shoah, Churban, or Judeocide, only a narrative about what the Nazis, or often simply what "the Germans" and "the war" did to her family. The diaries that I kept as a child confirm this memory. In the story my son wrote, based on his interview of his grandmother, the word "Nazi" does not appear; the perpetrators are always called "the Germans."

3. Jim Keegstra, a Canadian teacher, was found guilty in 1985 of teaching high school history students in Eckville, Alberta, Holocaust denial and hatred of Jews. See Bialystok (236-39).

4. My father, George Haas, immigrated to Canada from Czechoslovakia one month before World War II began. His story is also one of ironic luck, the bad luck of injuring his thumb in a train door so that he could not take engineering exams and become the engineer he wanted to be. Going to agricultural college and gaining experience as a farm manager instead likely saved his life and that of the eight Jews who came to Canada with him. Frederick Charles Blair, director of the Canadian Immigration Branch at the time, did not believe that Jews could be farmers and permitted the national railways to select only 50 Jewish farm families a year (Abella and Troper 16); my father and the group that accompanied him were accepted under this plan. As a child I knew nothing of Canada's restrictive immigration policies in the 1930s; the story of my father's thumb was simply a taken-for-granted good-luck story. I never dwelled on the "luck" of those who could not emigrate or that the actual date my father entered Canada—July 28, 1939—was so close to the beginning of the war.

5. Yet this appalling story appears in the essay my son, Joshua Kertzer, wrote about his grandmother, an essay based on his interview with her. I include the essay (see p. 40-43), not as an accurate record of my mother's experiences, but as another form of evidence to indicate both how children make sense of Holocaust stories and how my mother spoke once about this event to a specific child. In the face of my mother's uncertainty about what she was willing to say to her daughter in the 1950s is a child's written response to what she was willing to say to him 40 years later. The interview took place in December 1992; the essay was subsequently written as a school assignment at University Elementary School, Calgary, Alberta, in spring, 1993. One of Joshua's teachers, Pat Clifford, has told me that neither she nor Sharon Friesen, his other teacher, guided

the shaping of his narrative. Except for using the Czech spelling for Trutnov, I have resisted my maternal instinct to alter the essay in any way.

6. Even now I find myself very nervous watching Holocaust films and have, on occasion, phoned my mother the next day as though I am still seeking the magic reassurance of her voice. This visual terror may also explain my fascination with picture books that deal with the Holocaust.

7. Adolf Eichmann, the Nazi in charge of the Hungarian transports, was captured in 1960. Was it his capture and subsequent trial and the way this allowed discussion of what happened in the camps that makes my mother now say that she did not talk about Auschwitz until 1961 when I was 12?

8. My grandmother, Josephine Fodor, remained in mourning until she died in 1989. She left instructions that on her tombstone, a tombstone my grandfather does not have, be written "Beloved wife of Dr. Adolf Fodor, born December 14, 1886, perished during the Holocaust, October 25, 1944."

9. When I read memoirs by other survivors, I catch myself looking for confirmation of my mother's story in narratives that emphasize sisters surviving because they stayed together; e.g., Isabella Leitner's *Fragments of Isabella: A Memoir of Auschwitz*.

10. In the original draft of this essay, I wrote *"Das ist schön ja"* (that is beautiful, yes). After she read the paper, my mother observed that Mengele had not praised Magda's beauty but rather her impressive stature, *"Das schon ja."* The adjective, *schön*, means beautiful; the adverb, *schon*, means already or certainly. In my mother's words, Mengele recognized that Magda was "really something." I note this as yet another example of the distance between what a child hears and what a mother says.

11. Like all stories, "Six Years of Terror" has taken on a life of its own and has been used by a classmate of Joshua's as source material for her own Holocaust story. At least one student teacher has challenged its authenticity as a story written by an eight-year-old because "this is not what a child sounds like."

2

"Do You Know
What 'Auschwitz' Means?"

The question of my title is asked by the mother of Piri Davidowitz in the penultimate sentence of Aranka Siegal's fictionalized memoir, *Upon the Head of the Goat: A Childhood in Hungary 1939-1944*. The reader never hears the answer to the mother's question; in Siegal's final sentence, before Mr. Shuster can respond, the German guard yells, and the train door clanks shut. The sequel, *Grace in the Wilderness: After the Liberation 1945-1948*, begins in Bergen-Belsen at the end of the war. Presumably Piri, having survived Auschwitz, now knows the answer to her mother's question, but the reader is never given this answer; coherent, conclusive statements are not part of the meaning of Auschwitz. That meaning is not just hidden from the reader; it is denied. If Piri cannot know for certain what Auschwitz means for her mother, in that Piri survives and her mother does not, what meaning can the reader possibly construct? The unanswered question, in effect, becomes the meaning, for it is what is left with the reader: Do you know what Auschwitz means? Auschwitz is what I cannot narrate.

Part of what Piri cannot narrate is the death of her mother, a death that she guesses occurs shortly after the arrival at Auschwitz. Piri's need to understand the mother's final words to her two older daughters as "her last act as our mother"

(*Grace* 70) is itself ambiguous, for she had come to notice in the ghetto what a good actress her mother was. Are the mother's final words—"Be brave and look after each other" (70)—part of a continuing act of motherhood, a mother acting as though maternal gestures make sense on the ramp of Auschwitz? The very idea of motherhood as protective, powerful, and nurturing cannot survive the boarding of the trains, as is evident when Mrs. Davidowitz orders the German soldiers not to touch her daughters; despite her ability to speak in both German and Hungarian, her maternal voice is powerless. She can protect neither Piri nor herself. Even as the train door clanks shut, Mrs. Davidowitz must pull "her head back [...] to avoid being struck by the door as it closed with a loud metallic clank" (*Upon* 214). It is the sound of machinery, not the human voice, that triumphs in the final sentence of *Upon the Head of the Goat*.

What bears notice is that this brutal diminishment of maternal power and maternal voice happens before the train door shuts. It represents the end of what can be narrated. The mother's head pulls back to avoid being struck by the train door; what happens when she is pushed, the reader assumes, into the gas chamber? Siegal's two subtitles are deceptive; appearing to cover a nine-year period, they omit the time between June 1944 when the train door shuts, and spring 1945, the moment of liberation. Piri may say in the sequel that she cannot stop thinking about Auschwitz, but the narrative focus on postwar events indicates that, as a traumatized survivor, she can neither express nor consciously think about what her mind dwells on. In *Grace in the Wilderness*, fragments of memories, details of nightmares, will occasionally convey that Auschwitz is synonymous with the mother's death: "I choked up at the mention of Mother. I could not get my mind away from Auschwitz" (69), but the mother's question remains unanswered, as impossible to narrate as the moment of her death.

Memoir, like fiction, is obviously constructed; the writer in retrospect gives a shape to her experience; she recalls or gives emphasis to events that she now sees as significant. Yet to do so is not necessarily to explain those events, or to conclude that there is a lesson about the triumph of the human spirit in the words of her story. The writer may see a pattern and a redemptive meaning in her experience, but she need not. It is as though the religious and legal sanctity inherent in being a witness frees her from the need to explain her testament: I saw this; it may make no sense to you or to me, but this is what I saw. In *Grace in the Wilderness*, when Piri returns to her memory of the Auschwitz selection, the moment when she last saw her mother, she refers to her mother as the one to whom the daughters look "for an explanation" (69). Her sister, Iboya, may see a spiritual meaning in their survival—that is, the guiding hand of the mother's spirit—but Piri remains confused and uncertain, as though the possibility of explanation vanishes with the mother's selection.

In removing the necessity for an explanation, memoir disrupts a commonly recognized boundary between children's and adults' reading about the Holocaust, in that children's books seem to function primarily as explanations of what adult texts often claim is ultimately inexplicable. Disrupting this boundary, memoir also offers the possibility of presenting to children a Holocaust topic many adults can barely tolerate, that which is conveyed by the word, Auschwitz. Conveyed, yet not conveyed, for the word, Auschwitz, has become for many adults the location of the unbelievable, the incommunicable, the place where no well-argued explanation ever seems complete enough to make those of us who were not there fully understand what it means. Auschwitz, the place supposedly beyond the descriptive capacity of everyday language, has itself become a synecdoche for all the death camps, as well as a metaphor for all the places that Terrence Des Pres insists are beyond metaphor. It is as if full understanding is available only to the dead; even the survivor often admits that what she witnessed in the death camps was witnessed by a different self, and only that self fully understands what the survivor/narrator now speaks of. Often in adult Holocaust memoirs, the narrator testifies to inhabiting a double self, the deeply buried one who lived in Auschwitz and the surface one who can talk to us and herself about it:

> No, it is all too incredible. And everything that happened to that other, the Auschwitz one, now has no bearing upon me, does not concern me, so separate from one another are this deep-lying memory and ordinary memory. I live within a twofold being. (Delbo "Days and Memory" 331)

But to write thus for children, to suggest that the narrator has problems believing, comprehending, and narrating her own story, that the sensations and memories accessible only through dreams are fortunately not accessible through ordinary language, goes against our understanding of the function of children's historical literature, a function that David L. Russell, in "Reading the Shards and Fragments: Holocaust Literature for Young Readers," alludes to when he says that "art of the Holocaust is necessarily didactic art" (268).[1] How can this art be didactic, what exactly does it teach, when the memoirist herself writes from a different impulse, a need to convince herself as well as the reader that the words she writes testify to an experience she still finds "incredible"? The memoirist often claims that she does not comprehend her own experience. How then can she take on the explanatory function so essential to the child protagonist who often narrates Holocaust fiction for children? Memoir appears to inscribe an impermeable border to our knowledge, presenting through its fragments not so much a "whole [that] becomes greater than the parts" (Russell 268) as a questioning whether full comprehension of Auschwitz is either possible or desirable. In its insistence upon a limit to understanding, memoir sometimes betrays our conviction that children need a Holocaust fiction that is very different from the fiction that adults read. Identifying when a Holocaust memoir is intended for children is a tricky business. Are we not likely to assume that the memoir with the hopeful lesson must be the memoir that is most appropriate for children, and that the more hopeful the lesson, the younger the reader?

Yet this is not always the case. That Siegal's memoirs are marketed as children's books demonstrates not only the ineptness of publishers in recognizing the features of age-specific reading, but the way that the Holocaust mocks our belief in any clear relationship between maturity and understanding. In another memoir, *What Did You Do in the War, Daddy? Growing Up German*, Sabine Reichel ridicules her initial belief that she was taught about Hitler and the Third Reich when she was 14 as "the result of a carefully calculated estimate by the school officials—as if German students were emotionally and intellectually ready to comprehend and digest the facts about Nazi Germany at exactly the age of 14.3" (104). German history, she comes to realize, was taught chronologically; no consideration was given to the age of the students. And what permits *Upon the Head of the Goat* to become a highly regarded children's book (winner of both the Boston Globe/Horn Book Award for Nonfiction and the Janusz Korczak Literary Award) appears to be the decision to close the train door, a narrative strategy that, like the religiously connotative titles, fools us into thinking that Siegal's memoir has the other chief characteristic that we tend to associate with children's books, the consolation of shaping narrative order. But think about that ending and its unanswered question. Where is the triumph of the human spirit, the heroic rhetoric that reassures us, not just in children's books, but even in Holocaust memoirs directed at adult readers?

An example of an adult memoir that is far more hopeful is Eva Brewster's *Vanished in Darkness: An Auschwitz Memoir*. At the end of the book (published, not by Puffin, but by a small western Canadian publisher, NeWest Press), the narrator recounts how her heroic mother, who has repeatedly saved her daughter from extermination, instructs her at the end of the war in her future role as a survivor: "You [...] will see to it that young people will not ever again be persecuted" (Brewster 134). The narrator accepts this heroic task, promising her mother "that, never again [...] would a dictatorship rob [her] children of their birthright, their freedom and their happiness" (135). This is the meaning that the narrator gives to her experience; this is the task that will lead Brewster years later to write her memoir.

The marketing of Brewster's and Siegal's books indicates the difficulty memoir raises for our deeply held beliefs regarding age-specific Holocaust reading. Looking for a way to explain how certain memoirs become children's books, Elizabeth R. Baer suggests that "It is almost as if the publishers decided that if one wrote an autobiographical book about being a child during this era, then the book would be marketed for children; if one were an adult [...] then one's book is marketed for adults" (393). Although many bibliographies appear to support this insight, there are some childhood memoirs that remain resistant to being marketed primarily or initially for children. This suggests that a theory of memoir in Holocaust children's literature that looks only to the age of the protagonist is inadequate. If the voice of the child in the memoir is too incoherent, if it does not produce either the knowledge or the hopeful lesson that we wish to give the readers of children's books, how many adults will encourage their children to read the memoir even if it is in a children's bibliography? If we are surprised that *Vanished in Darkness* is marketed for adults, it can only be because we take for granted that hopeful lessons drawn from Holocaust material are what young children require, as though the very proof of our maturity is our willingness to give up childish things, in this case the hope, lessons, and clarity which we require as children.

I see several inconsistencies in this model of developmental understanding, and many are evident in Russell's essay, an essay that concludes urging us to tell children "the truth" (279). Implicit in Russell's argument that "children [...] ages of ten or twelve and up are fully capable of dealing with the fundamental issues of the Holocaust" (267) is the belief that these issues need only be treated the right way, that is, "sensitively handled" (268), for children to "achieve a measure of perspective" (267). Only by ignoring other "truths,"—that historical events never come with ready-made singular meanings; that post-Holocaust, we continue to argue over the meanings of this particular historical event; that the work of Judith Miller, as well as that of many others, demonstrates how nations make different meaning of the Holocaust—can Russell refer to a singular meaning, consistent perhaps with how he refers to "fundamental issues," but he never clarifies what those issues are. Yet Russell also concedes that there are obvious limits to children's ability to understand the Holocaust, limits he contains too easily with dashes, "The Holocaust—its incomprehensible nature aside—" (268).

At what age then do child readers become adults, for whom we permit a larger "perspective" that paradoxically includes the possibility that there is something "incomprehensible" (268) about the Holocaust? How do we frame our child-directed explanations so that children do not sense the deception in our not telling them this? And of most concern, how do we ensure that children who have learned that the Holocaust is a subject like any other, one that can be "sensitively handled," do not remain forever insensitive to the kind of troubling knowledge accessible in memoir? Fearing that we will brutalize children by a bluntness of language regarding the murder of millions of people, we tell stories whose delicate and sensitive language persuades us that, despite the Holocaust, human values remain the same. The Holocaust was an aberration; our humanistic values remain strong.

Despite Russell's hyphenated aside and the shards and fragments named in his title, his own language reveals an adult who clearly does believe that there is a singular meaning, an "ultimate significance" (268) to the Holocaust. Perhaps he is right, but his choice of diction—for example, "the besieged human spirit" (277) and "the baseness of humanity" (278)—differs strikingly from those who do not share his belief that the "ultimate significance" of the Holocaust is a universal lesson about human nature. His conclusion sounds very much like the kind of universal human lesson we are used to finding in children's books. Comparing children's books about the Holocaust to Puritan tales, Russell applies to Holocaust fiction a religious sensibility in which such reading will "lead us out of the darkness and toward the light" (279). Such redemptive language mocks the "incomprehensible" and undercuts once again the very distinction between what the child can understand and what Russell, the adult, understands. It assumes that once we reach the light, God will explain the Holocaust to us; it also assumes that we will be satisfied by that explanation.

Unlike *Vanished in Darkness* and Russell's essay, *Upon the Head of the Goat* contains no heroic exhortation, and even *Grace in the Wilderness* is far more tentative in its hopeful conclusion, as Piri comes to understand that she will have "to live with the Fritzes of the world" (220). Her memoir gives a meaning to her experience, but a meaning in which hope is minimal and the lesson far from obvious. Siegal's work thus fits uneasily into our usual expectations of children's books; instead of offering a closure that has the heroine reach a moment of "insight, reconciliation, maturity, or moral triumph" (Langer, "Fiction" 237), she disrupts her narrative and thus creates a memoir that comes close to the fragmentary nature of Holocaust testimony as described by Shoshana

Felman: "composed of bits and pieces of a memory that has been overwhelmed by occurrences that have not settled into understanding or remembrance" ("Education and Crisis" 16).

Even admitting that a written memoir is not oral testimony and that Siegal's work does show multiple signs of remembrance, I still find it remarkably free of the usual heroic lessons that accompany many children's books on the Holocaust; for example, consider the heroic self-sacrifice of Chaya who dies so that another may escape extermination in Jane Yolen's *The Devil's Arithmetic*. Just before Chaya dies, she insists that there is a lesson, "That we *will* survive. The Jews. That what happens here must never happen again" (157). Siegal's work is suspicious of such eloquence. References to a lesson emerging from Piri's survival are rare: the dedication to *Upon the Head of the Goat* may state "Auschwitz could not sever the bonds of love and friendship which contributed to my survival," but its moral implications are more than balanced by the numerous descriptions of the child narrator's confusion, her inability to understand the newspapers or the conversations of the adults around her. Siegal's narrative emphasizes Piri's confusion and unanswered questions: "pogroms, scapegoats—was this what being a Jew meant?" (13). Over and over again, the same line appears: "I felt confused" (38).

Piri's confusion resembles that of the adults around her. Having seen early on the bodies of dead Ukrainian soldiers floating in the river, Piri chastises herself for imagining such fates for her father and brother-in-law: "Why did I think of such terrible things" (41). In repressing her fears, in trying to live life as normal, she resembles her mother far more than Babi, the grandmother who disapproves when her daughter gets pregnant in such terrible times. It is Mrs. Davidowitz who ignores until it's too late her mother's advice to send her older daughters to the United States. In stressing the shared confusion of Piri and her mother, Siegal implies how the adult victims of the Nazis were like innocent children; the child narrator that Siegal constructs never exhibits the wisdom of hindsight. Writing only what she witnessed and thought then, she remains loyal to the voice of the dead mother. Yet such loyalty seems less a sign of conscious moral choice than of her inability to understand what has happened to her.

It is left to the reader with historical knowledge to see ironic patterns: the repetition of Passover Seders at which one or more family members are absent; the contrast of trains in 1939 that do not run when the borders are sealed and so keep Piri apart from her family versus the trains that in 1944 do run and produce a final separation; the gentleness of her mother's bathing her in a setting where only her younger brother and niece can laugh at her nakedness versus the later undressing and showers of Auschwitz. Piri merely reports, and the reader, too, gets confused. When Piri tells her mother of testing God by eating grapes on the Sabbath, her sister scolds her that the lack of divine punishment does not mean God does not notice; God is just too busy. Is God too busy to see what is happening in Europe? A Slovak refugee fleeing deportation does not know her intended destination: "Only God above knows" (64). Piri never says that God is absent; she only asks questions that demonstrate her growing distance from her grandmother's faith: "'We are all God's children,' Babi used to say [...]. Did she mean Germans, too?" (211).

Piri's questioning of her faith brings her closer to her mother's position. The goat that the mother buys is, initially, just a goat that can provide the children with milk. When it is confiscated by the local authorities, Piri's mother ironically revises the Old Testament scapegoat reference, saying that the goat is sent into the wilderness bearing the sins of the Nazis. This revision of the story in *Leviticus* emphasizes her critique of traditional religion, and the inadequacy of religion to explain what is happening. Piri does not initially understand her mother's reference to the scapegoat; when Mr. Shuster later suggests economics might offer a better explanation, "very bad to be a Jew during depressions" (205) and then explains what a scapegoat is, Piri is even more "confused" (205). While she now understands her mother's reference, a reference which provides the title of the memoir, the title itself implies a question: "'But these are not our sins,' I said [...]. Why should we have to carry them?'" (205). The title is a tribute to the dead mother's voice, but the question remains and seems to provoke only more questions.

The challenge of writing about the Holocaust in children's literature lies precisely here: resisting the well-intentioned impulse to construct an unambiguous hopeful lesson; considering instead whether there are ways in which even young children's texts, and certainly young adult texts, can include a space for such questions. These questions, left unanswered in the sense that there is still no consensus about what the answers should be, are more likely to be unsettling when children's books include strategies that bring readers within the barbed wire of the concentration camps. I recognize that much can and should be explained to young children about the Holocaust—for example, the ideology of antisemitism; the nature of racism; the historical, economic, cultural, and religious events leading to genocide (no list of causes is ever comprehensive)—and all of these topics do appear quite regularly in children's books, including picture books. Yet most children's books are justifiably reluctant to take on the task of coherent explanation written from within the perspective of the concentration camps. The Jewish protagonists usually escape (through immigration before the war, through hiding or resistance during; it often seems that the only two Holocaust stories for children are about Anne Frank or the Danish resistance), or the stories are told from an outsider's perspective (for example, post-Holocaust American Christian as in Cynthia Voigt's *David and Jonathan*, or German bystander as in Roberto Innocenti's *Rose Blanche*, or Hans Peter Richter's *Friedrich*). Such narrative perspectives permit the powerful telling of stories (whether of resistance or of acceptance of Nazi ideology), but still avoid the more difficult writing of a story told from the perspective of the concentration camp victim. Carol Matas's *Daniel's Story* (discussed in Chapter Five) is a rare exception.

An examination of Margaret Wild's *Let the Celebrations Begin!* indicates the difficulty of creating a picture book set in a concentration camp. The epigraph—"[a] *collection of stuffed toys has been preserved which were made by Polish women in Belsen for the first children's party held after the liberation*"—forms the impulse behind a very hopeful story, which ends in the liberation of the camp, "and so the celebrations begin!" (n. pag.). Yet many have found *Let the Celebrations Begin!* offensively hopeful in its seeming disregard for the many children who died in the camps and in the absence of historical context (not only are there no pictures of Nazis or dead bodies, but, except for one double-spread illustration of the barracks, the women and children are drawn on a white background). To speak of a longing for toys seems to trivialize the reality of a place where admittedly "there are no toys" (n. pag.), but to say only this seems so inadequate. Is the focus on toys a way of resisting the Nazi perspective on these children? Do the repeated references to four-year-old David wrapping himself in his "mama's old black shawl" (n. pag.) and the mockery of old Jacoba who complains twice "that it will be our fault if she gets rheumatism in her back this winter" (n. pag.) provoke young readers to ask questions that the dominant narrative does not mention? Where is mama, and why does David have her shawl? Whose fault is it really if Jacoba gets rheumatism? There are other questions: why do the children look so thin and have no hair? Why are their clothes only rags? Why are they in this place? These are all important questions for young readers to consider, but the likelihood of their asking such questions seems to depend on a historical awareness that the book dares not present.

In comparison, in the picture book *Rose Blanche*, children view events from the German child's perspective, a child who holds a Nazi flag in the first illustration. Children see the Holocaust victims, including an illustration that includes the vulnerable, unnamed little boy with hands held up, which is based on a famous Nazi photograph taken in the Warsaw ghetto. Even though the book's title alludes to the anti-Nazi White Rose student movement, and the heroine, Rose Blanche, ends up following the little boy, discovering and aiding the starving Jewish children behind the electric barbed wire, and dying for her heroic actions, it is her death (shot because she is part of the resistance or because of an accident—the text leaves this uncertain) that captures the reader's interest. What happens to the concentration camp children, who, like Rose Blanche, are missing in the final illustrations is not the subject of narration.

Staying outside, such texts can both explain and provide the hero and hope so necessary to children's books. For instance, Alex, the 11-year-old protagonist in Uri Orlev's *The Island on Bird Street*, survives five months in the ghetto on his own and is then reunited with his father and ready to join the partisans. Compare Alex to Robinson Crusoe, Orlev instructs readers—and readers do—for we already know how to read such heroic adventure stories; others will disappear, or be shot dead, but not our hero: "You sure are lucky, Alex" (30). It is only the dust jacket that implies another comparison: one with Orlev himself, a child who also hid in the Warsaw ghetto, but was captured and sent to Bergen-Belsen. Alex may question his luck, may long to be in a fairy tale where animal helpers assist him, may even realize that "real wars weren't like the ones in adventure books" (102), but the Robinson Crusoe metaphor keeps us hopeful. What child will question Alex's conclusion, "That's really the end of my story. They took me to the forest to be with them, among the partisans" (160)? Yet is it not the end of Alex's story only because the camps are what cannot be narrated?

Books directed at young adult readers insist less on the necessity of hope and happy endings, yet they also hesitate to take readers into the concentration camps. Cynthia Voigt's *David and Jonathan* is set in America immediately after World War II and later during the Vietnam War. Voigt distances and contains the narrative of the survivor by focalizing the action through the naïve American innocence of the non-

Jewish Henry, who must have Jewish customs and post-Holocaust anxieties explained to him. Although the novel's title refers to the two Jewish protagonists—David, a Holocaust survivor, and Jonathan, an American Jew—the reader's point of entry remains Henry, who realizes in horror that he finds it "easier to imagine" (148) being a Nazi than being a victim and that "he [doesn't] want to understand" (150). David, the traumatized Jewish survivor who ultimately commits suicide, remains unknown, operating more as provocation to Henry's questions about his own sexual desires than as a character whose trauma leads to further insight about the Holocaust. The little that David tells about the camps is more than Henry can stand. In his conflict with David over Jonathan, Henry comes to wish that David—that is, the past—"never [...] happened" (185). David forces an unwilling understanding upon Henry:

> How the Jews could stay in Germany [...] . How non-Jews [...] could refuse to believe or discover what was going on, and feel innocent. How the Nazis, the SS, could treat people [...] . None of it was more than Henry could imagine. He knew himself. (185-86)

Exploring issues of responsibility, and postwar American antisemitism, as well as parallels between Vietnam and the Holocaust, David and Jonathan repeatedly struggles with "the futility of questioning the unanswerable" (228), but in a manner that implies that young adult American readers can only approach the concentration camp world indirectly and in very small doses. After David's suicide, his uncle insists that Christians and Jews must ask different questions and must derive different lessons from the concentration camps. American Jews must ask how and whether they will live in this world; American Christians must learn another lesson, about the link between the genteel antisemitism of old money in Boston and the atrocities in the camps. Just hearing the camp names makes Henry despair.

If too much knowledge of what occurred in the camps leads only to despair, it is no surprise that we avoid narrating Auschwitz, preferring to celebrate hope and heroism, spiritual victory over physical slaughter, by telling children and young adults stories about the Holocaust that we can ourselves tolerate. Yet to do so is to embrace a comforting delusion Lawrence L. Langer identifies when he argues that the Western tradition that finds tragic enlightenment in suffering is merely ironic evidence of our inability to understand, and reluctance to confront, what concentration camp life was really like. In his essay "On Writing and Reading Holocaust Literature," Langer argues that we need a different language. Given that camp victims had no agency, to speak of tragedy is inappropriate; to find heroism misleading: "Those who would convert death in Auschwitz or Bergen-Belsen into a triumph of love over hate feed deep and obscure needs in themselves having little to do with the truth" (7). This quotation is part of a passage in which Langer explains why he has not included the writing of Anne Frank in his anthology, *Art from the Ashes*. In writing on Holocaust literature, Langer always speaks of the need to unlearn our literary assumptions, to eschew "the comforting notion that suffering has meaning—that it strengthens, ennobles, or redeems the human soul" (4). Langer is scathing on the consequences of focussing on the uplifting, heroic story, our need "for reassurance that mass murder had its redeeming features" (7).

Similarly, Elie Wiesel and Claude Lanzmann are hesitant to view their own work on the Holocaust as fitting within the category of explanation. To explain is dangerous, for it runs the risk of understanding. In "A Plea for the Dead," Wiesel concludes that the need for understanding relates to our need for closure: "We want to know, to understand, so we can turn the page: is that not true? So we can say to ourselves: the matter is closed and everything is back in order" (144). Lanzmann, director of *Shoah: An Oral History of the Holocaust*, speaks of the obscenity of understanding, of the way grand theories explaining the Holocaust are a way of escaping the reality of the camps and endorsing the perspective of the killers ("The Obscenity of Understanding" 207). In his documentary, *Shoah*, survivors repeatedly conclude their accounts with the word, "unbelievable." It is SS *Unterscharführer* Franz Suchomel in his account of Treblinka who keeps asking Lanzmann if he understands. To understand, to make sense of the process of extermination, is for Lanzmann to speak as a Nazi. Lanzmann refuses to understand. Asked by Roger Rosenblatt, at the end of the televising of *Shoah* in 1987 on the American Public Broadcasting System, what he understood after the 11 years he took to make the film, Lanzmann hesitates. He finally replies, "I cannot tell you."

Certainly many writers, both historians and novelists, have criticized Wiesel and cautioned about the danger of mystifying the Holocaust, warning that sacralizing the systemic murder of millions of people does nothing to ensure that such murder does not occur again. Yet the wide acceptance of the capitalized if problematic word, Holocaust, indicates how culturally difficult it is to find a language appropriate to this particular systemic murder. It is revealing that the critique of mystification has been voiced by those who have decided to set their fiction outside the Auschwitz boundaries. Thus Aharon Appelfeld, child survivor and Israeli novelist, whose fiction is so often about the Holocaust, places his stories before and after what happens in the concentration camps, even as he warns against "the tendency to speak of the Holocaust in mystical terms, to link the events to the incomprehensible, the mysterious, the insane, and the meaningless" (Appelfeld 92). Seeing this "tendency [as] both understandable and dangerous, from every point of view," he rightly reminds us that "[m]urder that was committed with evil intentions must not be interpreted in mystical terms" (92).

Not only can children's books not afford the luxury of refusal of understanding, the refusal seems itself to be an explanation, in that Lanzmann's very insistence on the "machinery of murder" (Lanzmann, "The Obscenity of Understanding" 213), on the question—*How* was extermination carried out?—cannot avoid implicitly asking the question, *Why?* As context for his refusal, Lanzmann likes to quote Primo Levi, "*Hier ist kein Warum*" [Here, there is no Why] ("The Obscenity of Understanding" 204), the answer an SS guard gave when Levi asked this question on his arrival in Auschwitz. Yet this in itself is unsatisfactory, for to quote the SS guard is to endorse the Nazi point of view, something that, in fact, Levi does not do when he includes the anecdote in *Survival in Auschwitz*. Levi insists even as he analyzes the laboratory that was Auschwitz that there is an immense distance between the behaviour produced in the camps and the behaviour of humans outside the camps. And part of human behaviour outside the camps is to ask why. Lanzmann insists that his own refusal of understanding is based on the gap between all the possible explanations of the Holocaust and the reality of what took place in the camps: "between all these conditions and the gassing of three thousand persons [...] there is an unbreachable discrepancy. It is simply not possible to engender one out of the other" ("The Obscenity of Understanding" 206).

Although on a moral level it may be true that no explanation can ever be complete enough, that no book will ever lead us to conclude, "Well, is it because of all these conditions that the children have been gassed?" ("The Obscenity of Understanding" 207), to decide that we should therefore not bother asking why the Holocaust happened or telling children about it is far from my intention. Wiesel's statement, "Who has not lived through the event, will never know it" (Fine 44), would be ironic indeed if it resulted in a refusal to tell children anything at all. Even if children's books can never satisfy the stringent premises of Langer, Wiesel, and Lanzmann, it may still be possible to write about the concentration camps for children in a way that acknowledges Lanzmann's insight and incorporates it as part of the explanation that the books provide. It may seem that our justifiable reluctance to have young readers witness the gas chambers means that most Holocaust children's fiction is inevitably ineffective, a failure through its very desire to protect, evoking in the child reader according to Hamida Bosmajian, "no more than a vague sense of sadness" (208). Yet, there have been more successful attempts to write such fictional witnessing for both children and young adults, and I will conclude by looking at the very different representational strategies of one of them, *Briar Rose*, by Jane Yolen.

Yolen's *Briar Rose*, intended for older readers, is a remarkably daring Holocaust novel.[2] In the Grimm Brothers fairy
tale, "*Dornröschen*" ("Briar Rose"), the heroine is cursed by a
fairy, pricks her finger, and then falls asleep. One hundred
years later, a prince who has heard of the sleeping Briar Rose,
kisses her awake. In Yolen's adaptation of this tale, a young
woman is gassed at a death camp, Chelmno, and left for dead
in a pit. Discovered by partisans, she is miraculously resusci-
tated through the kiss of life given to her by one of them, a
minor Polish aristocrat, Josef Potocki. When her only memory upon awakening is of the fairy tale, "Sleeping Beauty in
the Wood," Potocki names her Princess Briar Rose. Unlike
Yolen's earlier and more conventional *The Devil's Arithmetic*,
Briar Rose respects the narrative expectations of young adult
romance fiction, only to abandon those expectations in the
concluding "Author's Note." Her 23-year-old heroine, Becca,
has the requisite heterosexual romance that ends with a kiss,
a kiss that contrasts with the far more disturbing kiss with
which Potocki saved her grandmother, Gemma, at Chelmno.
It is this second kiss that gives us the "Hope and Happy
Endings" that Katherine Paterson requires of children's literature; but in the "Author's Note," Yolen deliberately takes
away both the kiss and the happy ending by reminding her
readers that the story of Gemma is a fairy tale: "Happy-ever-
after is a fairy tale notion, not history. [...] no woman [...]
escaped from Chelmno alive" (202). The lesson that emerges
in this sophisticated interplay between text and peritext is
not the consoling lesson of spiritual triumph but a much
harder one about the reality of historical facts and the difficulty such facts pose for representing this particular history
for young people. The difficulty is represented within the

narrative of Becca's childhood, for her friends, like Yolen's readers, are reluctant to listen to Gemma's version of "Briar Rose."

Like Becca's friends who want to hear the version of Sleeping Beauty that they already know, Yolen's readers want stories that they recognize, soothing tales that do not threaten their understanding of themselves. To get their attention, Yolen in essence must trick them, must risk telling Holocaust truth through telling a fairy-tale lie and then deconstructing that lie. This narrative approach is risky, but direct approaches to Holocaust truth seem even riskier. Certainly this is true in Poland where, according to Becca's translator/guide Magda, a teacher who tells her students the truth about the death camps does not return to work the following year.[3] Aware that her readers want happy endings, Yolen keeps warning them that happy endings take place only in fairy tales, just as her heroine keeps repeating the fact that no woman survived Chelmno. Neither fact proves easy to accept. As Magda tells Becca, and Yolen instructs her readers: "Truth is never tidy. Only fairy tales" (196). Manipulating our desire for the happy ending, Yolen teaches us why it is unavailable.

In her rewriting of "Briar Rose" as the fantastic story of how Gemma survives the death camp, Chelmno, Yolen begins by encouraging her readers to feel superior to conventional fairy tales and possibly also to feel disdain for the fairy-tale-like lives of Becca and her sisters. Clearly intended to evoke the stereotype (and casual antisemitism) inherent in the phrase "Jewish-American Princesses," the three sisters exist in an affluent world of brand-name possessions, expensive leather, mink coats, and excessively heavy luggage, a world that seems very remote from the Holocaust past the sisters (and Yolen's readers) know so little about. Not only does Becca's father ask her if she has heard of Jewish-American Princesses, but it turns out that Aron, the Jewish partisan who helped to rescue Becca's grandmother and then married her, was a medical student—a disturbing echo of the cliché about Jewish girls who want to marry doctors. Moreover, Becca learns this only after she determines to go to Poland, finds Potocki, and he tells her that Aron escaped being burned alive with the rest of his family, because he was away at medical school. Just as Becca's quest disrupts the stereotype of the "Jewish-American Princess," Potocki, who joins the partisans after he escapes from the labour camp, Sachsenhausen, does not fit the stereotype of the prince. Imprisoned by the Nazis for the "crime" of homosexuality, Potocki restores Gemma with a kiss, but the one he truly loves is Aron. Some might even call this prince who kisses the Polish Jewish Princess a fairy, the derogatory homosexual slang indicating Yolen's ironic distance from conventional fairy tales. The distance is necessary, for through it, Yolen gives us the heroic language Langer critiques, albeit parodied.

From a realistic perspective, the novel is absurd. Becca's mother never asks questions about her own mother's background; it is Becca, the youngest granddaughter, who, after Gemma's death, determines to make sense of her obsessive and peculiar retelling of "Briar Rose." Yet, as a fairy tale, *Briar Rose* makes perfect sense. Because Gemma's memories are obliterated by the gas at Chelmno, when she is revived, she has no memory of her past except for a fairy tale in which she, a princess in a castle, is the only one kissed awake. This loss of memory is less an exploration of trauma than a narrative strategy to protect Yolen's readers; we are distanced from the experience of being gassed, hearing of it through Potocki, a man himself persecuted by the Nazis, but someone on the periphery of Gemma's story, one of the partisans outside the gas van.

We are further protected because the novel's over-all focalization is Becca's, and we will learn and understand only as much as she is able to comprehend. Becca and Gemma may resemble each other, they may both be called Sleeping Beauties and princesses, but the granddaughter's naïve American perspective keeps us safe and keeps the narrative safely within the patterns of rescue celebrated by children's literature. Becca, Jewish-American Princess, actively seeks knowledge about her grandmother; Gemma, Polish fairy-tale princess, can barely speak or act. Rescued once by the partisans, now it is her story that will be rescued by her granddaughter. The partisans try to save other gassed victims; one woman before she dies tells them what it was like to be gassed: "I called my daughter's name over and over and over but she did not answer. Then the van started up" (176). In this way Yolen enters the gas chamber and tells the reader what Siegal cannot narrate. The mother remains loyal to the daughter, at least as far as she can remember; the amnesia produced by the gas allows Yolen a way to avoid what Lanzmann's *Sonderkommando* witnesses report: parents, struggling to breathe even as they were gassed, stepping on top of their own dying children.

Lanzmann begins *Shoah* at Chelmno, and viewers are told that only two men survived this particular death camp, one an adolescent in chains, who was often seen by the villagers. Lanzmann explains that one reason that the SS kept the boy

alive "longer than the others" (*Shoah* 1) was his beautiful
singing voice which could be heard as he went up the river to
get feed for rabbits. He also tells us that on January 18, 1945,
the Nazis shot "all the remaining Jews [...] with a bullet in
the head" (2). Among those shot was the child, Simon
Srebnik. He survived the shooting, and as a middle-aged
adult, is interviewed extensively by Lanzmann. Srebnik also
appears as an unnamed character in *Briar Rose* (169-70), one
sign that what is most interesting about the book is not
Yolen's reliance on a well-known fairy tale, but that her fairy-
tale Holocaust narrative is itself inspired by Lanzmann's
Shoah. The similarities to the film are numerous.[4] Picking up
on the resemblance between fairy-tale language and the language in Lanzmann's film—the references to barbed wire; the
Chelmno *Schloss* (castle), which the victims entered on their
way to gassing; Abraham Bomba's account in *Shoah* of how,
upon arrival in the camps, people vanished like magic: "There
was no trace, none at all, like a magic thing" (Lanzmann,
Shoah 37); the role of luck in determining who survived—
Yolen deconstructs the fairy tale. By doing so, she foregrounds the dilemma of the children's writer who wants to
challenge her readers' expectations, the writer who respects
Lanzmann's documentary, yet defies his artistic position in
her very attempt to write a fairy tale about the Holocaust.
Like Lanzmann, who ends his film with interviews about the
Warsaw Ghetto Uprising that resist traditional language
about heroic resistance, Yolen's embedded homodiegetic
narrator, Potocki, repeatedly instructs the reader to "Forget
every romantic notion [...] about the partisans" (153).[5] The
partisans he describes are neither romantic, heroic, nor particularly brave: "Wars do not make heroes of everyone" (146).

Although Potocki incorporates the heroic stories of resistance that the partisans tell each other as part of his narrative, he does so only to observe how the tellers never mention "that all the stories ended in death" (156).

Despite Potocki's warning, Becca insists that he and Gemma were heroes. Potocki objects to this language, first by quoting Emerson, "The hero is not fed on sweets but daily his own heart he eats" (194), and then by adding, "I have dined long and hard on my heart. And it is bitter" (194). This last statement echoes that of Itzhak Zuckermann, in an interview by Lanzmann near the end of *Shoah*. Zuckermann, second-in-command of the Jewish Combat Organization in the Warsaw ghetto, speaks totally outside traditional heroic discourse. Instead of the figure of a romantic resistance fighter eloquently describing the bravery he witnessed, the viewer sees a man with dark shadows around his eyes, a man whose four brief sentences end: "If you could lick my heart, it would poison you" (182).

Briar Rose incorporates numerous details from *Shoah*: the Nazi school teacher's wife who is interviewed by Lanzmann; the Chelmno villagers who continue to believe that the Jews deserved to die; the constant reminders that the beautiful Polish landscape is both mask and byproduct of the corpses that fertilize it. Yet *Briar Rose* differs not only in Yolen's reliance on fairy-tale discourse, but in several additional ways that signal the need to deviate from Lanzmann's perspective in order to appeal to her North American adolescent readers. The first is her decision to create a Chelmno priest who speaks to Becca, one who counters the antisemitism of the villagers interviewed by Lanzmann; in her "Author's Note" Yolen states, "There may be good people [in Chelmno]. I have never heard them interviewed" (201). The second is her transformation of the protagonist/quester of the film from a male director, accompanied by a translator who asks the questions he provides, to Becca, a young woman who, though still accompanied by a female translator, is far less certain about the object of her quest or the questions she should ask. But it is the third difference that is most revealing of the self-censorship that often occurs in Holocaust fiction for children; it appears here when Yolen clearly refers to a moment in *Shoah*, but does so in such a way that her readers are protected from the knowledge provided by Lanzmann's account.

The passage occurs in Chapter 23, when Gemma tells the very young Becca that, as the prince goes through the castle, no one is "stirring" (128). Becca, perplexed by her grandmother's choice of the word "stirring," becomes distraught: "What is stirring, Gemma? [...] Why would they have soup spoons when they were sleeping? Why would they want to be making soup when they're lying down?" (128). The more excited Becca becomes, the less willing Gemma is to answer her question. Unless the reader knows Lanzmann's film, the child's anxiety is inexplicable. In *Shoah*, "stirring" appears in the context of Filip Müller's difficulty in understanding the orders he was given the first time he entered the Auschwitz I crematorium. Müller, who remarkably survived five liquidations of the Auschwitz *Sonderkommando* (the special detail of prisoners who were forced to burn the bodies and normally were killed after a few months), tells Lanzmann of his disbelief when he first saw the corpses: "I couldn't understand any of it" (*Shoah* 49). He describes how an SS man rushed up and told him to go "stir" the bodies; still Müller didn't understand. Like Becca, he asks Lanzmann, "What did he mean,

'Stir the bodies'?" (49). Only when another prisoner told Müller to imitate his action, poking the burning bodies with a steel poker, did Müller learn what stirring meant in the crematorium.

In *Briar Rose*, this horrific context remains hidden, a knowledge that the author possesses and reinscribes in her choice of the word "stirring," but one which she refuses to share with her readers. For similar reasons, even as Yolen incorporates *Shoah* into her text, she abandons its factual brutality through the invention of a fairy tale in which a female survivor is resurrected by the partisans. Srebnik tells Lanzmann a far bleaker story of unloading the Chelmno gas vans: "I remember that once they were still alive. [...] They were all moving, they were coming back to life, and when they were thrown into the ovens, they were all conscious" (Lanzmann, *Shoah* 91). Srebnik speaks of how, as a 13-year-old who had already seen so much horror, he didn't react and possibly didn't understand what he was seeing. Yolen takes his memory of the bodies coming back to life and gives it a happy ending. Despite this ending, she also gives her readers a secondary narrative, one whose lesson lies outside the text, in the final paragraph of her "Author's Note," and its blunt refusal of the story she has just told: "This is a book of fiction. All the characters are made up. Happy-ever-after is a fairy tale notion, not history. I know of no woman who escaped from Chelmno alive" (202).

The history that makes us wish fairy tales did happen, that life were like a children's book and we all lived happily ever after, is not an easy history to read or write. If we persist in thinking that children need hope and happy endings (and I must confess that I believe that they do), then the stories we give them about the Holocaust will be shaped by those expectations, and we will need to consider narrative strategies like Yolen's that give child readers a double narrative, one that simultaneously respects our need for hope and happy endings even as it teaches us a different lesson about history.

Yet when I think of my mother's story, I hesitate, torn between my adult understanding of history and my childhood memory. Even as *Briar Rose* makes me question my childhood belief that my mother was never really at risk and acknowledge how like a fairy tale that belief was, I also recognize how consoling I found it. The story she once told me about the day she was marched into a "shower" room in Birkenau increasingly disturbs me. Her explanation—"They pretended it was the gas chamber to scare us. It wasn't."— gave me the hope and happy ending that we both wanted. But was the room a gas chamber? Were orders given to gas the women and then revoked? Did she survive only because some bit of machinery broke down? The more I learn about what Auschwitz means, the more I question her narrative and my understanding of it. An alternative in which the Nazis were not pretending is just as plausible. What does it say about the questions raised by Siegal's memoir and Yolen's fairy-tale novel, that I now find the story that my mother was not gassed more incomprehensible than the fact that my grandfather was? But how can I say that as a child I would have appreciated a double narrative? The implications of that double narrative frighten me still.

NOTES

1. While the title, "Reading the Shards and Fragments: Holocaust Literature for Young Readers," and focus of his article suggest that Russell is talking about Holocaust literature as a didactic art only in so far as it is presented to young children, there is very little in his argument that allows for the possibility of a Holocaust writing that is not didactic.

2. On Yolen's Website (http://www.janeyolen.com), *Briar Rose* is listed as an adult work; nevertheless it has also been named an ALA Best Book for Young Adults. The Website also contains a link to a high school in Australia that places the novel on the grade 12 curriculum.

3. Yolen's decision to narrate much of the story through the voice of Josef Potocki, a homosexual portrayed sympathetically, may have led to the book being burned in Kansas City, Missouri. On her Website, Yolen discusses the ironies of this burning in relation to the Holocaust subject matter of the book; she also describes her own childhood reading and how she was not harmed by reading books which some might regard as more appropriate for adults.

4. Yolen's Website confirms that she wrote *Briar Rose* after watching *Shoah*: "It suggested the fairy tale 'Sleeping Beauty' in a horrible way." The relationship between the two texts is striking to anyone who reverses this pattern, as I did, when I watched *Shoah* after reading *Briar Rose*.

5. A homodiegetic narrator is a narrator who is also a character. Although such a narrator often speaks in first person, in the section of the novel in which Potocki tells Becca how he saved her grandmother, he refers to himself in third person, "as if he were only a storyteller and not one of the main characters" (136). Through this narrative technique, Yolen emphasizes not only that Potocki is telling Becca a story, but also that as narrator, he is objective about the inadequacy of his character.

3

A Daughter's Endless Mourning:
Maternal Representation in
Isabella Leitner's Memoirs

"We spoke of our houses, of Strasbourg and Turin, of
the books we had read, of what we had studied, of our
mothers: how all mothers resemble each other!" (Levi 101)

Primo Levi's comment on mothers in *Survival in Auschwitz:
The Nazi Assault on Humanity* is a throwaway line, part of a
conversation that quickly moves to his central narrative concern, his attempt to teach a fellow prisoner Italian by reciting
Dante's poetry, as the two men fetch soup one day. By speaking of how "all mothers resemble each other," Levi claims a
human bond that momentarily challenges the world he is in.
In contrast, he turns to Dante, not because the poet resembles other poets, but precisely because the poet is exceptional. Mothers resemble each other; Dante is unique, the one
poet whose language resonates so powerfully, defiantly, and
paradoxically within the *Lager* (camp).[1] Although the memoir's original title in Italian, *Se questo è un uomo* (*If This Is a
Man*), draws attention to the ambiguity concerning Levi's
sense of his identity during this time, reciting Dante, even in
fragments, reminds him that he is still a man and allows him,
if only for a moment, to forget where he is. Levi is both aston-
ished and bewildered; he does not know why Dante has come
to mind, and he soon discovers that he is unable to recite the

entire canto. The resulting chapter, "The Canto of Ulysses,"
remains one of the most moving and disturbing episodes in
the book. When Dante's Ulysses says that men were made to
seek knowledge and excellence, these lines condemn him to
one of the lowest circles of the *Inferno*; in the *Lager* Levi hears
the lines anew. He becomes convinced that they convey
something necessary for "all men who toil" (103).

For Levi, who so rarely sentimentalizes, mothers can
remain part of an unanalyzed comic discourse because he
places them outside the *Lager*: "His mother too had scolded
him for never knowing how much money he had in his
pocket" (101). His own mother remained in Italy; in "The
Canto of Ulysses," he does not consider the reality of what
happens to mothers in the *Lager*.[2] Aware that in the death
camps mothers are killed precisely because they are mothers,
Levi describes what he sees, and what he sees for the very
reason that men and women are separated in the *Lager* is a
world of men, not women.[3] A reader of Holocaust memoirs
written by women sees what Levi does not describe and
learns, perhaps, to be more hesitant about generalizations
regarding mothers. Although one brutal generalization
remains unquestioned—Jewish mothers with small children
are murdered by the Nazis because they are mothers with
small children—the memoirs written by women complicate
the representation of motherhood and daughters' construction of themselves both as daughters and as mothers. In
women's memoirs, mothers do not all resemble each other.

Gender remains a controversial category of Holocaust
analysis. For instance, Yehuda Bauer in his recent collection
of essays, *Rethinking the Holocaust*, titles one chapter, "The
Problem of Gender." His other chapters also examine prob-

lems of thinking about the Holocaust, but in no other chapter title does the word "problem" appear. Bauer concludes that a gender-studies approach is valuable so long as we remain cognizant of the context of Nazi policies that ultimately "did not differentiate between the fate of women and the fate of men" (184).[4] Lawrence L. Langer in "Gendered Suffering: Women in Holocaust Testimonies," similarly questions what role could be played by gender during the extreme conditions of the Holocaust and warns against reading memoirs to draw conclusions about "why some women survived and others did not" (43). While such conclusions would be mistaken, attention to gender can respect the reality of women's experiences and how they represent those experiences. The circumstances under which women were more likely to survive—in hiding, in the ghettos, in the camps—is part of the historical record, one which gender studies can help to clarify. In addition, an attention to gender foregrounds representational issues about why some memoirs are read and others are not, issues that touch on both the larger category of Holocaust memoir and the subcategory of memoirs that we give to children. Reading gender and the shaping of gender to fit the narrative requirements of children's literature on the Holocaust, we become more aware of how women's narratives are rewritten for child readers and how little space there is for trauma narrative in children's texts. We also see how attitudes towards gender and concern about the impact of traumatic discourse upon child readers come together to produce a coherent, non-traumatized voice in children's books, one which says that gender does not matter even as it deletes the specific, if limited, ways that it did.

An analysis of a recent Holocaust bibliography for children immediately raises two gender-specific post-Holocaust facts. The first is that in contrast to the male-authored memoirs that dominate the canon of adult Holocaust discourse —for example, Elie Wiesel's *Night*; Primo Levi's *Survival in Auschwitz*—in children's literature on the Holocaust, women's memoirs far outnumber male memoirs. The second is that the emphasis on women's narratives in memoirs, biographies, and autobiographies for children is not matched by a similar pattern in children's fiction. The basis for this observation is Edward T. Sullivan's *The Holocaust in Literature for Youth*. Sullivan includes 129 works under the heading "Autobiography and Biography": 51 works are about male subjects; 78 are about females. Sullivan's subject index to his entire bibliography lists a total of 17 titles that relate to Anne Frank; 12 appear under "Autobiography and Biography," the others under "Drama" and "Non-fiction." This number of titles about one person is matched only by the number of works about Adolf Hitler. If we exclude the titles that are either by Frank or about Frank from the autobiography and biography list, we are left with 51 per cent indicating female subjects whereas only 39.5 per cent indicate male subjects. If we include the titles about Frank, 60.4 per cent are about female subjects. In contrast, under the heading, "Fiction," Sullivan lists 143 books; excluding the 29 that are either about both men and women or not clearly identified in gender terms, an equal number (57 titles each) are about men and about women.

How do we understand these statistics? Is the difference between the percentage of female subjects to be found in autobiography/biography and the percentage in fiction an indication that when women write Holocaust fiction for children, they tend, like male writers, to write about male subjects? Certainly more women novelists in Sullivan's fiction list write about male subjects than vice versa. Should we conclude that the statistics merely reflect that women have written more memoirs? If they have, how does this relate to other statistics that indicate that fewer women than men survived the concentration camps? If women have not written more memoirs, does Sullivan's list indicate that when women write memoirs, their memoirs are more likely to be regarded as appropriate for children?

Theorizing the reasons behind Sullivan's choice of works is not a futile academic exercise, for it raises other issues about gender and Holocaust representation. In his explanation of the choice of texts, Sullivan rightly acknowledges that "[j]udging what adult titles will have appeal for older teens is tricky business" (9). Yet choosing adult titles that might appeal, he excludes disturbing female adult memoirs, such as Charlotte Delbo's *Auschwitz and After*, thereby indicating that some female adult memoirs are not appropriate for children. What accounts for these decisions? Why does Sullivan include male adult memoirs such as Filip Müller's *Sonderkommando* account, *Eyewitness Auschwitz*, and Rudolf Vrba's *Escape from Auschwitz*? Are the latter two included just because they are memoirs well-known to adults familiar with Claude Lanzmann's *Shoah*? Both Müller and Vrba have major roles in Lanzmann's film. Or are they included because they are graphic and exciting, appealing to already-established gender codes and conventions of children's literature, whereas an equally compelling memoir of a young boy in hiding, Saul Friedländer's *When Memory Comes*, does not, and so is not included?

Certainly biographies and autobiographies about well-known male figures, either adult canonical texts or narratives about rescuers, escapists, and Nazi hunters, dominate the stories about male subjects in Sullivan's autobiography and biography list. For example, 15 out of the 51 titles about male subjects are by or about Primo Levi (2), Elie Wiesel (3), Raoul Wallenberg (4), Janusz Korczak (4), and Oskar Schindler (2). Does the difference between the percentage of female memoirs and female-subject fiction indicate that there is something about female experience in the Holocaust that resists traditional conceptions of children's fiction? Do women write memoirs because the Holocaust stories they want to tell do not fit the narrative patterns of children's fiction? An examination of the narrative choices made when women-authored memoirs are rewritten for children further suggests that the Holocaust memoirs women write also do not always fit the patterns of memoirs read by children, that one major point of resistance is when traumatic narratives refuse to come to terms with the death of the mother.[5] Like Bauer, who considers the "problem of gender" by writing a case study of the life of Gisi Fleischmann, I examine the "problem of gender" through another case study, a detailed reading that focuses on the representation of the maternal in the four Holocaust memoirs published by Isabella Leitner between 1978 and 1994.[6]

The Endless Mourning of Isabella Leitner

In *Saving the Fragments: From Auschwitz to New York*, the second of four Holocaust memoirs written by Isabella Leitner, the narrator questions her obsessive need to return to "that terrible terrain again and again" (*Saving* 49). Not only has her physical liberation not produced an equivalent liberation of memory, but she recognizes also the psychological burden of her memories of Dr. Mengele and her impossible desire to be free of them. It was Mengele who, on May 31, 1944, separated Leitner from her mother and 13-year-old sister, Potyo. Leitner is not satisfied by reports of Mengele's death. The man who presumably drowned in 1978 (Epstein and Rosen 194) is still alive in her mind, torturing her with the memory of his role in the murder of her mother, sister, and so many others. The narrator's frustration turns her to the complexities and challenges that confront the survivor who wishes to tell children about the Holocaust: "Will our children be able to forget what we shall tell them? Will we have the heart to tell them what we know? We will have to, because history cannot be trusted. It distorts. Will anyone believe the unbelievable?" (*Saving* 49).

In its five brief sentences, this quotation raises narrative and ethical issues central to the way the telling of the Holocaust functions as a border between adult and children's texts. Questions about what we should and can tell children about the Holocaust, the purpose behind our telling, and our understanding of what exactly children will find "unbelievable" are relevant in light of the very different narrative choices Leitner makes in each of her four texts. They are particularly resonant in light of the children's book Leitner published immediately after *Saving the Fragments*. Unlike the three memoirs directed at adults and young adults—*Fragments of Isabella: A Memoir of Auschwitz*, 1978; *Saving the Fragments: From Auschwitz to New York*, 1985; and *Isabella: From*

Auschwitz to Freedom, 1994—*The Big Lie: A True Story*, published by Scholastic in 1992, is clearly intended for young children. Not only do so many memoirs complicate the narrator's insistence on a simple opposition between the distortions of history and the truthfulness of the survivor's witness ("history cannot be trusted. It distorts"), the narrative choices of the most clearly identifiable children's book confirm that Leitner herself is unable or unwilling to tell children everything she knows. In *The Big Lie*, she chooses to tell children a very different story from the one that she tells adults.

One of the complexities that necessitates speaking about children without precise age references in Leitner's work is that her memoirs never directly say how old she was when she went to Auschwitz, an omission that is striking given her emphasis on the irony that her birthday—May 28, 1944—is the day she packs for deportation. A single reference to age appears in *Fragments of Isabella* immediately prior to the narrator's appeal to the dead mother to protect her from the threat of death. At the very moment when death seems imminent, perhaps because death does seem imminent, she refers to herself as a child. Although Leitner was 20 in 1944, she clearly thinks of herself as a child, and wants the reader to think of her as a child also. Given this, I do not think that her writing constructs the young adult reader as a category separate from the adult reader. Further evidence for this lies in the way that *Fragments of Isabella* and *Saving the Fragments* have been reviewed as both young adult books and adult books.

In contrast to my reading that sees *The Big Lie* as significantly different from the other three, Sullivan's age categories for the four memoirs indicate no difference and directly contradict information that accompanies the last two memoirs. In the author information provided in the most recent, *Isabella: From Auschwitz to Freedom*, and in *The Big Lie*, only the latter is called a children's book; the other memoirs are called books for adults. According to Sullivan, the first memoir, *Fragments of Isabella*, is appropriate for grades 7 to 12; its sequel, *Saving the Fragments*, is appropriate for grades 6 to 12. In keeping with my perception that the fourth memoir, *Isabella: From Auschwitz to Freedom*, is affected by the writing of the third, Sullivan places it as appropriate for only grades 5 to 10. Particularly puzzling is his decision to give *The Big Lie* the biggest range, grades 5 to 12. No rationale is provided for this.

Complicating what Leitner "knows" is her subject position as both daughter and mother. Although the maternal inspiration behind all her work is undeniable, that inspiration works in two contradictory ways. Writing as the survivor/daughter, Leitner in her adult texts incessantly mourns the murder of her mother, Teresa Katz. Writing as the teacher/mother whose task is to provide some clear knowledge for the child reader, she suppresses the pain of that ongoing mourning even as she attempts to write the future-looking text that her own mother might have written. Paradoxically, the act of writing maternally for children necessitates a muting not only of the dead mother's voice, but of the mother's symbolic role in saving her daughter's life. It is as though the only way Leitner can honour her mother and the values her mother represents is by constructing a maternal narrative voice that is appropriate for young children at the cost of suppressing her complex memories of her own mother, the one she still mourns.

The result of this narrative decision is not just a children's book radically different from the three adult memoirs, but an adult memoir itself influenced by the muting of the mother's positive role in the children's book. One sign of this is the deletion in *Isabella: From Auschwitz to Freedom* of a crucial line in the first memoir that links the narrator's acts of resistance to her listening "to my inner voices, to the infallible truth my mother had taught me" (*Fragments of Isabella* 54). In contrast, although *Isabella: From Auschwitz to Freedom* includes new material that speaks forcefully to the unresolved trauma of her mother's murder (and therefore refutes easy clichés about the healing effects of time), it omits this particular maternal tribute. Given that the omission comes in a book that merges the first two memoirs and deletes little else, a book published only two years after the publication of *The Big Lie*, I can only question whether the minimizing of the mother's role in the children's book has in turn affected the adult work. Regardless of whether this particular deletion was initiated by an editor, Irving A. Leitner (Leitner's spouse and co-author), or by Leitner herself, what is significant is that the deletion appears after Leitner published the children's book.

If the dead mother's legacy is faith in the human potential for goodness, dignity, and humanity, it is also a legacy that her children took for granted. To recall the mother's words is to risk recalling the children's failure to listen to her accurate prediction that Hitler would lose the war but would still destroy the Jewish people. It is to risk recalling what happens, first to the mother's voice and then to her body. Although Teresa Katz is still alive the day that the family prepares to leave the ghetto, her voice is already silent as the daughter remembers too late her mother's warning. To think of her mother's voice is also to recall what the daughter feels as she witnesses the destruction of that maternal faith in the future.

That trauma is recounted in *Fragments of Isabella* when the six children watch in horror as a boy younger than most of them, a 16-year-old SS officer, beats their mother; they know that if they move to defend her, they will only see her murdered in front of them. That this moment remains traumatic is confirmed by the persistence of paralytic language in the adult memoirs—for example, the reenactment of Leitner's traumatic paralysis in 1975 when she recognizes in the faces of German tourists in a Paris bar the possible murderers of her mother, and begs her husband and children to help her because she cannot move. In a new fragment added to *Isabella: From Auschwitz to Freedom*, the narrator similarly explains her inability to visit Kisvárda 34 years after her expulsion: "I was paralyzed by my emotions" (*Isabella* 205).[7]

Unwilling to burden children with the memories that provoke this sense of paralysis, Leitner omits such episodes and such quotations in *The Big Lie*. Yet, this narrative strategy is itself compromised, as she attempts to write a story for young children and is hard-pressed to come up with the lesson such books require. Without the memory of the mother's voice, there is no lesson; survival makes no sense. Attempting to simplify her Holocaust narrative for young children, Leitner presents a catalogue of the factual. But such facts on their own provide no lesson unless we conclude that the narrative's numb tone is itself a lesson, that the daughter who dares not let children know what she still feels about the murder of her mother does not know what else there is to say. The result is a book with a radical disjuncture, similar to that found in Puritan children's poetry in which the moral about the vanity of chasing the butterfly seems totally separate from the pleasure of the poem that precedes it. In the same way, Leitner's "Afterword" to *The Big Lie* functions to provide the lesson and to explain the book's title, a lesson and explanation that are not at all evident in the narrative proper.

The "Afterword" explains that the title is a reference to the big lie repeatedly propagated by Hitler that Jews were responsible for German unemployment. The connection between this abbreviated history lesson (six years of war summed up in six pages) and Leitner's account of her Hungarian family's deportation, imprisonment, and liberation is puzzling. An "Afterword" that spoke about the historical deportation of Hungary's Jews in the spring and summer of 1944 might make sense, but Hungary is not even mentioned; the reluctance of the United States government to grant visas to European Jews, a reluctance that made it impossible for Leitner's father to free his family, is similarly omitted.

In view of all that Leitner omits in *The Big Lie*, the book's title inadvertently hints at a more complicated lying, the lying a mother/writer/survivor must engage in when the very act of remembering her own mother inhibits her from endorsing fully her dead mother's faith in the future. A quote from Elie Wiesel on the dust jacket of *The Big Lie* testifies to the value of survivors' voices; his words assert that survivors speak a truth that is unavailable elsewhere. As true as this may be, the truth of *The Big Lie* is radically different from the truth Leitner expresses in her other texts. And the truth of the "Afterword" is itself framed by a self-consciousness about language, a questioning that also appears elsewhere, such as in "*Lager* Language," a chapter added to *Fragments of Isabella* in the Laurel/Dell 1983 paperback and also included in *Isabella: From Auschwitz to Freedom*. In this chapter, which Leitner says she wrote in Hungarian in 1945, she records "the one language even God cannot understand" (*Isabella* 227). The "Afterword" to *The Big Lie* is equally self-conscious about its diction, first telling us what "[h]istory calls the years 1939 to 1945" (74) and then telling us that we now use the word, Holocaust, to describe what the Nazis did to the Jews. Such language alerts us to the difficulty of finding the right words for the events Leitner is describing. If history cannot be trusted, one reason is the inadequacy of its language. What are the right words for talking to children about the murder of mothers and sisters?

What the terms, "World War II" and "the Holocaust," elide is the specific gendered experience and ongoing suffering of a woman who loses two sisters and a mother. At any time finding the right words for telling children about the death of mothers is a challenge, but how do we tell children about the maternal deaths occasioned by Nazi policy? If we have to tell children about such deaths, are we more or less responsible if we choose not to tell them everything? Leitner implies that she is fulfilling a survivor's painful moral duty; we "have to" tell children "what we know," but the fact that she structures this duty as a question indicates a profound hesitation about it. Children should not forget what we tell them. The exhortation "Never forget" is so familiar, but the narrative voice in *The Big Lie* forces herself to forget, or at least forces herself not to say, what she does not want children to know. For if we tell our children what we know, do we not run the risk of burdening them too, making them inheritors of our nightmares? Are there some things that it is necessary to forget, not to tell children?

The example of Leitner's own mother is useful here, for it is not at all clear that the inspiring final words Leitner attributes to her in the adult memoirs were even spoken by the mother on the train to Auschwitz. Are they words imagined by the daughter who reads in her mother's silence the words she needs to hear? Similarly the mother never says that she knows that she is going to her own death. Preparing for deportation, Leitner remembers her mother's smile and how she is tormented by that silent smile: "deep inside I know she knows" (*Fragments of Isabella* 6). Would Leitner really have preferred that her mother speak the truth that they both suspect? Or is it part of the mother's heroism that she remains silent? Leitner's own silence in *The Big Lie* regarding her response to her mother's death may then be read as a tribute and imitation of her mother's behaviour. The narrative problem relates to a key difference. Leitner can read her mother's silence, but the child reader of *The Big Lie* cannot know what Leitner omits from her text.

Central to these narrative difficulties is the question of belief. How can Leitner convey her personal knowledge of "the unbelievable" to anyone, let alone to children? In a new introduction written in 1993 for her fourth memoir, she alludes to the difficulty she faced in 1945 of needing to speak about her experiences but not knowing who her audience was: her sisters already "knew everything" (*Isabella* 15), and those who were not there could never understand. That she initially wrote her fragments in Hungarian hints that her ideal readers can only be her mother and the other dead. For the rest of us, "Auschwitz was—and is—unfathomable"

(*Isabella* 15). The language that refers to Holocaust events as both "unfathomable" and "unbelievable" is common in survivor memoirs directed at adults, a narrative strategy by which survivors express both their impossible communicative task and their moral resistance to events that they know are all too real.

But to call these events "unfathomable" and "unbelievable" is to indulge in a language of mystery and incomprehension that children's books about the Holocaust do not permit. Why tell children about the Holocaust unless we think that such events can be understood—understood and then avoided? When Leitner writes for children, she excludes the "unbelievable"; orders that the Hungarian Jews could not believe in 1944 are presented as fact in *The Big Lie*. The one time that Leitner uses a word of disbelief, "incredibly" (68) in *The Big Lie*, it refers to the surviving sisters' discovery of a train station that will enable them to leave Germany for Odessa. This exclusion of the "unbelievable" has radical implications for the lesson that Leitner thinks is necessary to market *The Big Lie* as a children's book and suggests that there is an unresolvable contradiction between her own understanding of her life and what she thinks children will and should believe. Are children unwilling to believe that daughters never get over the murder of their mothers? Or is that endless mourning a fact that we do not want to tell children because it is too terrible, because it implies that the Holocaust is not simply an event that happened long ago?

Although Isabella Leitner is the primary author of all four books, her husband, Irving A. Leitner, is named as general editor and author of the Epilogue, "This Time in Paris," in *Fragments of Isabella* and as co-author of the other three texts. Leitner dedicates *Fragments of Isabella* to her husband. The same dedication appears in *Isabella: From Auschwitz to Freedom*, supplemented by a dedication to the United States Holocaust Memorial Museum. The extent of the husband's role in three of the books is uncertain; the smaller font size of "with Irving A. Leitner" that appears on the title page of *The Big Lie* may imply a lesser role, but the copyright page acknowledgment implies something greater. Such complexities of authorship prohibit any simple conclusions that assume that the different narrative choices of the adult and children's texts are Isabella Leitner's alone.

But these choices may be reflective of North American cultural attitudes about what is appropriate in children's reading about the Holocaust and in the way a woman survivor speaks about her Holocaust experience, whether to children or to adults.[8] Despite the truth of Judith Miller's ironic conclusion, "the Holocaust does not 'teach'" (279), there may well be (as there is in the material that Miller examines) a "lesson" in Leitner's multiple tellings. It is a lesson about the challenges of Holocaust representation and the difficulty of telling children about the Holocaust. Above all, it is a lesson about the complications that ensue when the daughter who mourns and the mother who teaches are one and the same, but our genre distinctions—children's literature; adult memoir—and the psychological suppositions that support them demand that we treat them separately.

There are numerous differences between *The Big Lie* and the three adult memoirs—for example, the shift from fragments and present tense in the adult memoirs to the coherent chapters and past tense in *The Big Lie*—but the most striking is the erasure of the anger, fury, and grief of the daughter-survivor who cannot forget the murder of her mother in the gas chambers of Auschwitz, and how this erasure in turn affects the very possibility and nature of a lesson. This anger and grief infuses the adult texts with the memory of the mother's voice, eyes, and smile as a never-ending torment. Despite the uplifting title of the most recent memoir, *Isabella: From Auschwitz to Freedom*, and the more coherent organization presenting a chronological narrative that seemingly celebrates the move from Auschwitz to Liberation to America, the additional fragments, in particular the three new entries at the end, reinforce the adult memoirs' focus on the traumatic loss of the mother. Indeed, the clarity achieved in *Isabella: From Auschwitz to Freedom* by the chronological reorganization of the material covered in *Fragments of Isabella* and *Saving the Fragments* does not fit the accompanying complicated textual apparatus that remains as fragmentary and contradictory as the multiple memoirs themselves. Preceding the three "books" of the memoir proper is a new poem, "May 31, 1944,"—the day that the mother and sister are murdered—and a new introduction; following it is both the epilogue of the first memoir and the introduction, now renamed an "Afterword," to the second.

With the exception of the "Afterword," such narrative confusion and complex textual apparatus are notably absent in the children's version. *The Big Lie* begins with an autobiographical voice that provides necessary facts, the narrator's first name and the name of the town where she lived. The narrator soon shifts to first person plural, a voice that accompanies the way that *The Big Lie* excludes the numerous gendered details of the adult memoirs. Such details include not only the narrator's incessant mourning of her mother, but also her relationship with her sisters and the many observations about other mothers and babies. They include her memory of menstruation in the cattle car, her fear of rape by Russian soldiers, her sister's love affair after the war, and their father's opposition because the young man is not an orthodox Jew.

Instead, the first person plural voice in *The Big Lie* calmly and carefully controls all personal references, particularly references to the mother. In Chapter Two, more facts are provided. Since everything happened, nothing is "unbelievable." Orders are given that the Hungarian Jews cannot believe, but they comply. The order to wear a yellow star is followed by a factual reference to the mother sewing such stars. When the family arrives in the ghetto, the mother calmly tells her six adolescent children to clean their space so that they do not get sick. The narrator does not pass judgment on the wisdom of her mother's advice; she simply reports. Similarly in Chapter Three, describing the train ride to Auschwitz, the narrator allows herself only one brief reference to her mother: "Mama held Potyo close to her body" (*Big Lie* 34). A double-spread map of the train journey from Kisvarda to Auschwitz separates Chapters Three and Four. It is a highly stylized map in which there are, with the exception of Budapest and Odessa, no towns except for those that the train drives through. No other towns matter.

The unnamed mother (she is identified as Teresa Katz only in the adult texts) and Potyo, the youngest sister to whom Leitner dedicates *The Big Lie*, are gassed upon arrival in Auschwitz. This traumatic memory obviously torments the author, for, in every text she writes, she repeats the dates she cannot forget: May 28, 1944, her own and her mother's birthday; May 29, 1944, departure to the ghetto; May 31, 1944, arrival in Auschwitz. In *Fragments of Isabella*, the late fragment, "May," acknowledges that, since 1944, the scent of May is "the smell of burning flesh. The burning flesh was your mother" (94). The narrator in the adult memoirs states bluntly that time does not heal. If she now has moments in May when she does not smell burning flesh, "That is not happiness, only relief" (94). The book that she wishes to write but cannot is the one that would address the dead mother unambiguously: "I want to tell my mother that I kept her faith, that I lived because she wanted me to" (94-95). She wants to, but the daughter's anger and grief keep getting in the way. It is always one of her siblings whom Leitner praises for behaviour that reflects the mother's values; for Leitner herself, the tension between her mother's values and the counter-values of her own memories problematize any simple endorsement. The answers that mothers teach are unbalanced by the questions daughters learn in Auschwitz.

On the train, Leitner imagines the mother instructing her children to see beyond the world of Auschwitz, to look forward and have faith: "You can nourish your children's souls and minds, and teach them that man is capable of infinite glory" (*Fragments of Isabella* 16-17). Despite these imagined words, the tone in the adult texts is coarse, bitter, and ironic. The first night in Auschwitz, Philip (Leitner's brother) finds his four surviving sisters and tells them: "Eat. If they give you shit, eat shit. Because we must survive" (*Fragments of Isabella* 27). When Leitner and two of her sisters escape during a forced march to Bergen-Belsen, the harshness of Philip's language returns: "the cycle of eating and shitting does not stop" (82). Even the American visas that Leitner's father obtains too late are understood this way: "They could be framed ... or used for toilet paper" (9).

In Chapter Four of *The Big Lie*, it is not just Philip's excremental language that is softened and modified, but the inscribing of the mother's words and the mother's faith as essential to how Leitner understands and remembers her own survival. For example, Leitner gives two versions of messages that Philip sends his four sisters in Auschwitz. In *The Big Lie*, he sends his love and urges the sisters to survive. In *Fragments of Isabella*, he adds two reasons for them to survive—revenge and the determination to "build a future free of bloodshedding" (29). Leitner repeats Philip's final exhortation in the memoir's concluding sentence when she vows to her dead mother that she will teach her children "to love life, to respect man, and to hate only one thing—war" (98). Yet, despite this vow and the way she implies that its content links her to the teaching and voice of her mother, Leitner elects not to pass this maternal tribute on to the child readers of *The Big Lie* and then deletes the sentence containing the vow to the mother in *Isabella: From Auschwitz to Freedom*.

Similarly, Leitner mentions in both *The Big Lie* and *Fragments of Isabella* that in the workcamp, Birnbaumel, as a form of resistance she would stop digging as soon as the guards turned away. But it is only in *Fragments of Isabella* that she links this resistance and her survival to the words of her dead mother: "My mother had told me not to aid my enemy. In that forest in Birnbaumel in December, I remembered her. I honored her and kept myself alive" (53). Significantly, *Isabella: From Auschwitz to Freedom* qualifies Leitner's conviction that it is the daughter's obedience to the mother's words that keeps her alive. The confident causal relationship between honouring the mother and keeping herself alive is replaced by the more tentative, "I honored her and tried to keep myself alive" (62). Such omissions and revisions indicate more than the different choices Leitner makes when writing for children in The Big Lie; they indicate how the need to suppress traumatic memories about the mother in the children's text affects in turn the presentation of the mother in the final adult text. There, Leitner still honours her mother, but the positive connection between that tribute and her own survival seems less evident even as the trauma remains.

What is even more apparent is that the never-ending horror of losing the mother cannot be represented in The Big Lie, as though its suppression marks the border between the coherent knowledge of the children's version and the traumatized adult texts. In The Big Lie, the mother's words are minimally reported: the futile shout to her children upon arrival in Auschwitz that they stay together, and then, after Mengele sends the mother and younger sister, Potyo, to the left, a final maternal statement, "Be strong [...]. I love you" (42). In Chapter Five where the narrative voice must calmly explain to the child reader what Auschwitz was, the mother's death is reported only in the context of, and as illustration of, the method of the general killing: "Those sent to the left by Dr. Mengele, like Mama and Potyo, were led directly to their deaths" (46). There are no further references to the mother.

The extent of the erasure, the deliberate omission of Leitner's personal grief and anger in The Big Lie through a controlled maternal voice that teaches children the facts that they need to know, is striking when one reads the adult memoirs. Even in Isabella: From Auschwitz to Freedom, in which the two earlier adult memoirs are put together, Leitner can generate at most only "a measure of peace" (16). The three adult memoirs fit her work within the traumatic realism described and praised by Michael Rothberg, a traumatic realism whose pedagogy "refuses both to supply a redemptive ending [...] and to give up on attempts to communicate the extreme" (155). The pedagogy of *The Big Lie* works more conventionally, through an erasure of the personal voice to achieve the placidity that explains to young children what Auschwitz was. Such placidity can only be achieved by excluding the tormented self-definition of the adult memoirs: "We were born of mothers the smell of whose burning flesh permeates the air" (*Fragments of Isabella* 49). This tormented self-definition also explains "what Auschwitz was," but it is an explanation that terrifies, more in keeping with how, "traumatic realism produces knowledge, but not consolation" (Rothberg 156).

Most would agree that such exclusions are necessary to the way Holocaust literature is presented to young children. Hazel Rochman in her review of *The Big Lie* praises Leitner's discretion, her emphasis on "[o]nly the facts" (982), and her narrative decisions: "There's no rhetoric, no tears, no hand-wringing about 'atrocity' and 'horror.' The book is short, the type spacious. Just facts. The telling has the elemental power of the best children's literature, in which the simplicity is poetic and speaks volumes" (982). The casual reference to poetic simplicity and speaking volumes indicates how easily we accept the minimizing of the impact of the mother's death as a necessary feature of the best children's literature. How does this silence speak? Do we really believe that children can hear in silence what we imagine would traumatize them if written down? The surprising implication that it is adults who need more than facts, whereas for children facts alone are sufficient, fails to recognize that unresolved grief and anger over the death of one's mother could itself be considered a "fact." It also ignores another cultural "fact," that adults too are uncomfortable when women mourn their mothers too long (and that maybe this "fact" is reinforced in the children's books that they once read).

In the adult memoirs, it is the obsession with her mother's death that marks them as adult. While the title of the second memoir, *Saving the Fragments: From Auschwitz to New York*, implies a resolution to the story begun in *Fragments of Isabella*, that shaping and chronology are false to Leitner's incessant and traumatized return to what the adult writer clearly regards as the central event of her life, the loss of her mother. *Saving the Fragments* begins with an epigraph about May 31, 1944, the day that Leitner cannot forget because it is the day her mother was murdered. The narrator is still tormented by that fact. This epigraph appears in an even more forceful manner in *Isabella: From Auschwitz to Freedom* in that its original reference to a period of "forty years" is now too brief and the word "decades" (11) must take its place. The smoke of her mother burning will remain forever. In all the adult memoirs, Leitner mentions that she can no longer recall the names of key individuals. Their names have disappeared, but the memory of the physical loss of the mother—the scent of burning flesh—never disappears.

Such a relentless vision is troubling even in an adult text and very remote from the vision of the female author constructed by Howard Fast's introduction to *Saving the Fragments*, an introduction that complicates any simple binary relationship between what can be said in children's and adult texts about the Holocaust. What can be said by a woman is also at issue, for Fast's introduction is remarkable in its deliberate refusal to acknowledge the extent of Leitner's anger and grief. Fast calls Leitner "an innocent. [...]A young girl" (*Saving* x), whose "very existence is an affirmation of life, a song of hope, [and, tactlessly] a clear bright flame that defies the murderers of mankind" (x). But where are the hope and innocence in the narrator who rejoices at the chaos at the end of the war and arrives in the United States resentful of the pressure to provide hope for others? Insisting on reading her story as one of love and redemption, Fast infantilizes and feminizes Leitner's account, discounting the possibility that her stylistic choice of fragments is deliberate and offers its own analysis of her experience. Instead, he insists that the book is better for not being analytical—how could a young girl analyze? Given such authorial innocence and youth, Fast concludes that it is up to him to draw the lesson and direct the reader to the purpose of Leitner's book, a pointing that inadvertently and ironically shows that such a lesson is not apparent, that Leitner's memoir is not so easily reduced to the hopeful lessons many North American readers wish to take from Holocaust writing. Fast must tell us the lesson in case we miss it and falsely think that young girls or older women have a right to their anger: "These fragments are a [...] a sermon on the wonder and goodness and value of life. All is possible if men and women deal in trust and love" (*Saving* 12).

How can Fast derive this lesson from a book that begins with the torment of the narrator's smoke-filled eyes, that continually refers to her pain and anger, that calls into doubt the very possibility of healing? Simple faith in "wonder and goodness and value of life" is not conveyed by the narrative voice that mourns her mother, grieves over the death of two sisters, and recognizes the alienation between the surviving sisters and their father. To find a sermon when the adult memoirs deliberately avoid any simple explanations for the narrator's survival—was it the support of her sisters? Her prayer to her mother? Chance? The unnamed attaché who arranged that the three surviving sisters leave for America on the next available military ship?—is a further demonstration of Fast's determination to make Leitner's memoir say only what he thinks it should. That his reading of *Saving the Fragments* is now reprinted as part of the textual apparatus of *Isabella: From Auschwitz to Freedom* is further evidence of the cultural need to direct the reader away from Leitner's unresolved trauma. Simply repeating the titles of the additional three concluding chapters, "I went home … I did not," "Scents and Images," and "Fear" indicates how this final memoir ends with a woman who can never be free, but is always trapped in two times, the present, and 1944.[9] In the final chapter of *Isabella: From Auschwitz to Freedom*, Leitner explains that in 1990 she attended a concert given by German musicians, for she reasoned that the players were born "decades after their elders melted down my mother" (210). Yet as soon as she heard German spoken by older people at a reception after the concert, she suddenly questioned her American freedom, a questioning that changes the way we read the title of the memoir. When the final chapter is called "Fear," the freedom promised by the title is fragile.

Fast is not alone in his insistent cheerfulness. A *School Library Journal* review of *Saving the Fragments* is clearly relieved that Leitner's "upbeat style [...] assures readers of her desire to put the past behind her and get on with her life" (Spencer

114). Another more astute reviewer in *Kirkus Reviews* recognizes that Leitner has not been able to put the past behind her and therefore pans the book for its subjectivity and failure to give North American readers the kind of moral and affirmative ending that they look for in Holocaust stories: "Basically it falls flat at the end. [...] Leitner went through hell and lived to tell about it, and nobody doubts the nobility and goodness of her instincts. But it takes more than good instincts to make a vital book" (702). There is nothing "upbeat" about Leitner's concluding reference to the silences that accompany the surviving daughters' reunion with the father who had escaped to the United States in 1939, but was unable to obtain visas for his wife and children. The chapter in which the daughters are reunited with the father is called "Lying to My Father."

In contrast, the epilogue to *Fragments of Isabella*, "This Time in Paris" written by Irving A. Leitner, refuses to find a hopeful lesson and insists upon Leitner's continuing torment. Towards the end of *Fragments of Isabella*, the fragments become increasingly brief and inconclusive as though Leitner is struggling and failing to find the closure that readers demand. Arriving in the USA on May 8, 1945, the very day that the war ends in Europe, she speaks of the giant and invisible Sorrow that accompanies her, her vision of the dead that a year later keeps her from seeing her own face in the mirror. "May" becomes an annual reminder not of her birthday, but of the time "The world ended" (94); "Peter" is the son whose birth she announces to her dead mother; "Richard" is the second son who is "the sound of [the mother's] soul" (98). But not even the birth of two children gives closure, for Leitner still begs the mother to help her, "Help me, Mama. Help me to see only life" (97).

The Epilogue that follows with its account of two vacations in Europe (1960 and 1975) confirms that, for her husband, the only lesson in *Fragments of Isabella* is the one that refuses closure, that acknowledges the survivor's continuing anger, fury, and paralyzing grief. The last night of the Leitner family's second trip to Paris, in the Café Cristal (another *Kristallnacht?*), Leitner is overcome when a group of German-speaking tourists surround her table. The sound of the German they speak, their appearance and age, paralyze her: "He could be the one who killed my mother" (110).

The function of this epilogue in which the spouse and the son, Peter, come to the aid of the still traumatized survivor is very different from the "Afterword" that replaces it in *The Big Lie*. Like the striking difference conveyed by the two titles, the one speaks to the shattering of the self, the other strives to give the child reader a coherent explanation for the Holocaust. It is fitting that in the Epilogue it is the adolescent son, Peter, who wants to help his mother. Back in their hotel, he prints the words, "AUSCHWITZ, BERGEN-BELSEN, DACHAU" (111), but he is unable to reenter the café to give his note to the Germans. In the end, his father enters the café, places the note on a tray, and delivers it. Whether the tourists are indeed affected by the accusation of these words is left unsaid. What is important is the father's recognition that he must do this for his children, for the final line of the epilogue refers to his emergence from the café and walking back, not to his wife, but to his children.

What the "Afterword" and epilogue do share is a structural similarity, one in which the "lesson" is detached and

separate from the survivor's narrative, a separation that problematizes the very idea of a lesson and the ability of the sur-
vivor/memoirist to write it. The difference between the two
endings indicates that it is not enough to say piously that we
must tell children about the Holocaust. What we tell them
and how we tell them (let alone what they hear when we tell
them) is far more complicated. When children's books
demand a narrative voice whose primary function is to explain
events, the writer whose adult texts dispute the possibility of
such coherence, clarity, and explanation is faced with difficult
narrative decisions, decisions that may necessitate excising
the very daughterly grief that motivates her writing.

Hence when David L. Russell concludes "Reading the
Shards and Fragments: Holocaust Literature for Young
Readers," by rhetorically asking, "What is appropriate for
young readers?" and then answers, "The truth, the truth, the
truth" (279), I find the force of his wishful thinking beside
the point. What is "the truth" in Leitner's multiple tellings?
The dust jacket's claim that *The Big Lie* will give children
hope for the future is hardly descriptive of a book whose only
reference to the future is the concluding sentence, "We were
ready to start life anew in America" (72), and whose factual
narrative gives the young reader no advice on how to achieve
that desired end. Similarly, Russell's well-intentioned exhortation elides the difficulty of reconciling the "truth" we tell
children and Leitner's tormented vision of the dead mother.
The truths that Leitner cannot tell children are multiple and
maternal. They include the painful, far from hopeful, truth of
Saving the Fragments: "But my pain and anger keep intruding,
however hard I try to fix my gaze on the road that is supposed to deliver me into the future" (*Saving* 41). They also

include the "unbelievable" possibility that Leitner escaped the bullet of the *Oberscharführer* on January 23, 1945 because of an intercession from her dead mother. Having appealed to an indifferent God, the terrified daughter prays to her mother as the *Oberscharführer* approaches the daughters' hiding place. Suddenly he is gone: "What happened?" (*Fragments of Isabella* 71).

In the world of "the unbelievable" that constitutes the Holocaust universe, this question, with its obvious suggestion that Teresa Katz did save her daughters' lives, can only be written in an adult text.[10] Adults may question whether the mother did intercede, but such questions are themselves further evidence of an adult text. When we insist that children's texts must explain the Holocaust, we are quite able to tell them that six million Jews died (that horrific fact is believable). However, questions about survival that find their answer in a place for the dead mother remain in the realm of "the unbelievable," part of the daughter's story that Leitner must omit as she struggles to tell children what she knows and to keep faith with her dead mother's promise: "wherever I'll be, in some mysterious way, my love will overcome my death and will keep you alive" (*Fragments of Isabella* 17). It is unclear if Teresa Katz spoke these words in the cattle car, or if Leitner heard them through her mother's silence and gave them voice when she wrote her adult memoirs. What is clear, however, is that these are words that are not said in *The Big Lie*.

NOTES

1. An *Arbeitslager* is a work camp. Levi rarely uses the word Auschwitz; interested in analyzing the world that the Nazis create in the camps, he uses the words that he heard in the *Lager*.

2. Mirna Cicioni indicates that after Germany in September 1943 made Mussolini head of a puppet Italian Social Republic in northern Italy, many Italian Jews went into hiding. Levi's mother hid in the mountains north of Turin (14-15).

3. Soon after they arrive at the *Lager*, the men ask what has happened to their women. Levi does not trust the answers he hears and is convinced that the Germans will kill all of them.

4. In Myrna Goldenberg's terms, women's memoirs document "different horrors within the same Hell" (327).

5. Another memoir about a daughter and her mother that exists in multiple versions is by Livia Bitton-Jackson. Sullivan includes two and states that *I Have Lived a Thousand Years: Growing Up in the Holocaust* is an adaptation for younger readers of Bitton-Jackson's first memoir, *Elli: Coming of Age in the Holocaust* (17).

6. Gisi Fleischmann was one of the leaders of the Working Group, an underground organization in Slovakia that attempted through bribery of Nazi and local officials to stop the deportation initially of Slovak Jews, and later, through the Europa Plan, of all Jews. Fleischmann was deported to Auschwitz in October 1944. Bauer indicates that "No one knows how she was killed" (183).

7. Leitner's birthplace, Kisvárda, appears with the accent in the adult memoirs; in *The Big Lie: A True Story*, Kisvarda has no accent.

8. Editorial choices and publishers' views on how to market the Holocaust are a further complication.

9. The reprinting of Fast's misleading introduction is parallel to the continuing inclusion of François Mauriac's problematic Foreword to Elie Wiesel's *Night*.

10. The role of a dead mother in protecting the daughter by making her invisible appears frequently in women's memoirs. See, for example, Rena Kornreich Gelissen's *Rena's Promise: A Story of Sisters in Auschwitz* in which we are told that the enraged camp elder is unable to see the injuries on the narrator's face because the mother's spirit masks them.

PART TWO

◆

The Voices of Children

4

Reading Anne Frank Today: Lessons, Innocence, and the Voices of Children

"The absolute, however, is a treacherous place to seek lessons." (Gourevitch, "Behold Now Behemoth" 62)

Near the beginning of *We Wish to Inform You That Tomorrow We Will be Killed with Our Families: Stories from Rwanda*, Philip Gourevitch asks why anyone would read his book. Imagining a reader who hopes "for some understanding, some insight, some flicker of self-knowledge — a moral, or a lesson," Gourevitch hesitates: "I don't discount the possibility, but when it comes to genocide you already know right from wrong" (19). By questioning the necessity of reading for "a moral, or a lesson," he separates the motive of his implied adult reader from the didactic framework that governs much writing for children. Adults do not read about genocide to learn that genocide is wrong: "you already know" this. Examining his own motivation for writing about Rwanda, Gourevitch similarly concludes that he is not really looking for the right way "to behave in this world" (19). Such words seem too positive: "The best reason I have come up with for looking closely into Rwanda's stories is that ignoring them makes me even more uncomfortable about existence and my place in it" (19). He then probes his motives even further: "The horror, as horror, interests me only insofar as a precise

memory of the offense is necessary to understand its legacy"
(19). Although words like "memory" and "legacy" often
appear in the rhetoric of children's lessons, here they resonate
differently, more as questions than as answers. What is the
legacy? Uncertain of the answers, Gourevitch's language
remains deeply and self-consciously moral. Repeatedly he
challenges the reader: what does justice mean when we are
talking about genocide?

Elsewhere Gourevitch has contrasted his personal
response to images of horror with the widespread insistence
that in viewing such images we (and particularly children)
will find useful lessons. In "Behold Now Behemoth: The
Holocaust Memorial Museum: One more American theme
park," a review that appeared in *Harper's Magazine* in July
1993, he turns away from an exhibit to write in his notebook
that the images come with a context that may not be the one
that is intended by the museum staff: "[s]nuff films. Naked
women led to execution" (60). Knowing that the images are
meant to function pedagogically, he objects: "The problem
was simply that I could not make out the value in going
through this" (60). That Gourevitch is himself the child and
grandson of refugees who fled the Nazis might lead us to
expect him to see some possible "value in going through this,"
but it is the very memory of his childhood nightmare of running away, the nightmare occasioned by his family's own
history, that contributes to his dilemma.' Even as a child, he
realized that "Nothing could be learned" (55) from his nightmare; now, as an adult, he is equally unable to see any complex lesson emerging from a museum precisely designed, he
can only conclude, so that children can walk through nightmare. The only lesson that the adult Gourevitch is willing to

derive from the Holocaust is the simple fact of its occurrence. Thus, he repeatedly interrogates the museum's educational premise that links the Holocaust with lessons about American civic responsibility. Categorizing the museum as a "monument against absolute evil," Gourevitch warns that "[t]he absolute [...] is a treacherous place to seek lessons" (62) and insists that "political and ethical madness [...] teaches nothing about political and ethical sanity" (62).

Questions about the cultural function of the museum reoccur in *We Wish to Inform You That Tomorrow We Will be Killed with Our Families*, particularly when Gourevitch describes a later visit to Washington (dated May 1994). Standing in line at the museum, identified in the text only as "an immensely popular tourist attraction" (151), he contrasts the lapel buttons that urge visitors to remember with the front-page newspaper photograph of contemporary genocide victims. The tension between the rhetoric of "never again" and what Gourevitch sees in Rwanda is central to his project: "for all the fine sentiments inspired by the memory of Auschwitz, the problem remains that denouncing evil is a far cry from doing good" (170).[2]

Gourevitch's frustration with fine sentiments and his questions about the lessons invoked by the memory of Auschwitz cast a useful light on our obsession with explaining, defending, challenging, and revising Anne Frank. In asking why we read about historically real horror, why we believe that children will profit from exposure to the artifacts of horror, and in writing about other children destroyed by genocide, Gourevitch may seem far removed from recent questioning regarding Frank. Yet his questions are not that different from those expressed by Holocaust scholars concerned about Frank's central role as the voice of the child who speaks the lessons which govern the books we give to children. Such scholars are disturbed by the way that her voice has come to speak some essential truth about the Holocaust, a truth that appears not only misleadingly hopeful but that for that very reason is acceptable classroom material. This chapter frames the debate over Frank with Gourevitch's words, but it also positions the debate in the context of the different lessons offered by other voices of childhood. In Cynthia Ozick's "The Shawl," Binjamin Wilkomirski's *Fragments: Memories of a Wartime Childhood,* and Zlata Filipović's *Zlata's Diary: A Child's Life in Sarajevo,* the voices of childhood are strikingly different from Frank's voice; what remains constant is the adult need to hear in those voices a lesson about innocence.

The Voice of Anne Frank

Within the classroom, a narrowly framed pedagogical debate controls both Anne Frank's *The Diary of a Young Girl*[3] and the Frances Goodrich and Albert Hackett play, *The Diary of Anne Frank.* The young diarist who, on March 29, 1944, responded to a radio broadcast about a possible postwar publication of diaries by imagining publishing a novel whose very title, *The Secret Annex,* would mislead readers into "think[ing] it was a detective story" (Frank 240), who told her diary in the same entry, "Although I tell you a great deal about our lives, you still know very little about us" (240), who wrote on April 14, 1944, "I seriously doubt whether anyone will ever be interested in this drivel" (259), has been for many years the subject of lesson plans and educators' conferences. A 1964 high school edition of the play (an edition I cannot recall using, but one still available for purchase in 1999) comes complete with 11 pages of "Notes and Questions" including a list of 22 "General Questions." The final one asks, "Could the story of the Frank family ever be enacted in Canada? Discuss" (Goodrich and Hackett 101).

The much more detailed *Diary* guides available today include comparable questions, which often, despite their initially open-ended nature, quickly limit the range of acceptable answers. In a recent guide, the author instructs the teacher to reassure students "that you are going to be learning *with* them as you embark on your study of the Holocaust" (Moger 8). Nevertheless, here too, the parenthetical information following supposedly open questions determines the parameters of the permissible answers: "Can you think of times in American history when to speak out was a matter of life and death?" (28). Before the child can respond, the parenthesis begins: "(In the 1960s, for example, civil rights activists were murdered. But [...] the federal government did finally step in. No national policy of annihilation existed as it did in Nazi Germany)" (28). The possibility that a child might successfully challenge the final statement seems as unlikely today as that I, in 1964, might have argued that the story of the Frank family could well have taken place in Canada.

The lesson that the *Diary* offers today may not be identical to the hopeful lesson about spiritual triumph celebrated in the 1950s or to the counter-lesson castigating Otto Frank that is implicit in Bruno Bettelheim's 1960 essay, "The Ignored Lesson of Anne Frank." Yet as soon as we give children the *Diary*, we seem compelled to frame their reading with our pedagogical expectations.[4] Our underlying anxiety about children's reading about the Holocaust—an anxiety inscribed in Ursula F. Sherman's title, "Why Would a Child Want to Read about That? The Holocaust Period in Children's Literature"—inevitably produces the need for a clear educational outcome in which the lesson gained somehow compensates for the innocence lost, and we engage in endless debates over how to tell children about the Holocaust and to what degree this telling will and should affect their innocence. And such pedagogical conversations continue; the *Stratford Festival of Canada Visitors' Guide 2000* advertises a teachers' conference on Shakespeare and the Holocaust, a conference that will feature performances of *The Diary of Anne Frank* and *Hamlet*. The brochure says that the Goodrich and Hackett play has been "newly adapted" by Wendy Kesselman, but the novelty of the adaptation is not apparent in the well-known quotation that the brochure highlights, "I still believe, in spite of everything, that people are really good at heart" (*Stratford* 13).

Following the many scholars who object to the dominant role played by the *Diary* in children's reading, and writers, such as Cynthia Ozick, who asserts that the *Diary* is not a Holocaust book at all ("Who Owns Anne Frank?" 78), educators and librarians have either emphasized that children should not read just the *Diary*[5] or they have produced detailed teachers' guides that supplement the relatively reassuring story it tells. With elaborate titles like *Understanding Anne Frank's The Diary of a Young Girl: A Student Casebook to Issues, Sources, and Historical Documents* and *Teaching the Diary of Anne Frank: An In-Depth Resource for Learning About the Holocaust Through the Writings of Anne Frank*, the lengthy subtitles alone indicate the problems of an approach that places the weight of a child's Holocaust understanding on a single book. Their approach also presumes that the role of the *Diary* as a primary source of children's understanding is not likely to change.[6]

For this reason, the guides are meticulous in providing contextual historical information that is either statistical (how many Dutch children survived in hiding? How many returned from the camps?) or narrative (other victim and survivor stories), as well as biographical information regarding Anne's life and death beyond her final diary entry. In *Understanding Anne Frank's The Diary of a Young Girl*, Hedda Rosner Kopf not only includes her own mother's account of Bergen-Belsen as a way of imagining the final days of Anne Frank, but she also acknowledges that the "diary has often been appropriated by those who wish to turn [Anne Frank's] thoughtful adolescent musings into truths for all of us to live by" (58). In contrast, Susan Moger in *Teaching the Diary of Anne Frank* is less willing to separate the *Diary* from its optimistic pedagogical function. Instead, she balances the famous uplifting *Diary* quotation, "In spite of everything I still believe that people are really good at heart" with another, less optimistic, and less well-known one, "There's in people simply an urge to destroy, an urge to kill, to murder and rage" (82).[7] Yet the hopeful pedagogical framework does not alter, despite a hesitancy that leads Moger to write, "By learning about the Holocaust, we *may* [my italics] prevent it ever happening again" (8). In a later section called "Teaching About the Unthinkable," she abandons her initial doubt regarding the impact of such study and reassuringly spells out what is the "essential lesson to take away from this saddest of stories"

(87), a lesson about the power of "ordinary people" to carry out the Holocaust and their equal power to "prevent [its] horrors [...] from sweeping the world again" (87).

However accurate Ozick's critique of the ways that the *Diary* has been misused,[8] many North American parents continue to object to their children reading it. Anticipating this, Moger includes a sample letter for teachers to send to families to justify its pedagogical relevance. Like the image of a gigantic Anne and her diary hovering over the world that appears as the concluding illustration in the picture book, *Anne Frank*, by Yona Zeldis McDonough, and like the continuing popular interest in theatrical revivals or newspaper reports of the discovery of a few unpublished diary pages, Moger's careful letter undercuts any likelihood that other Holocaust children's books will replace its central importance.[9]

Paradoxically, one reason for this centrality is that we seem reluctant to abandon our belief in innocence. As soon as we speak about children and war, references to the loss of childhood innocence are predictable.[10] Despite the ease with which a postmodern age acknowledges the ideological basis to our notions of childhood, the concept of innocence not only determines how we imagine the voices of children, but the lessons that we demand are frequently, though problematically, contingent on that innocence. A good example is Karen Shawn's excellent guide for grades 8 and up, *The End of Innocence: Anne Frank and the Holocaust*, designed as a one-week curriculum, with a chapter "Lesson" for every day of the week. Shawn's questions are far more open-ended than those in many other guides. Reminding adolescents who may desire "simple solutions to complex problems" (39) that,

according to Erik Erikson, Hitler displayed a similar adolescent need, she seeks to provide a "counterpoint to Anne's
voice" (1), one through which students reach a knowledge
that the "pure, clear voice" (1) of Anne could never speak."
Not only does Shawn advise the student "For the end of
innocence is the beginning of knowledge" (3), but she also
subtitles her fifth and final lesson, "Beyond the Diary—the
End of Innocence" (ix). After quoting a passage in which
Frank is hopeful of the future, Shawn contrasts Frank's ignorance with the knowledge of the post-Holocaust child:
"When she wrote those words, she did not know what her
fate was to be. When we read those words, we do know" (39).

But where does innocence reside? Clearly Shawn's lesson
plans indicate that children's Holocaust pedagogy values
knowledge over innocence. Despite our desire to protect the
child reader and to imagine children's literature as an innocent space, the end of innocence is the goal of any pedagogy.
In contrast, innocence in adult texts functions in a very
different way; the child protagonist in adult texts sees far
more than the child protagonist in a children's book, yet the
former tends to remain incapable of understanding what she
sees. Describing the child's mind in adult books as "at once
open and uncomprehending" (13), Naomi B. Sokoloff argues
that in such texts "the young character's incomprehension
serves to indicate the incomprehensibility of the catastrophe"
(*Imagining the Child* 15). In contrast, in children's books, whatever the limitations on what the child protagonist sees, the
narrative moves towards giving the child (both protagonist
and reader) clarity of insight. The child reader reads in order
to know. To use the figure of the child "as a way to sidestep
trying to formulate an interpretation of evil that defies

understanding" (Sokoloff, "Childhood Lost" 262) suits the demands of adult readers far more than child readers.

A further irony is that, despite how adult texts conceive the child's mind as innocent and uncomprehending, many adults insist that in their own childhood they were far from innocent. Defining adulthood by their distance from both the lessons imposed in childhood and the innocence that supposedly defined them as children, they protest, as does Nina Auerbach, "When I was Anne Frank's age, I hated Anne Frank, and so did other disaffected American Jewish girls in the 1950s" (8). In her review of Melissa Müller's *Anne Frank, the Biography*, Auerbach recollects a very different collective identity from the one often taken for granted in accounts of the *Diary*'s "universal" appeal. She qualifies her dramatic dislike by further confessing, "but some of us used her too, to escape from lives we thought were awful, and for this callowness I still cringe" (8).

Although I do not share Auerbach's adolescent memory of being "haunted" by Anne Frank (Auerbach 8), I agree with her questioning of the *Diary*'s "universal" appeal.[12] Unlike Auerbach, I have no childhood memory of having read the *Diary*, seen the play, or the film. My diary entry for May 3, 1960, tells me that I did see the film, but in its minimal reporting of three apparently equivalent events, it reveals little else: "We saw 'Ann [sic] Frank' at the Plaza. We took our balls to school. The two Patsys and I played Monkey." Not only have I forgotten, but I notice now that the same diary contains ample evidence that I appreciated other films and television specials far more. How do I read my minimal reference to the film and my subsequent failure of memory? Do they suggest that the survivor/immigrants' child was less likely to be chastened by parental reminders of the moral example of Anne Frank, or that my disaffection differed significantly from Auerbach's? The evidence is ambiguous, since my sister can recall not only seeing the film but being taken out of school in order to see it. It is the latter fact that impressed her at the age of nine, for she understood it to mean that our parents believed that seeing the film was very important. Yet my mother, like me, has no recollection of seeing it. Did I simply not know what to say in response to the film (if you can't say anything nice, don't say anything at all)? Did my diary preference for romantic dramas and television comedy indicate that I was not fooled by the comic incidents of the film, that far in advance of recent critics who label the play and film perfect examples of American sentimentality, I knew it all along?

I doubt it. My other diary entries for 1960 definitely appreciate non-Holocaust films and television more (on April 16, I wrote that *Mrs. Miniver* was "real exciting"; on May 7, I regarded the *Phil Silvers Special* as "really funny"); yet what does this prove? To read my silence as a 10-year-old's anxiety regarding the darker meaning of Anne Frank's story seems a desperate attempt to prove that I was traumatized. My diary shows no signs of the precocious voice or writing talents of Frank and makes no reference to my mother's story. Perhaps, Frank's *Diary* simply did not matter to me. In comparison, my diary tells me that Princess Margaret's wedding on May 6, 1960 clearly did matter, as did the birthday present that I received a few weeks later. One sentence for Anne Frank; four sentences for Princess Margaret; three sentences for a bra.

But why was I writing a diary, and why was I given the first one on my ninth birthday? I can remember receiving it; it was regarded as a suitable present for a girl about to go to summer camp.[13] Does the voice of my 1960 diary demonstrate how I was unconsciously imitating the tone of a diarist whose words I had not read? Certainly Frank's tone appealed to cultural expectations regarding the appropriate style of the female child's voice in the 1950s and early 1960s, and such needs could have so valorized her voice during my childhood that I sounded like her even when I had not read her. Yet my inability to remember the film, let alone to understand the context for my diary entry, foregrounds more than the trivial question about what I was thinking when I saw "'Ann Frank' at the Plaza," or a wry observation about the inadequacy of my memory compared to that of so many recent memoirists who claim a total recall of childhood. It also speaks to the folly of reducing Frank's complex diarist's voice to a simplistic message. On December 24, 1943, Frank wrote, "I sometimes wonder if anyone will ever understand what I mean" (152), words that are often forgotten by those who argue over which sentence in the *Diary* best represents her message. Is it not possible that even diaries revised by adolescent girls thinking about possible postwar publication are not primarily intended to produce messages?

Adults who claim to be too sophisticated for Anne Frank continue to look for messages and find them in childhood voices that pointedly demonstrate their own reluctance to face historical facts. They berate readers who fail to recall that Frank's hopefulness reflects her unavoidable ignorance of her terrible death in Bergen-Belsen; sometimes the snide tone unfairly implies that she also should be faulted for not knowing. Yet it is not children, but adults, who gave awards to Binjamin Wilkomirski's *Fragments: Memories of a Wartime Childhood*, a "memoir" whose historical credibility any adult familiar with the dismal facts regarding childhood survival during the Holocaust should have suspected long before the scandal regarding the book's authenticity arose.[14] Perhaps fearing that to question the author's identity would inadvertently support Holocaust deniers, few did suspect *Fragments'* legitimacy as memoir. I did not suspect; in a June 1998 e-mail to a colleague, I noted that "what is truly astonishing in *Fragments* [is] that the narrator claims that he was in a camp from the time he was a toddler and somehow he survived." I accepted Wilkomirski's claim. After all, so much about the Holocaust was "unbelievable": "somehow he survived." Any suspicions that I had regarding the book's legitimacy as memoir were diverted by my disbelief that anyone would regard *Fragments* as a book appropriate for children's reading. When *Fragments* was alleged to be a fraud, many readers were angry with the publisher and the writer, for they had read in good faith and now felt betrayed. In very different circumstances, Frank wrote in good faith, with far better excuses for her ignorance. Where does innocence reside?

The Lesson of a Complex Voice

In view of the deaths of Frank and so many others, to argue that she matters because of her complex voice seems to favour style over historical facts. Yet the *Diary* remains contentious and worth reading because of the ambiguity of that voice, which is so much more complex than the voice of the child often depicted in adult texts. We may argue whether Wilkomirski really was a child survivor; there is little space to debate the nature of the traumatized voice in his text. In contrast, the Anne Frank who writes is a child experimenting with voices; for instance, on January 22, 1944, she criticizes her words of November 2, 1942, "*I wouldn't be able to write that kind of thing anymore*" (59). What I now value in Frank's voice is its self-censorship, its careful construction: "What will we do if we're ever ... no, I mustn't write that down" (301). When Frank is angry, she self-consciously requests the reader: "please take into consideration that this story was written before the writer's fury had cooled" (118). Determined to create a cheerful voice, not only because the adults need her to sound that way, she correctly perceives that to be otherwise would serve no useful end, "I could spend hours telling you about the suffering the war has brought, but I'd only make myself more miserable" (82).

While Lawrence L. Langer is correct to insist that both children and adults need to read the *Diary* in the context of other Holocaust narratives ("Opening Locked Doors" 190), we might also consider how Frank's complex narrative voice resists being constrained by the requirements of children's pedagogy. Indeed, one reason that we continue to argue about the value of reading her *Diary* is that there is so much more to her voice than the single line that has come to represent her. The famous line, "I still believe, in spite of everything, that people are truly good at heart" (Frank 327), is part of a lengthy passage recorded July 15, 1944, which begins in reaction to the self-critique Frank perceives in a library book titled, *What Do You Think of the Modern Young Girl?* Claiming to have a great deal of self-knowledge and to have hidden her true self from her father, she distances herself from her parents and expresses her disappointment in Peter, "I soon realized that he could never be a kindred spirit" (326). The famous faith in people is framed by a reference to living in a time "when ideals are being shattered [...] when the worst side of human nature predominates, when everyone has come to doubt truth, justice and God" (327). The uplifting sentence actually concludes a paragraph full of references to "the facts" and "grim reality" and the way that they make any ideals "seem so absurd and impractical" (327). The play may turn these despairing lines into the equivalent of an adolescent developmental stage: "I think the world may be going through a phase, the way I was with Mother" (Goodrich and Hackett 84), and perhaps this is appropriate given the play's subsequent reference to how Anne's time in hiding has allowed her time to mature, but in the *Diary* the famous line is followed by an existential acknowledgment that Frank chooses to believe in spite of the facts: "It's utterly impossible for me to build my life on a foundation of chaos, suffering and death" (327).[15]

The facts of which Frank is fully aware include a world "being slowly transformed into a wilderness" and one which "one day, will destroy us too" (327). Her faith is so tentative: "and yet [...] somehow [...]. In the meantime, I must hold on to my ideals" (327). The "must" is desperate. In the next entry, July 21, 1944, she mocks herself: "For once, I'm not rattling on about high ideals" (328). In the *Diary's* final entry, August 1, 1944, the supposedly naïve optimist calls herself a "bundle of contradictions" (329) and concludes, "I [...] keep trying to find a way to become what I'd like to be [...] if ... if only there were no other people in the world" (331). Frank could not know that this would prove to be the final entry, so it would be a mistake to read the sentence as a grand conclusion, yet arguments over her "message" and her relevance tend to forget that writers of diaries rarely organize their entries around a theme.

Despite the complexity of Frank's voice—heard in her references to gassing, lines of people marched to their deaths, the "doomed" Hungarian Jews—and quite likely as a consequence of the *Diary's* early success, we tend to relegate it to childhood.[16] It becomes a kind of fairy tale for children and others who are not able or willing to confront the full horror described in adult Holocaust texts, a border text that signals the difference between childhood and adulthood, the site where we act out the multiple tensions between children's reading and literature valued by adults. Signs of this tension are evident, for instance, when Harold Bloom includes the *Diary* in the Modern Critical Interpretations series, but then barely mentions it in his introduction, preferring instead to praise Philip Roth's *The Ghost Writer*. Regarding the *Diary* as "more of a historical emblem than a literary work" (Bloom vii), he insists that "criticism is irrelevant. [...] One cannot write about Anne Frank's *Diary* as if Shakespeare, or Philip Roth, is the subject" (1).[17] The series is meant to include the best current criticism, but given his view of the *Diary* as outside the realm of literature, how can there be any real literary criticism of it? In his Editor's Note, Bloom categorizes the essays he anthologizes as "essentially exercises in morality and history" (vii).

Many adults demonstrate a comparable ambivalence that reduces Anne Frank's *Diary* to childhood Holocaust lessons. Like Gourevitch, Holocaust historians frequently write as though the lessons we find and the questions we ask to justify Holocaust children's literature are exactly what professional maturity puts aside. Thus, historian Michael R. Marrus carefully distances himself from Holocaust children's literature when he confesses to a skepticism regarding "the so-called 'lessons' of history" ("Good History" 24). Although he concedes that Holocaust lessons "have their place in shaping primary or secondary school exposure" ("Good History" 23), he does not specify what that place is or what the lessons are: "if good history revealed commonly agreed-upon, useful lessons, we would have extracted and put them to use a long time ago" ("Good History" 24).[18] The most the historian can hope for, he writes, is a deeper "appreciation of human reality [... one which] in a very general sense [...] can make us more mature, wiser, more 'experienced' observers of the human scene" ("Good History" 24). Marrus's is the lead essay in *Lessons and Legacies II: Teaching the Holocaust in a Changing World*. His skeptical comments foreground the tension between the understanding of a professional historian regarding the purpose of his work and the lesson-driven agenda that frames that subject when the reader is a child.

In contrast, Holocaust history in children's books is supposed to teach a lesson. What that lesson is depends upon the particular way adult writers perceive the ethnic, religious, and national identity of their child readers; however, the need to construct a lesson, some lesson, remains constant. In *Learning About the Holocaust: Literature and Other Resources for Young People*, the authors quote George Santayana—"Those who cannot remember the past are condemned to repeat it" (Stephens, Brown, and Rubin 7-8). Santayana's words appear with predictable regularity in works on Holocaust education for children, often in a context that seems to prove the very opposite, as they do in the same book when the authors state that "Lessons from the Holocaust provide us with a framework to *view* [my italics] ongoing atrocities" (7). The unfortunate choice of verb inadvertently suggests that such lessons are more likely to produce a reaction common to television viewers, who know when to switch the channel because they have seen it all. Like the authors of *Learning About the Holocaust*, Edward T. Sullivan quotes Santayana on the first page of *The Holocaust in Literature for Youth* and then proceeds in the succeeding paragraph to list the numerous genocides that have occurred since the Holocaust. Are we seriously to conclude, therefore, that those genocides occurred because our Holocaust education was inadequate, or that Hitler would have been stopped if the world had indeed remembered "what the Turks did to the Armenians" (3)? What then are we to make of Sullivan's admission that "More has been written about the Holocaust than any other genocide" (4) or that, in his bibliography, he annotates close to 500 Holocaust books and over 100 related books?

In contrast to Marrus, who insists that deep questions about human nature are outside the historian's province—"the answers—if there are answers—are tied up with notions of humanity itself and its capacities for good and evil" ("Getting It Right" 151)—Sullivan is convinced that "The primary goal of Holocaust education" is the teaching of "important lessons" (5) about human nature, lessons "about hate, the hate that is within all of us" (5). Yet Sullivan acknowledges that the main aim of his book is bibliographical: "I want [...] to make teachers aware that there is a lot more to the Holocaust than Anne Frank's *Diary*" (5). In making this statement, he mirrors the current and widespread consensus among Holocaust scholars and other adult readers that to read only the *Diary*, or even worse, just to see or read the play, is to produce a very peculiar and partial understanding. It is this understanding that Jason Sherman satirizes in his play, *Reading Hebron*, in a scene in which a non-Jewish character, thrilled to be at her first Passover *seder*, confesses that she once longed to be Anne Frank.

When Sullivan objects to the centrality of the *Diary* in children's literature, he attributes to it a remarkable power. Disturbed that it is likely to be the only Holocaust literature read by high school students, he leaps to the surprising conclusion that this may explain why "neo-Nazi groups are having such an easy time recruiting young people" (6).[19] The implication, that a different book (perhaps the kind Anne Frank might have written had she had pen and paper in Bergen-Belsen) would be more effective in combating Holocaust denial, reveals both the persistent faith in the transformative power of the books we give children and the powerful impact Holocaust denial has had in establishing the need to tell children about this particular genocide.

Other Voices, Other Lessons

While I share Gourevitch's suspicion of drawing lessons from the Holocaust, the cultural debate over the *Diary* encourages me to see several such lessons. The first concerns the source of adult dissatisfaction with Anne Frank. Does it really derive from the commodification and sanctification of her story and speak to readers' greater awareness of Holocaust realities? Or does it derive from a change in the way many adults now imagine how a Holocaust child looks and sounds? Alvin Rosenfeld notes that the first public reference to the *Diary* was in a 1946 Dutch newspaper article titled "A Child's Voice" (246-48).[20] The early reviews of the Goodrich and Hackett play repeatedly invoke the delicacy of both Anne's appearance and her voice. Twice in Brooks Atkinson's "Foreword" to the play, he reassures us of the play's "delicacy" and pointedly connects this delicacy to the play's "triumph" (v). The stage production is "lovely" (v); the performance is a thing of "beauty" (ix). And should we care to look, Anne's photograph "shows a beautiful maiden with an oval face, black hair in a jaunty bob, lively eyes and a sweet mouth" (vii). With this "delicate" image to screen the memory, still vivid in 1955, of newspaper photographs of the liberation of the camps, photographs that no sentiment can make delicate, the viewer is free to imagine a spiritual triumph; Walter Kerr "reviewing the play for the *Herald Tribune* [... describes Anne as] soaring through the center of the play with the careless gaiety of a bird that simply cannot be caged" (Rosenfeld 252).

Today this image will strike many as terribly and offensively false. The image of the Holocaust child that we now accept is grounded in the brutal facts of Holocaust reality— the children died, the babies died, the goodness of people's hearts had nothing to do with it and certainly could not be heard in their dying voices. If children "soar" in adult Holocaust literature, they are most likely being kicked by SS boots, thrown out windows, or hurled against walls. And if we praise their voices, we do not speak of delicacy. The paradigmatic voice of the Holocaust child for many contemporary adult readers is the cry of the powerless, the cry of the baby Magda in Ozick's "The Shawl" that signals her inevitable death as she rides on the Nazi guard's shoulder, "swimming through the air. [...] splash[ing ...] against the electrified fence" (9-10).

In this compelling short story, Ozick, for once breaking her rule about fictionalizing the Holocaust, pares its details to a narrative of constant hunger, unquenchable thirst, impossible choices, and failures of voice. We know neither the name of the camp in which the 15-month-old Magda dies, nor the identity of her father—"You could think she was one of *their* babies" (4). We know only what Rosa, Magda's mother, knows: "Magda was going to die very soon; she should have been dead already" (5). Ozick provides no lesson other than the text's reminder of the impossibility of speaking: "Magda was defective, without a voice" (7). When Magda finally utters a sound, "Maaaa ...aaa" (8), her cry only reinforces what Rosa has known all along: her baby is going to die. And the mother's voice proves equally impossible as Rosa first flies, searching for the shawl to quiet her daughter, and then forces herself into silence as the voices of the electric fence hum and go "mad in their growling" (10) when Magda is electrocuted. Stuffing her daughter's shawl into her mouth, Rosa silences herself—"swallowing up the wolf's screech" (10)—so that the guards do not shoot, as Ozick silences any readerly impulse to find in the Holocaust some narrative of coherence or hope.

Even when Ozick breaks her own rule about not fiction-alizing the Holocaust, she is careful to focalize "The Shawl" from the mother's perspective. We see only what Rosa sees; there is no attempt to imagine what the toddler sees. My sec-ond example demonstrates that, when we focalize the child's perspective, even if the child's voice is radically different from the uplifting coherent voice of the Anne Frank celebrated by Goodrich and Hackett, that voice too can be turned into a lesson, one which may initially cater to adult longing to celebrate the traumatized child's "innocence" under "unbelievable" circumstances. Ultimately the lesson is a more sober one about the naïveté of adults who are so eager for "the truth of the Holocaust through a child's eyes," that they forget how few children survived—that any child who could witness such events died in doing so.[21]

Both lessons are evident in the astonishing literary reception of Binjamin Wilkomirski's *Fragments: Memories of a Wartime Childhood.* There is no doubt that the paradigmatic voice of the Holocaust child for many adult readers between 1995 and 1998 was the brutalized voice of the child in *Fragments.* Over and over again the narrator in *Fragments* returns to a young child's incoherent memory of how Nazi guards threw or kicked him, sometimes into walls, sometimes over walls. Familiar with Ozick's crying child whose flight is met with death, or with the statistics regarding young child mortality in the camps, we can only read with amazement as this terribly tortured child survives. Adults should know the brutal facts—the children died, the babies died—but preferring to set aside such facts, they accepted Wilkomirski's story and expressed their awe at the child's voice. Readers who might well mock the final line in Goodrich and Hackett—Otto Frank's statement, "She puts me to shame" (87)—accepted the double shame produced by Wilkomirski's words: how could the Nazis do such terrible things to young children? How could postwar adults not listen? "I grew up and became an adult in a time and in a society that didn't want to listen" (Wilkomirski 153).

There is no doubt that the sadistic events described in *Fragments* fit our knowledge of Nazi brutality, even as our belief that they happened to this boy demonstrates our reluctance to accept the historical facts regarding young child survival. In the scandal that has arisen since the Swiss journalist Daniel Ganzfried first questioned Wilkomirski's identity in an August 1998 article in *Die Weltwoche*, we can see how adult readers' belief in the traumatized child's voice allowed them to suppress any questions regarding how a child so young, so vulnerable, and so brutalized could have been not only present at so many Holocaust situations, but survived to tell the tale.[22] The lesson that we might draw today from our willingness to ignore historical fact (children that young simply did not survive the camps, and certainly not children who experienced so many acts of violence) would be very different from the lessons about innocence that many adults once saw in this text.

If *Fragments* continues to disturb adult readers, it does so now for very different reasons, since most have come to regard it either as a deliberate fraud or as the work of a troubled individual who honestly believes that he is a Jewish Holocaust survivor. Stefan Maechler, the Swiss historian commissioned to investigate the authenticity of the memoir, rejects Ganzfried's depiction of the author as "a coldly calculating man systematically executing a fraud" (269).[23] He concludes that the man born in Switzerland in 1941 as Bruno Grosjean, subsequently adopted and renamed Bruno Dössekker, gradually came to believe in the child survivor story he told. Maechler also suggests that the fantasy of being a

Holocaust child survivor gave Wilkomirski a recognizable language for narrating his trauma as "an unhappy, illegitimate, adopted working-class child" (278), a language which guaranteed him a far larger and more sympathetic audience than he would have had if he had written a memoir recalling the real traumatic experiences he had as a child in Switzerland.[24] The language was familiar because readers approached the text having already concluded that an ideal Holocaust memoir would contain certain episodes and would be narrated in a certain way. They understood what the traumatized voice in *Fragments* could barely express because they had read such episodes elsewhere; they approved the incoherence of the voice because they already believed that the Holocaust was inexplicable. The memoir thus served the needs of the public as well as the needs of the writer: "As a victim who could not have been more innocent and more ill treated, [Wilkomirski] was met with worldwide solidarity and boundless sympathy" (Maechler 272). The memoir was praised for its profound insight; what made it successful, Maechler concludes, was its reliance on well-established conventions for narrating the Holocaust.

One of the many strengths of Maechler's analysis is his attention to the reasons for the enthusiastic acceptance of Wilkomirski's claim that he was a child survivor.[25] The focus in the early investigative articles by Elena Lappin in *Granta* and Gourevitch in the *New Yorker* has been on the author's identity. In contrast, Maechler draws attention to the role played by the child's voice, the public's willingness to believe in Wilkomirski's literary voice simply because it was so well-suited to our current understanding of what a Holocaust child's voice should sound like. Observing that "a reincarnat-

ed Anne Frank" (118) was one of the many fans to write to
Wilkomirski, he suggests that Fragments gives us Anne Frank
with a happy ending: "[a]t the point where Anne Frank left
us, we take up the path and go farther with Binjamin" (291).
Other readers agree, but would be surprised by Maechler's
insistence that central to Fragments' appeal is its fairy-tale
happy ending. Don't they claim to be attracted by the brutal
honesty of Binjamin's voice? Would they not say that it is the
Diary that is the fairy tale and that Fragments takes them on a
different path? More than one reader has contrasted the voice
of Anne Frank with the voice of young Binjamin and insisted that Fragments is the perfect antidote to the "sanitized"
idealism of Anne Frank.[26]

Despite the brutality it speaks, adult readers perceive the
Holocaust child's voice as innocent in some sense. Writing on
the scandal, Ozick notes how Fragments appeared to give us
"in a child's pure voice, a narrative of German oppression to
set beside the classic accounts of Elie Wiesel and Anne
Frank" ("The Rights of History and the Rights of Imagination" 25). A publisher's blurb on the dust jacket of my copy of
Fragments quotes Mary Karr on how Wilkomirski's moving
"innocent" voice describes "horrors an adult mind can barely
fathom." Binjamin knows what Anne Frank could not yet
know when she wrote the Diary; he appeals to adults precisely because his horrific knowledge is precariously framed by
his toddler status. Adults may read Fragments now as a disturbing parody of the Holocaust child's voice; what is equally pertinent is that the child's voice in this book suits the
construction of childhood innocence necessary to adult texts.
Adult readers believed in Wilkomirski's voice because they
already knew that this is what the child's voice would sound

like if the child had survived. What they were willing to forget is that adults use childhood voices to express what "the
children themselves could not voice for a variety of reasons:
because they were killed too young to speak for themselves;
because they were overwhelmed by trauma" (Sokoloff,
"Childhood Lost" 262). As Sokoloff notes, such voices exist
"only in a realm of the imagination" (263).

Even if the questions regarding Wilkomirski's identity
had not been raised, it is unlikely that *Fragments* would ever
have replaced the centrality of the *Diary* in children's reading.
Long before serious questions arose regarding the book's
legitimacy as Holocaust memoir and likely as a consequence
of its stunning success in the adult market, *Fragments* did
appear on several children's recommended book lists.
Sullivan recommends it for grades 9 to 12, and includes it in
his list of "must have" titles, which school librarians should
"purchase immediately" (223). *Fragments* also appears on several Internet children's recommended book lists, including
"Sixth through Eighth Grade 'Essential' Fiction" list, a list
that was posted to the international school librarian's listserv
LM-NET: *http://www.wcsu.k12.vt.us/~wardsboro/list67.htm*.[27]
It is identified as a translated children's book by the Cooperative Children's Book Center at the School of Education,
University of Wisconsin-Madison, *http://www.soemadison.
wisc.edu/ccbc/trans96.htm*, and as one of the best books for
young adults (12 to 18), American Library Association,
http://www.ala.org/yalsa/booklists/bbya/bestbooks97.html.[28]
Despite the perplexing and contradictory assertions of these
lists—is *Fragments* suitable for the child in grade 6 or is the
book more suited to the older adolescent?—the voice of the
child narrator in *Fragments*, whether the book is read as

memoir or fiction, remains highly problematic in terms of the narrative expectations of children's books. It is not simply a question of the brutality of Wilkomirski's text, but the way that brutality combines with the narrative's total resistance to the children's literature requirement of coherent knowledge.

If and when children read beyond Anne Frank's *Diary*, they will likely be given books that fulfil that need for precise information. This is the lesson I draw from the attention given to *Zlata's Diary: A Child's Life in Sarajevo*, published just prior to *Fragments* and lauded for a very different and far less innocent child's voice. It is a voice more suited to the pedagogical needs of children's reading, speaking in a way that suggests that the main impact of Anne Frank's *Diary* has been to teach other children to sound like her. If Binjamin does not understand what he sees, Zlata understands only too well. Hence, the need to find an "Anne Frank of Sarajevo" (Filipović v), who can draw the world's attention through her child's voice, is accompanied by the paradoxical characterization of Zlata Filipović as a child diarist who "seemed more adult [...] than most of the adults I knew" (Filipović ix). Filipović herself uses this child/adult reversal not only when she characterizes the adult politicians as "kids" (Filipović 167), but also when she repeatedly writes self-conscious entries that appeal to adult expectations regarding war, childhood, and the loss of innocence. A long list of full cap., triple exclamation-marked nouns is followed by the diarist's ironic summation, "That's my life! The life of an innocent eleven-year old schoolgirl!! A schoolgirl without a school.[...] without games, without friends [...] without nature [...] without chocolate or sweets [...]. In short, a child without a childhood" (61).

To say that the very banality[29] of most of the diary entries makes Zlata Filipović sound more like a child than Anne Frank only raises the question yet again of what "a child" sounds like and what is the cultural use we make of that voice. Filipović is both conscious of the comparison with Frank—"Hey Diary! You know what I think? Since Anne Frank called her diary Kitty, maybe I could give you a name too" (27)—and frightened by the implications—"I don't want to suffer her fate" (160). When a book based on a selection from her diaries is first promoted, she reads a speech whose penultimate sentence expresses a longing to return to "the shores of my childhood" (156).[30] In the very next entry, she reports being filmed "for American TV as the 'person of the week'" (157). Such diary entries suggest that, even if giving children Frank's *Diary* does not stop a war, it may well produce children who will learn how to imitate her voice. And adults will value their writing, even if such children bear little resemblance to the diarist they supposedly imitate. Not surprising except for those who actually believe the lessons to be found in children's books, Zlata's message to the world does not produce peace.

The Voices of the Brave Hutu Girls

If innocence is less a property of childhood than a literary device through which adults imagine childhood, it is also apparent that the adult desire to protect children through the books that we give them accomplishes very little in terms of actual protection. Even when we have doubts about the meaning of innocence, we continue to write about historical horror and construct lessons that invoke the voices of children. Although Gourevitch warns the reader not to look for a lesson, the way he ends *We Wish to Inform You That Tomorrow We Will be Killed with Our Families* speaks to the difficulty of refusing this narrative pattern, and in this difficulty I find my final lesson. According to Katherine Paterson, children's books are supposed to end with hope; after 350 pages, Gourevitch leaves it up to his adult reader to decide "if there is hope for Rwanda" (352). Yet in this book, that is so obviously not a children's book, Gourevitch's final story is about the murder of 17 schoolgirls who were ordered to separate themselves into Hutus and Tutsis, but refused. In this report of yet another massacre lies the only hope he can offer his readers, "But mightn't we all take some courage from the example of those brave Hutu girls who could have chosen to live, but chose instead to call themselves Rwandans?" (353). Although the words of "those brave Hutu girls" seem so different from the words of Anne Frank, in ending with this story of massacred schoolgirls who chose to speak in opposition to the dominant voices around them, Gourevitch shows how dependent we remain on the way we imagine the voices of children for remembering history and teaching the lessons that help explain how and why we read Anne Frank today.

NOTES

1. Gourevitch provides this family background in *We Wish to Inform You That Tomorrow We Will be Killed with Our Families*.

2. This quotation appears more than once in Gourevitch's work. See "Behold Now Behemoth" (57).

3. In future references, called the *Diary*. Unless otherwise specified, all quotations are from *The Diary of a Young Girl: The Definitive Edition*.

4. Bettelheim's essay in which he blames Otto Frank for hiding his family together rather than hiding separately or emigrating to a safer country is a perfect example of what Michael André Bernstein calls back-shadowing. Bettelheim insists that he does not wish to criticize the Frank family, "only the universal admiration of their way of coping" (Bettelheim 250). Yet he continually does criticize their behaviour and implies that Otto Frank's failure to "draw the right conclusions" (255) is responsible for the deaths of his family. Nevertheless, Bettelheim's objection to the play's cheerful ending: "If all men are good at heart, there never really was an Auschwitz" (251) remains valid.

5. See Rochman, "Should You Teach *Anne Frank: The Diary of a Young Girl?*"

6. This premise is also operative at the United States Holocaust Memorial Museum. Their children's exhibit, "Remember the Children: Daniel's Story," and the accompanying book, *Daniel's Story*, certainly expose children to information not available in Anne Frank's *Diary*, but their reliance on the diary form implies the likelihood that child visitors will already have read or studied the *Diary*. The exhibit functions as a supplement to the *Diary*.

7. Moger is quoting from B.M. Mooyaart's translation of *The Diary of a Young Girl*. In the Definitive Edition published more than 40 years later, the translation by Susan Massotty is slightly different: "I still believe, in spite of everything, that people are truly good at heart" (327) and "There's a destructive urge in people, the urge to rage, murder and kill" (276).

8. Ozick provides a long list of misuse. The *Diary* "has been infantilized, Americanized, homogenized, sentimentalized; falsified, kitschified, and, in fact, blatantly and arrogantly denied" ("Who Owns Anne Frank?" 78).

9. In his cogent discussion of Anne Frank, Peter Novick notes that it is exactly what appealed to audiences in the 1950s, "Anne's 'universalism' [... that] outraged writers in the 1990s" (117). Given the Canadian Stratford's decision to produce the play in 2000, we might conclude that such outrage is not widely shared by those who attend summer theatre festivals.

10. See for example Sokoloff's reference to "genuine childhood" (*Imagining the Child* 9). Advertisements for memoirs about children and war nearly always refer to the innocent voice that speaks in the text.

11. In the Bryan Singer film, *Apt Pupil*, Todd Bowden also receives one week's instruction in the Holocaust; however, the film, and the Stephen King novella that inspires it, have a very different reading of the end of innocence.

12. Auerbach's reference to being "haunted" echoes Philip Roth's use of Anne Frank in *The Ghost Writer*.

13. On July 1, 1958, I arrived at camp and wrote my first entry: "I ~~hate~~ don't like it here."

14. I refer to the author as Wilkomirski since that is the name under which he published *Fragments*.

15. In their stage directions preceding the shattering of the door, Goodrich and Hackett imply that the secret annex has functioned to hide Anne while she matures: "She is no longer a child, but a woman with courage to meet whatever lies ahead" (Goodrich and Hackett 86).

16. Hilene Flanzbaum calls *The Diary of Anne Frank* "the most important landmark in the Americanization of the Holocaust" (1).

17. One cannot, but others have demonstrated the value of doing so. See, for example, Brenner's reading of Frank in the context of four Jewish women intellectuals. Judith Tydor Baumel begins her historiographical overview in *Double Jeopardy: Gender and the Holocaust* with the statement, "In the beginning there was Anne Frank" (39). Baumel's book also includes a useful essay on "Teaching the Holocaust Through *The Diary of Anne Frank*." Baumel does not concentrate on Frank, but she does not ignore her either.

18. Novick is equally skeptical about Holocaust lessons in *The Holocaust in American Life*.

19. I find Sullivan's assertion astonishing, given how questioning the authenticity of the *Diary* has been a mainstay of Holocaust denial. See Lipstadt, 229-35.

20. The article by Jan Romein, professor of Dutch history at the University of Amsterdam, appeared in *Het Parool* on April 3, 1946 (Rosenfeld 248).

21. Quotations are taken from customer comments on amazon.com regarding Binjamin Wilkomirski's *Fragments*. Noted February 13, 2001, posted March 29, 1999, by a reader from Lisle, Illinois, in response to reports that the book was not written by a child survivor.

22. Discussing how few readers raised objections to the critical acclaim that *Fragments* initially received, Stefan Maechler points to Gary

Mokotoff, a member of the Jewish Book Council board, as a rare exception. Mokotoff, not convinced that the book was written by a survivor, protested when *Fragments* received the National Jewish Book Award, and in his letter to the jury observed that the events in the book "seem to be the sum of the experience of all survivors" (115).

23. Maechler's report was commissioned by the literary agency of Liepman AG in April 1999; in October 1999, he sent an interim version to the agency and the publishing houses concerned. Suhrkamp Verlag immediately announced that it was withdrawing all hardcover copies of *Fragments* from German bookstores and removing the title from the backlist of its publishing imprint, Jüdischer Verlag. Within a few weeks, Schocken (Wilkomirski's English publisher) issued a similar announcement. In 2001, Schocken published an English translation of the report, *The Wilkomirski Affair: A Study in Biographical Truth*; the publisher includes the complete text of *Fragments* and explains that this will help the reader assess the report's findings.

24. Maechler notes that *Fragments* was never a bestseller; even the English translation sold only 32,800 copies (119). He focuses on the book's significance as "a media event," in which reading tours are more important than the number of books sold. During such readings, Wilkomirski did not always read from his memoir, but, according to Maechler, he always performed the role of traumatized child survivor, and the people in the audience became his humble and adoring fans.

25. Although I agree with Maechler's reading of the role played by the traumatized child's voice in the popularity of *Fragments*, our conclusions were reached independently. They also differ in that I am primarily interested in the relationship between the enthusiasm for Wilkomirski's traumatized child's voice and the objections to Frank's very different voice. I also question Maechler's observation that it is "extraordinary" for a child's perspective to be adopted in an autobiographical work about the "terror of the Nazi regime" (279). Anita Lobel's *No Pretty Pictures: A Child of War* (discussed in Chapter Six) is just one example. If by "terror of the Nazi regime" we mean more than what occurred in the camps, and if by "[t]he rigorous adoption of a child's perspective" we do not necessarily mean a narrative "beyond all subjective understanding" (279) there are many other texts that offer a child's perspective. As I argue throughout this book, our understanding of "a child's perspective" is not stable.

26. See customer comments on Binjamin Wilkomirski's *Fragments* in amazon.com (noted February 13, 2001): April 24, 1998, Agnieszka from New Brunswick, New Jersey, contrasts the "sanitized" view of the Holocaust provided by Anne Frank with the "unpretentious child's voice" of Wilkomirski; April 22, 1998, Jennifer Quail of Lexington, Virginia, similarly praises Wilkomirski for offering a young person's view that "sanitizes nothing" in comparison to Anne Frank.

27. The Website for this particular list no longer exists. My e-mail attempt in 1999 to learn why the book was recommended in December 1997 for a reading list for such young children and why it was categorized as fiction, not memoir, long before questions arose regarding Wilkomirski's identity, proved unsuccessful.

28. I am indebted to Steve McCullough, in May 1998 a graduate student at Dalhousie University, Halifax, Nova Scotia, for bringing these internet lists to my attention after I confidently asserted that *Fragments* would never appear on children's book lists.

29. Or is this banality produced by the reader's awareness that Zlata escapes Sarajevo?

30. A small press in Sarajevo published a selection from the diaries in summer 1993 (Filipović viii). Zlata read the speech at the promotion for this publication, and then included the speech as part of her diary entry for July 17, 1993. The last entry for the diary in its current form is October 17, 1993; there is also an epilogue dated December 1993.

5

A Multitude of Voices:
The Production of Daniel's Story

On November 22, 1991, Daniel Weiss, a producer of books for children and adolescents, wrote to Susan Morgenstein, director of special exhibits for the future United States Holocaust Memorial Museum.[1] As head of Daniel Weiss Associates, Inc., someone both professionally and personally committed to educational children's books, and interested in the development of the museum, he told her how moved he had been by the "Remember the Children" exhibition which he had just seen in New York.[2] Aware of plans to open "Daniel's Story" as a special exhibition concurrent with the museum's opening in April 1993, Weiss proposed various publication possibilities, including a historical novel based on Daniel's Story (USHMM.2000.061.21).[3]

This was not the first time that linking books with the exhibition had been suggested. In July 1990 Morgenstein had been advised by Jeshajahu Weinberg, the museum's director, to delay meetings with potential publishers because such decisions were premature. Now, however, if the museum wanted to offer visitors a companion novel to the special exhibition planned for children when the permanent site officially opened on April 22, 1993, they had to act promptly. In January 1992, meetings were scheduled to select a publisher and an author; two months later, Carol Matas began work on the novel. By early February 1993, Morgenstein showed colleagues and donors a favourable review of *Daniel's Story* in *Quill & Quire*; later that year, she congratulated Matas on the book's nomination for a Governor-General's Award in Canada. The intense editorial and content debates of July 1992 were now in the past; there was even talk about a possible sequel (USHMM.2000.041).[4]

The illustrations and cover design of *Daniel's Story* tell a far more complex story. In a letter written on July 28, 1992, regarding details of the front and back covers, Ronald Goldfarb, on behalf of the museum, informed Susan Kitzen, executive director of Daniel Weiss Associates, that no historic photographs would be permitted (USHMM.97.014.23). This refusal is consistent with the ambiguous and strategic use of photographs in the novel. Each of the novel's four parts—"Pictures of Frankfurt," "Pictures of Lodz," "Pictures of Auschwitz," and "Pictures of Buchenwald"—refers to photographs, either real or imagined.[5] Yet there are no photographs in the book. The photographic record of the Holocaust acts as a witness, but what it records is not necessarily what we are willing to show children. By making her character, Daniel, a photographer, Matas can explain to the reader the historical context required to understand the photographs; why, for example, the people photographed are terrified (*Daniel's Story* 25).[6] By having him recall photographs that the reader cannot see, she avoids the difficulty of deciding what Holocaust photographs are appropriate for young readers. By allowing him to describe photographs that are taken from him and scenes that he is not allowed to photograph, she addresses the limitations of the photographic record.

Despite Goldfarb's directive, photographs not only structure the narrative, they determine the design and content of
the three images on the front cover. The largest image shows
a child wearing a peaked cap and a yellow star on his back; his
hands clutch a wire fence. We cannot see what he is looking
at. Based on a photograph taken in the Lodz Ghetto, in
which a child looks through a wire fence at an adult woman
whose sorrowful face is half-hidden by the child's arm, the
painting respects the authority of photographs for telling the
story of the Holocaust even as it signals that it is a painting,
not a photograph. The copyright page identifies it as a
"Cover painting by Paul Henry, based in part on a photograph by Mendel Grossman" (DS ii). The two smaller paint-
ings placed on top of this image—one of a Nazi with an SS
banner in the background, the other of a group of people
wearing Jewish stars and presumably being deported—are
framed to resemble photographs. What is the relationship
between these figures and the novel? Are we to read the child
in the largest painting as Daniel? The back cover crops this
child's image so that we see only his head and shoulders;
beside this image, we are asked, "Can Daniel survive history's
deadliest moment?"

Mendel Grossman took several photographs of the fatal
deportation of children under the age of 10 from the Lodz
Ghetto in September 1942 (Adelson and Lapides 356-57).[7]
In The Children We Remember, Chana Byers Abells glosses the
specific photograph that most closely resembles the cover
painting: "Sometimes they took them away from their families and sent them far from home" (n. pag). In a different photograph included in both Lodz Ghetto: Inside a Community
Under Siege (Adelson and Lapides 357) and The Diary of

Dawid Sierakowiak: Five Notebooks from the Łódź Ghetto, we see the child, or perhaps another child standing in exactly the same pose, taken from the other side of the fence (Adelson 225). The painting that is and is not a photograph, the painting that obscures what the child is facing, permits a more hopeful story than that told in accounts of the deportation. So too do the words on the back cover that assure us that Daniel "finds hope, life, and even love in the midst of despair."

In contrast, Arieh Ben-Menahem says of Grossman's photographs: "He did not seek beauty, for there was no beauty in the ghetto" (Grossman 96). If the need for hope partially explains why the museum requires a fictional protagonist, the cover also suggests that fiction is acceptable only if it is historically grounded but discrete in the history it tells—the equivalent of the painting that blurs the background details of the photograph. The correspondence regarding the cover also demonstrates the museum's insistence that every detail of *Daniel's Story* be subject to their approval. Evidence of this approval still appears on the front cover above Matas's name—"Published in conjunction with the United States Holocaust Memorial Museum"—and in more detail on the back cover. A cover that gives the author's name only once but the museum's name twice is as unusual as the information that appears on both the copyright page and back cover: "Produced by Daniel Weiss Associates, Inc." The story of that production—the multitude of voices that debated the relationship of history and fiction, the nature of a child's voice, and the requirements of the child reader—is the subject of this chapter.

A Team Approach

That no other Holocaust novel by Carol Matas lists a "producer" as well as a publisher speaks to the exceptional circumstances governing the writing of *Daniel's Story* and illustrates why the production story told by the archival material at the United States Holocaust Memorial Museum and the Carol Matas papers housed at the Department of Archives and Special Collections, University of Manitoba Libraries, is so central to my analysis of Holocaust representation in North American children's literature. Despite its surface accord, the correspondence reveals deep disagreements regarding the writing of history for children. All agreed that children's books on the Holocaust must teach a lesson, but the lesson that the correspondence demonstrates is how difficult it is to reconcile the differing demands of historical accuracy, representative narrative, and Holocaust pedagogy. To navigate through all the records—memos, faxes, manuscript revisions, and annotations—demonstrates that when a book like *Daniel's Story* is "produced," it must also accommodate the conflicting demands produced by the authority of established scholars, the standing of the United States Holocaust Memorial Museum, and the expectations of its visitors. The theoretical issues addressed are helpful not only in tracing the "production" of *Daniel's Story*, but also in clarifying how much is at stake whenever we produce a children's book about the Holocaust.

In response to Weiss's proposal, Morgenstein asked him to set up a meeting. In a January 14 memo to Daniel Weiss, Elise Howard, and Betsy Gould (a publisher of Bantam Books for Young Readers, who had seen the exhibit with

Weiss and was interested in developing books on the topic for children), Leslie Morgenstein reviewed the background to the meeting that would take place at Bantam six days later.[8] He informed them that four museum representatives— Weinberg, Morgenstein, Ronald Goldfarb (a literary agent and attorney), and Michael Berenbaum, project director— would attend (USHMM.2000.061.21). This number of people is the first sign that the novel for which Weiss saw his company playing a key liaison role would involve complications far beyond those usually encountered between a children's novelist and her editor. Since all parties wanted the book in print by the time of the museum opening, the short timeline necessary would only exacerbate such complications.

The museum team that had been planning the special exhibition since May 1991 regarded the travelling exhibition as a work-in-progress and also expected the special exhibition to evolve, subject to the feedback of children who visited it and the professional expertise of child psychologists and educators.[9] Morgenstein's commitment to a team approach and her belief that continuing assessment would result in the best exhibition are evident in her speeches on the subject. In one, she explained that both the travelling and special exhibitions were designed as lessons on history and moral issues that 8- to 12-year-old children would understand (USHMM.2000.041). As an example of the continuing evaluation and the planners' sensitivity to child visitors' responses, she told her audience that the Remember the Children Team learned that children did not relate to Daniel until they added a diary written in script.[10] The team had also learned that children regard diaries as private, but journals as something that teachers can read. Further evidence of the exhibition's evolution is found in an April 6, 1992 memo to her Remember the Children Team, in which Morgenstein informed them that outside educators brought in to assess the planned exhibition had observed that children would have studied Anne Frank's *The Diary of a Young Girl* in grade 7, and would therefore be receptive to the diary concept. Although the educators realized that the museum conceived their target audience as stopping at age 12, they told Morgenstein that they believed that many older children would also attend (CM.A.95-64.4-1).[11]

Not only did the differing responses and expertise of children, psychiatrists, educators, and Holocaust scholars serve to develop both exhibitions, but the process of development continues to be regarded as crucial information for teachers. In "Things to Know About *Remember the Children, Daniel's Story*," teachers are told: "The exhibition was created with the help of a team of experts and has been reviewed by child psychiatrists, educators, and museum interpreters" (*Teacher Guide* 3). However, in commissioning a companion children's novel, the museum encountered a form that could not be altered since the book could not be published as a work-in-progress. In addition, not only might the collaborative approach of exhibition development conflict with the method of the author, but the very possibility of collaboration was diminished when the novelist chosen at such a late date entered the process after many of the experts had already established their authority and given their views.

What space was left for the legitimacy of the novelist's expertise, her sense of how children read, her understanding of the best way to represent Holocaust issues for the child reader? The travelling exhibition already provided feedback from children; the museum staff included Holocaust scholars and had access to educators involved in Holocaust pedagogy. Under these circumstances, it was unlikely that the museum would regard the expertise of the children's novelist as at all equivalent to the authority of the child visitor and the Holocaust scholar. The museum had the power of final approval, of withholding the words "published in conjunction with the United States Holocaust Memorial Museum"; if the parties involved wanted that validation on the cover, the pressure on the novelist to comply with the museum's views would be intense. That Matas's novel portrays a Daniel whose voice remains distinct from the voice of the *Daniel* in the exhibition speaks to her remarkable ability to comply with the museum's demands while simultaneously working to retain her conception of the narrator.

Not only did the short timeline for the production of the book intensify pressures on Matas to comply with what the museum required, it also suggests that the museum never considered either that a children's novelist who took seriously their demand for historical accuracy might require more time to do her research and transform it into a novel—in early planning notes on the novel, Matas wrote "Sounds too much like history lesson" (CM.A.95-64.3-15)—or that she might claim her own expertise regarding child readers and children's historical fiction. In the draft of a July 22, 1992 letter to Morgenstein, Matas, who had accepted the challenge of writing a book in only a few months, showed signs of the time pressures. Writing of her great respect for all those working at the museum and her own determination "to both tell a good story and be historically accurate," she added a brief postscript: "Doing a book like this in four months, when I would normally take a year (*at least*) to research and another to write is extremely difficult" (CM.A.95-64.4-2). Years later, Matas would answer the letter of a child fan curious about another novel, *Jesper*, "Writing *Jesper was* difficult, but since writing *Daniel's Story* everything else seems easy" (CM.A.95-64.7-43).[12]

Matas believes that she was chosen to write *Daniel's Story* because Scholastic had bought the paperback rights to her first two Holocaust novels, *Lisa* (1987) and *Jesper* (1989). The former was published in the USA as *Lisa's War*, the latter as *Code Name Kris* and *Kris's War* (Matas, e-mail, 19 Dec. 1998). The sales and critical acclaim of these two books support this belief; however, Weiss's correspondence indicates that he had Matas in mind even before Scholastic Press became involved. She is first mentioned in a February 20, 1992 letter to Jean Fiewel of Scholastic Press (USHMM.2000.061.21). It suggests that the museum was willing to consider offers from more than one publisher, and that Weiss, frustrated by the time Bantam had taken to make an offer, now thought that Scholastic might be more appropriate than Bantam. With that in mind, Weiss asked Fiewel if she was interested in publishing several exhibition-related books, including a novel intended for middle-graders. He praised Morgenstein's enthusiasm for the project and then stressed the market potential for such books given the many children who would be visiting the special exhibition each year. Mentioning Goldfarb, Weinberg, and the many others who would be involved, Weiss accurately predicted a complex and sensitive committee process, which would benefit from his role as producer. Functioning as a liaison between the museum and publisher, he anticipated freeing the publisher of this task.

Concerned about the short timeline, the fact that he had already lined up Matas to write *Daniel's Story*, and the likelihood of an offer from Bantam, Weiss suggested that if Scholastic were interested, Fiewel should provide him quickly with something appropriate about the company to show Goldfarb.[13]

On March 9, 1992, Morgenstein sent Susan Kitzen a package of materials related to the special exhibition. This included a draft storyline for the exhibition, a floor plan, a historical timeline, a chronology of events that would have affected a family such as Daniel's, a packet of historical photographs used by the exhibition team, and a very tentative draft script. In her cover letter, Morgenstein emphasized both the confidentiality of the material and its in-process nature since the special exhibition was still being developed. Ten days later Kitzen forwarded the material to Matas; meanwhile, several people at the museum, including Weinberg and Morgenstein, read Matas's first Holocaust novel, *Lisa's War*. On March 30, Matas, Weiss, Kitzen, and Kate Waters of Scholastic met with Goldfarb and Morgenstein to obtain an overview of the museum project and the progress on the exhibition.

All parties wanted the novel to be historically accurate. With this in mind, on March 31, the museum faxed Matas a bibliography on children and the Holocaust that included Alan Adelson and Robert Lapides's *Lodz Ghetto: Inside a Community Under Siege*.[14] In May, in response to further questions, Alex Zapruder, another member of Morgenstein's team, sent Matas research material that included another list of recommended books and photocopied excerpts, including Lucy Dawidowicz's *Hitler's War Against the Jews*. In her thank-you note, Matas mentioned that she was reading Leni Yahil's *The Holocaust*. Clearly, she used these sources, especially Adelson and Lapides's compilation. Later, one reader at the museum questioned the manuscript phrase "wedding invitations" as a way of referring to deportation orders; she apparently did not recognize that the source was Jozef Zelkowicz, one of the Lodz Ghetto writers excerpted by Adelson and Lapides (246). Although Matas kept the phrase, she was frustrated at having to confirm its source. Similarly, when Sybil Milton, the resident historian at the museum, questioned the way Matas depicted the awfulness of the rations in Lodz, Matas backed up her description by citing Oskar Rosenfeld, quoted in the same historical text (CM.A.95-64.4-1).

But long before readers could assess the historical accuracy of manuscript details, the difference between a novelist working independently in Winnipeg, Manitoba, and an exhibition team working as a group in Washington, DC, proved problematic. On April 6, Morgenstein wrote to Weiss, Kitzen, and Matas that, having assigned *Lisa's War* to all members of the exhibition team, she was now forwarding the comments of one of the exhibition evaluators (USHMM. 2000.099). Kitzen replied the very next day with her own questions regarding the implication of the evaluator's comparison of the protagonists Lisa and Daniel. She also requested that future editorial comments not be sent directly to Matas, reminding Morgenstein of their prior understanding that all editorial suggestions would be sent first to her office, but that Matas would be free to contact the museum if she had any research questions (USHMM.2000.099). On April 8 Morgenstein confirmed her understanding of this process and was careful to honour it. Whatever editorial comments were later seen by Matas, they were always forwarded to her by Kitzen. But even in accepting Kitzen's request, Morgenstein insisted on the benefits of the team approach used in exhibition development and continued to consult widely on the appropriateness of Matas's work. The reason for cooperative assessment remained clear; the exhibition team believed that this process would produce the best book (USHMM.2000.099).

The Voice of a Representative Child

Weiss did not underestimate the challenges of producing a novel acceptable to the museum. The representational issues that proved most contentious and take up most space in the correspondence concern the voice of Daniel.[15] No questions arose about how a Canadian woman should write about the Holocaust for an American institution, whose intended visitors are Americans who in the course of their day on the Mall will visit other national tourist sites.[16] There is no evidence that Matas as a Canadian writer represented the Holocaust in ways that conflicted with the needs of an American institution, or that she questioned the museum's determination to present the Holocaust as a decidedly American lesson about the nature of democracy, the danger of bystander silence, and the moral imperative of individual choice.[17] In selecting Matas, the museum took for granted that she would share their pedagogical values, values apparent in the mission statement quoted at the beginning of the Teacher Guide: Remember the Children, Daniel's Story:

The mission of the United States Holocaust Memorial Museum is to inform Americans about the unprecedented tragedy of the Holocaust, to remember those who suffered, and to inspire visitors to contemplate the moral implications of their choices and responsibilities as citizens of a democracy in an interdependent world. (1)[18]

While Matas might not have seen these lessons as specifically American, her commitment to narratives of individual choice had much in common with the museum's goals. In *Daniel's Story*, the word "Canada" appears only as the prisoners' slang term for the Birkenau warehouse storing the deportees' goods, an ironic label that the museum felt needed more careful explanation in the text and glossary, but did not consider a problem.[19]

In 1992, Matas did not yet have a reputation for exploring feminist issues in children's fiction. Although she had examined the difficulties facing a female politician in *The Race* (1991), her reputation as a feminist author would not be established until the publication of *The Burning Time* in 1994. After *Daniel's Story*, her Holocaust novels demonstrated her strong preference for female protagonists, but this was not so in 1992. Her two previous Holocaust novels had both a female (*Lisa*) and a male protagonist (*Jesper*), so she was not perceived as a writer who might have invented a female narrator if she had been completely free to do so. In any case, since *Daniel's Story* was intended as a companion to an exhibit in which the name was already established, the question of gender did not come up.[20] Matas had to accept that certain narrative choices had already been made:

I was told that I must use the name daniel [sic], that he would have a family (which I would create), that he would live somewhere in Germany (again up to me), that he would go to the Lodz ghetto, then to Auschwitz, then to Buchenwald. That's it—the rest was up to me. (Matas, e-mail to the author, 19 Dec. 1998)

One obvious example of Matas's creative freedom is her development of Daniel's sister. In the exhibition plans that she was sent when she began work on the project, Daniel's mother and younger sister, Erika, die at Auschwitz. The mother is ill, and Erika is simply too young to survive. In the novel, Matas, aware that a 15-year-old girl might have survived the initial selection, extends Erika's life, has her play in the orchestra at Auschwitz, end the war in Gross-Rosen, and then die shortly after liberation in Waldenburg.

But Matas's freedom to invent her story proved far more restricted than "the rest was up to me" suggests. What made the process particularly contentious, far more than a matter of simply correcting historical details, were two central conceptual issues—the nature of Daniel and the nature of the child reader. Underlying all of the detailed responses to drafts of the manuscript was an underlying hesitancy regarding the legitimacy of fiction in Holocaust representation and an equally profound conflict about the nature and function of the child narrator. The museum's insistence on historical precision and research remained in uneasy balance with the creation of a fictional Daniel, who, within an accurate historical narrative, has to function as a representative child.

The child narrator of the special exhibition could have been a real child who did or did not survive. If the museum decided that young children need the hope provided by a narrator who does survive, there are certainly appropriate memoirs available. But, for whatever reason, most likely because such memoirs do not provide the comprehensive survey that the museum envisioned as suiting their pedagogical purpose, the staff preferred to use a fictional child. Thus the difficulty for Matas was twofold: her manuscript would be reviewed by museum staff far more impressed by historical accuracy than by the conventions of children's fiction, and they would come to her manuscript convinced that they already knew what a representative child should sound like. It should sound like the voice that they were collectively creating for the exhibition.

But how do we decide what a representative child sounds like when the subject is the Holocaust, and what exactly does that child represent? How can one voice represent the many voices of those who died and the few who survived? How does that child's voice fit within our contemporary understanding of how children speak and still respect the historical conditions of the Holocaust that we commonly assert destroyed the very possibility of childhood?[21] Can a representative child's voice imitate the voices of real Holocaust children and still fulfil its pedagogical purpose, or does pedagogy impose limits on what that voice can say and understand?

In order for Daniel to be representative, the museum invented a composite child, who could bridge the gap between the world of child visitors and the history that they saw in the exhibit. The narrative voice that guided children through the exhibition had to speak in terms that, the museum believed, they would comprehend. For example, Morgenstein repeatedly explained in her lectures on the exhibition that research revealed that children want to know practical things, that while children can understand the restrictions that gradually encroach upon Daniel's life, they cannot comprehend death (USHMM.2000.041). Clearly these generalizations apply more to the museum's target audience of child visitors between 8 and 12 than to the children who lived and died in Lodz, Auschwitz, and Buchenwald. Perhaps like child visitors, the 6-year-old Daniel cannot understand death in 1933 Frankfurt, but he is more likely to comprehend it when he begins to narrate his story as an adolescent in 1941 and when he concludes it in 1945.

Matas modulates the voice of Daniel very carefully; his voice begins as a conventional childhood voice speaking about events that the visitor will recognize, the world of family and games. In answer to the opening question of the novel, "What has happened to me?" (3), Daniel turns to the memory of a soccer ball hitting his head when he was 10. While he is allowed the occasional joke, he cannot be too silly. Neither can he be too angry or in any way too impassioned—that might conflict with the pedagogical purpose that requires a thoughtful, reflective voice, which will encourage child visitors to think as well. But requiring that Daniel's voice remain childlike according to the museum's understanding often means that it ceases to resemble the children's voices inscribed in the diaries that survived, even when the children did not. Collapsing the difference between child visitors and children in the Holocaust, the museum's conception of the childlike also overlooks how Daniel's voice changes as he grows up over the course of the war.

The museum seems not to have anticipated how often children would be confused by the invention of a representative child. The necessity of reminding visitors (and readers of *Daniel's Story* as well) that Daniel is invented remains. Even before opening the book, we read on the back cover that "Daniel is a fictitious character [whose] story was inspired by the real experiences of many of the more than one million children who died in the Holocaust."[22] In the same way, the *Teacher Guide: Remember the Children, Daniel's Story* acknowledges that some children "believe that *Daniel* [sic] is or was a real person, instead of understanding that he is a narrator who tells a story about real events that happened during the Holocaust" (3). The solution in the *Teacher Guide* is to print Daniel's name in italics "to serve as a reminder that *Daniel* is not a living individual" (2), but this strategy seems futile when visitors to the museum repeatedly see historical photographs that they are encouraged to interpret as depicting members of Daniel's family. While it is true that the exhibition carefully refrains from identifying one particular child as Daniel, its reliance upon photography does encourage visitors to imagine that one of the children they see in a group photograph must be him. And no visitors would hesitate about identifying either Daniel's mother or his sister. When Daniel says at the end of the exhibition that he will always remember his mother and Erika, visitors see photographs that they are likely to conclude must be of Daniel's mother and sister. Readers of the novel have proven to be similarly perplexed. Some write Matas asking why Daniel is invented if the events are true. Other children refuse to accept that he is invented. They urge Matas to write a sequel, but if she cannot, beg her to let them know what happened to him in real life (CM.A.95-64.7-36).

Revising Daniel's Voice

The reliance upon photography is evident in the first draft of the novel, a 243-page manuscript written in longhand. This version begins not with the train journey from Frankfurt to Lodz, but with Daniel en route to Auschwitz and imagining the possibility of a horrible, tortured death, a passage that Matas later moved to the beginning of "Pictures of Lodz." In the first draft, several of the key episodes exist but differ significantly from their final treatment: for example, Aunt Leah is really beaten up, not simply as part of Daniel's dream, and Daniel's grandmother gives him a Hitler Youth uniform, which he only stops wearing after his mother discovers it hidden under his mattress, not as a result of his own independent decision. Many of the minor characters have names —Moshe, Isaac, Zev—that Matas revised when informed that such names were not usual for German Jews; several companies that employ slave labour are also named. The draft also includes references to Mordechai Chaim Rumkowski, the Chairman of the Lodz Ghetto, which are deleted from the final version, as are references to the Jewish police in the ghetto, a discussion by Daniel and other adolescents regarding the behaviour of the Jewish police, and a lengthy exchange between the Jewish police and Daniel when he tries to escape deportation to Auschwitz. In the book, the latter passage is replaced by a much briefer one in which Daniel is quickly found by the Gestapo and put on the freight car. The second draft is typed, with an opening far closer to the final version, and includes the section headings that tightly structure the book.

The third draft was the first to be read by museum staff. On June 30 Morgenstein circulated copies to Sybil Milton, Jeshajahu Weinberg, and at least two other readers. On July 14, Milton sent Morgenstein the marked-up manuscript and a nine-page memo explaining in detail the factual errors and editorial revisions that required attention. For example, where Matas had written that all synagogues were burned during *Kristallnacht*, Milton noted that this was an exaggeration and gave the exact percentage of synagogues that were destroyed. Although Morgenstein's cover memo to Kitzen indicates that she forwarded Milton's copy of the manuscript and her memo at the same time, it appears to have arrived after Morgenstein had already discussed the manuscript with Kitzen. Thus Kitzen received Milton's response after she had summarized and discussed with Matas Morgenstein's response and that of two other museum readers.[23] As a result, Matas participated in a complex phone and fax discussion of her manuscript even as she was drafting revisions in response to earlier discussions and increasingly conscious of the tight deadline she was working against.

Although we cannot know what was said by phone, the archival records give clues to those conversations and indicate that the museum's suggested revisions involved more than historical accuracy. The records include, in chronological order, two readers' reports addressed to Morgenstein; Kitzen's memo to Matas summarizing her own response as well as issues identified by Morgenstein; Milton's nine-page memo to Morgenstein; three memos by Matas; still more memos by

Matas, Kitzen, and Morgenstein after Kitzen forwarded Milton's memo to Matas; and Morgenstein's seven-page memo to Kitzen.

Unlike Milton's mainly factual corrections, the written responses by the first two readers focused on the construction of Daniel. One reader observed with some dismay that the fictional Daniel seemed far angrier than the Daniel of the exhibition (USHMM.2000.061.22). Another reader sent Morgenstein a two-page memo on July 7 in which she summarized her concerns, as well as a marked-up copy of the manuscript where she noted passages in which Daniel's voice sounded too adult and episodes whose pedagogical point was unclear. She objected that Daniel's tone of voice differed from the tone used by the survivors she had met; she did not consider that the voice of a young person speaking during the war might not necessarily resemble the voice of someone much older speaking many years later. This reader also worried about how cynical Daniel was, and insisted that in a children's book evil cannot triumph (USHMM. 2000.061.22). Such responses indicate how the representation of history is affected by pedagogy; surely cynicism might be a valid response to this history and the murder of millions might well be interpreted as the triumph of evil.

Both readers were particularly troubled by the Hitler Youth uniform episode. Calling for a more linear development that included more historically significant dates to help the child reader comprehend Daniel's story, the second reader identified the central problem as Daniel's role as a representative child. She argued that giving Daniel too many exceptional experiences, whether in Frankfurt, the ghetto, or the camps, would only distract the child reader from the book's pedagogical purpose. Wanting a stronger emphasis on Daniel's role as representative child and on the function of his story as Holocaust pedagogy, she objected to aspects of the narrative that threatened to turn the book into an adventure story.

The reader's insistence that the book teach children was strongly framed by her equal concern regarding how much adults should tell children about the camps. She worried that the graphic and violent details obscured the central issue of the text, the loss of so many lives. Yet in expressing her concern that attention to graphic details might normalize the violence, the reader set aside what many historians and writers of memoirs accept as fact: in the camps, violence and horror *were* normal. This reader was not the only one to argue that Daniel's narration must function within limits regarding what is appropriate and tolerable for the child reader. Others would share her concern that elaborate descriptions of the burning pits and of soap made from the victims' fat are excessive and inappropriate.[24] Such objections foreground the aesthetic dilemma faced by any writer of children's literature on the Holocaust—how exactly does one write sensitively about genocide?

In keeping with the process Kitzen and Morgenstein had agreed upon in April, Kitzen summarized the museum's objections and discussed them with Matas. She also incorporated many of their comments on her own marked-up copy of the manuscript. In an accompanying memo, she encouraged Matas to develop Daniel's emotional response and introspection following various episodes and to give him "more childlike reactions" (CM.A.95-64.4-1). Although observing that the manuscript's emphasis on facts distances the reader from the story, she did not ask Matas to remove many of them. Instead she turned to the need for greater linear development and then summarized the museum's concerns regarding historical accuracy and moral issues too complicated for young readers. As examples of where historical facts make episodes improbable, Kitzen referred to the scene in which Daniel works in a Buchenwald photography studio late in the war, suggested that the Hitler Youth uniform episode is inappropriate and should be cut, and advised that the museum believed that "the concept of the Jewish police in the ghetto. [...] is much too complicated an issue for Daniel's youth group to discuss" (CM.A.95-64.4-1).

Perhaps not understanding, or unwilling to convey to Matas the full extent of the museum's objections to the discussion of the Jewish police, Kitzen simply asked if Matas could change it. In the margin of the manuscript where Matas refers to "Jewish police" during a Lodz Ghetto roundup, Kitzen suggested an alternate phrasing: "ghetto police" (CM.A.95-64.3-17). Beside the lengthy discussion of the Jewish police, where one adolescent calls Rumkowski "a brutal dictator" and another defends the actions of the Jewish police as preferable to the brutality of the German guards, Kitzen wrote, "too old and complex for our audience" (CM.A. 95-64.3-17). Then asking Matas to cut some of the "graphic, violent descriptions," she told her that she needed the revision by August 1.

Despite the tight timeline, or perhaps in response to it, and hoping to resolve quickly many of the larger issues by explaining her authorial choices, Matas faxed at least three memos on July 14. Their content clarifies her artistic intent. In a memo to Kitzen, she rejected concentrating on Daniel's feelings and explained her use of the present tense to evoke the different stages of Daniel's memory: "This book is about a 14-year-old, then 16-year-old, then 18-year-old character who is remembering what happened" (CM.A.95-64.4-2). The book "is not about *what* Daniel felt as he was living his experiences; it is about how he remembers these experiences and how he tries to make sense of them in the present" (CM.A.95-64.4-2).

This decision to write in the present tense, apparent in Matas's initial notes for the book, speaks to her belief that the intended child reader would be capable of understanding a sophisticated temporal structure. Whatever the ability of the child reader, the numerous places where the manuscript is annotated with questions about the child's voice demonstrate that the museum readers and Kitzen often misunderstood this structure. There are repeated queries indicating that readers confused the age of Daniel in his role as narrator and the age of the Daniel who is remembered. For example, Kitzen annotated one passage, "would an 11 year old think this?"; Matas responded in her own annotation that Daniel is 14 in that scene (CM.A.95-64.3-17). Insisting that Daniel remembering at 14 is different from Daniel remembering at 18, and recognizing the need to clarify the flashbacks but refusing to omit them, Matas also reminded Kitzen of a practical marketing consideration. Her intended readers would not welcome the thoughts of a six-year-old: "we all know that 10- to 12-year-olds have no interest in reading about a six year old. Therefore, it would be suicide to write the first section about a six-year-old, the second about a 14-year-old, etc., as you would create an audience who would only read certain sections" (CM.A.95-64.4-2).

In this memo, Matas also addressed the tone of Daniel's voice and explained that she deliberately chose "a cool, matter-of-fact" recollection. The alternative, a sensationalism in which children are encouraged to feel the horror with Daniel, she rejected as Stephen King-style horror, particularly gratuitous when the subject is the Holocaust: "Interestingly, in the few places where I do describe horrible things, you urge me to take them out" (CM.A.95-64.4-2). She reminded Kitzen that she rightly refused to describe Lisa's feelings when she shot the soldier in *Lisa's War*; she saw no reason to do otherwise now. Describing what Daniel feels at the very moment he shoots a Buchenwald guard—"As I pulled the trigger, triumph and hate coursed through my veins …"—would only "cheapen the work" (CM.A.95-64.4-2). And she concluded by referring to her judgment of what her child readers are capable: "I also believe that I am a good judge of what young readers can and cannot understand—they understand a lot! They are very clever and, I'm afraid, grossly underestimated too much of the time" (CM.A.95-64.4-2).[25]

In her second memo that day, faxed to Kitzen but addressed to Morgenstein and Zapruder, Matas drew on a contrast between history and imaginative literature familiar to readers of Aristotle's *Poetics*—"the historian relates what happened, the poet what might happen" (Aristotle 18). She argued for the right to retain incidents that are probable: "as long as the event could have happened, that is all I can be concerned with—not whether it usually happened. For you, Daniel is a general representation; for me, an individual character" (CM.A.95-64.4-2). She then proposed solutions to four of the museum's concerns through "reasonable compromises" (CM.A.95-64.4-2). The first concerned her unwillingness to abandon the episode in which Daniel's grand-mother gives him a Hitler Youth uniform; readers to whom she had shown the chapter liked it, and the episode reveals an important aspect of Daniel's character. Matas proposed rewriting the ending of the episode so that Daniel chooses on his own to stop wearing the uniform: "I think it worth illustrating that Daniel being a wild spirit *at first* thrived on the freedom and power he suddenly had" (CM.A.95-64.4-2).

The museum had also objected to the episode in which Aunt Leah is beaten up, because the readers regarded the incident as implausible in Germany prior to *Kristallnacht*. On this issue too, Matas was willing to compromise. Initially, she suggested a note explaining that it was not a common occurrence; later, she addressed the implausibility of the episode by rewriting it as a nightmare experienced by Daniel. On another point, the unlikelihood of Daniel's working as a Buchenwald photographer during the chaotic final weeks of the war, Matas agreed to emphasize the sense of chaos, but insisted that the structural integrity of the book demanded that she continue to refer to photography.

The only compromise that would prove absolutely unacceptable was the matter of the Jewish police. Apparently not realizing the full extent of the museum's opposition to any references to Rumkowski or the Jewish police, and thinking only of the episode in which their role is debated by Daniel, his new friend, Rosa, and other adolescents, Matas argued for retaining the discussion. She agreed that, "this is a complex moral issue and it is unclear what we should think about it. That is what I would like to convey to the reader" (CM.A.95-64.4-2). Asserting that "it is not my job as a children's writer to tell children *what* to think, but rather to *make* them think"

(CM.A.95-64.4-2), she proposed adding a scene in which Daniel discusses with his father the different views in the ghetto of the Jewish police. She could not "change 'Jewish' to 'Ghetto' police, as kids would assume they were Nazis or Poles" (CM.A.95-64.4-2). For Matas, the discussion of the Jewish police was integral to her construction of Daniel as an intelligent adolescent: "Daniel, because of who he is, would *have* to deal with this, puzzle over it, wrestle with it. He will not come to any conclusion but he couldn't be blind to it— he's too bright" (CM.A.95-64.4-2).

That same day Matas faxed copies of both memos to Amy Berkower, a literary agent at Writers' House Inc, and added the following:

> I feel strongly about the issues I've raised in my response and I hope that both Susans will see my point. This is *exactly* what happened with *Lisa's War*, but I stood my ground and it ended up on the *New York Times* Notable List. The editorial comments were identical, then and now, and my response must be the same. You cannot sensationalize a book about the Holocaust. I know Susan Kitzen doesn't want that, but that would be the result of following her suggestions. (CM.A.95-64.4-2)

On July 15, Kitzen faxed Morgenstein the memo Matas had written the day before to Morgenstein and Zapruder along with a cover memo indicating that she believed that Matas's proposed solutions would work. She also told Morgenstein that, with the pressures of the deadline, she was reluctant to forward Milton's lengthy response to the manuscript, since it included editorial comments as well as corrections to historical information. Instead, Kitzen requested that Morgenstein provide her as soon as possible with a list of the key historical inaccuracies that the museum believed needed to be addressed (USHMM.2000.061.21). Despite her hesitancy to send Matas the entire Milton memo, and with a cover note indicating that she had not yet heard from the museum regarding her July 15 fax, Kitzen faxed the nine-page memo to Matas on July 16, advising her to ignore any editorial comments and comments about matters that they had already discussed, but to concentrate on the "factual problems" that are identified. It is not surprising that the decision to forward this memo produced even more faxed exchanges, for Milton not only pointed out numerous historical errors, she also provided details that contradicted historical information given to Matas by a museum source in the spring.

The copious details provided by Milton indicate the difference between a historian and novelist's understanding of the child narrator and the child reader. Although check marks on the fax suggest that in many instances Matas corrected errors that Milton identified or agreed with her reading, at other times the novelist's frustration with the historian's suggestions is evident. For example, the first "substantial error" is the opening page reference to the number of Jews deported with Daniel from Frankfurt to Lodz. With scholarly precision, Milton provided two historical sources giving exact figures for the number of Jews deported from Frankfurt (CM.A.95-64.4-1). In the margins to the fax, Matas wondered just how a child would know the exact number of Jews deported with him. Her solution was to rewrite the passage in a way that dealt with Milton's comment but respected the knowledge available to her narrator: "I am on a train with [...] what looks like over a thousand other Jews from Frankfurt" (DS 3). Thus, the accuracy of the historical record and the impression of the child witness correspond. In other instances, Matas ignored Milton's corrections. While Milton gave precise figures for the numbers deported from Lodz in September 1942, Matas retained Daniel's reference to 20,000 people (DS 50). This number may not match the information historians now possess, but it more likely matches what someone in Lodz in 1942 might have believed since it is the number used by Rumkowski in a September 1942 speech: "they [the Nazis] requested 24,000 victims [...]. I succeeded in reducing the number to 20,000, but only on the condition that these would be children below the age of ten" (Adelson and Lapides 330).

On page 10 of the manuscript, Milton identified two other factual errors: the first concerns the date when Jews were expelled from German public schools; the second is Daniel's assertion that he could stay in school because his father was a World War I veteran. In response to the first Matas wrote in the margin, "According to Museum time line they were expelled gradually," and to the second, "this is from Museum" (CM.A.95-64.4-1). Evidence to support Matas may be found in the research material sent to her by the museum. Included in this material is a historical event timeline that states for April 25, 1933: "restriction of number of Jewish children in German schools; could not exceed 1.5% of all students. This law initially did not apply to children of war veterans and children with one Aryan parent" (CM.A.95-64.4-4).

Matas subsequently revised the passage on Daniel's schooling in accordance with Milton's comments; Chapter Two of the published novel begins with a reference to how Daniel's friends gradually and voluntarily left school in the years leading up to *Kristallnacht*. The *Daniel's Story Videotape Teacher Guide*, published by the museum in November 1993, more than a year after Milton criticized Matas's manuscript for this error, confirms that the historian is right about when Jewish children had to stop attending public school, but still continues to include the information that Matas used. In the "Timeline of Historical Events related to *Daniel's Story*, 1933-1945," included in the *Guide*, is the following entry for April 25, 1933: "The law against 'overcrowding in German schools and universities' is adopted, restricting the number of Jewish children allowed to attend. Children of war veterans and those with one non-Jewish parent are initially exempted" (22).

Matas took the critiques by the museum and Kitzen very seriously; on July 19 and 20 she drafted further memos to Kitzen and to Morgenstein.[26] Protesting that the short publication deadline was making it very difficult to create new episodes to replace major incidents such as the Hitler Youth uniform episode, she told Kitzen, "If I had an extra two weeks I could come up with another episode" (CM.A.95-64.4-2). Adding that changing the Hitler Youth uniform to a school uniform did not work—she had already tried writing the episode that way—she sent Kitzen a revised version of it and justified its inclusion by noting that it was taken from an incident in a memoir. She also indicated that, rather than including more dates, she was not only removing some of the dates Kitzen had inserted, but some of her own as well. Her justification was a consideration of the child reader and the difference between reading history and reading fiction: "The more we include the more kids will feel pressured to remember, organize and read as a history book rather than just following the story" (CM.A.95-64.4-2). For the same reason, she also passed on Berkower's suggestion that she write an afterword to explain the improbable episodes by discussing the difference between writing fiction and writing history.[27] In her memo to Morgenstein, Matas wrote that Milton's fax had left her confused in several instances; one example was the contradiction between Milton's description of the orderly life on German streets in the summer of 1938 and page 131 of Lucy Dawidowicz's *The War Against the Jews*. In the case of two incompatible historical views, how was Matas to decide which historian was right?

Morgenstein answered in a seven-page memo to Kitzen written on July 20. Intended to clarify the museum's views on the various issues raised by Matas, the memo was copied to Milton and Weinberg. When faxing the memo two days later to Matas, Kitzen omitted only the opening paragraph in which Morgenstein reminded her of their prior understanding that Kitzen would review all museum comments before deciding if they were appropriate to be passed on to Matas (USHMM.97-014.23). This was to be the last substantial memo Matas would see before submitting the revised manuscript to Kitzen on July 29. The memo carefully delineated the museum's position and the reasoning behind their critique, demonstrating how their key disagreements originated in their different understanding of the child reader, the role of the child narrator, the purpose of children's reading about the Holocaust, and an overriding concern about the dangers of fictional misrepresentation.

The first issue addressed was the Hitler Youth uniform. Morgenstein compared Daniel's wearing of such a uniform to a more recent, equally unlikely, and problematic American example, that of an African-American child putting on a Ku Klux Klan outfit. She used the analogy to demonstrate that the episode did not work. As soon as Daniel put on the Hitler Youth uniform, he became a participant, an act with moral implications far too complicated for children to address (CM.A.95-64.4-1). If the museum's critique of the episode derives primarily from their conception of child readers, both in terms of children's ability to comprehend complex issues and the pedagogical need for children to derive clear lessons, it is also premised on the museum's insistence that Daniel be a representative protagonist. Matas argued for the inclusion of the episode by citing a memoir that contains a comparable incident, but, given the museum's requirements, this was irrelevant. Their position that Daniel's story must be representative did not acknowledge that his very survival made his story exceptional.

The second issue came from the assumption that children's historical fiction should have the primary goal of teaching history to children. The objection to the beating of Aunt Leah and Matas's depiction of violence was rooted in historical accuracy and chronology. Supporting Milton's position on the unlikelihood of such an incident, Morgenstein argued that *Kristallnacht* had to be treated as a turning point in the history of the Holocaust. By placing the beating scene prior to *Kristallnacht*, Matas minimized the significance of that event and thereby prevented child readers from recognizing its importance (CM.A.95-64.4-1). This completely contradicted the museum's position on children's fiction.

The museum thought that children should not read about a protagonist who acts outside what historical facts permit. In her July 14 memo to Morgenstein and Zapruder, Matas had said, "For you, Daniel is a general representation; for me, an individual character" (CM.A.95-64.4-2). Now under the heading, "The Characterization of Daniel," Morgenstein responded that attention to the limits historical facts place on Daniel's behaviour would not lessen his character. She also objected to passages where Daniel moves from historical fact to speculation, as he does when he imagines what life would have been like if Hitler had not come to power. The passage reads, "If Hitler had not come to power they would have lived as usual—perhaps being mean to their wives and children, cheating a bit at businesses but in general leading a 'normal' life" (CM.A.95-64.3-15). Not only did Morgenstein assert that the irony of this passage is too complicated for children, but she categorized it as a possibly false assertion, for how can we know what would have happened without Hitler? Based on her understanding of how children read, she worried that children would take such statements literally (CM.A.95-64.4-1).

The construction of the child reader also underlies the museum's objection to Matas's inclusion of the Jewish police. Agreeing with Matas that her novel should challenge children, but citing the views of educators outside the museum, Morgenstein continued to insist that within the limitations of a children's novel Matas could not possibly enable her readers to understand the complex moral issues posed by the behaviour of Jews forced by the Nazis to administer the ghettos. She pointed out that ghetto inhabitants had different views on this issue, and that, if the topic of the Jewish police were to be included, its complexity would overwhelm the novel.

Despite this very clear statement of the museum's position, the revised manuscript that Kitzen received on July 29 still included references to the Jewish police. Feeling stymied at her inability to convince Kitzen and Matas that the subject could not be treated effectively in a children's book and concerned that the novel would be judged by a higher standard than other children's books because it was associated with the Museum, Morgenstein wrote Weinberg on July 30 for advice. His reply to Morgenstein on August 3 was short and to the point: he agreed completely that the role of the Jewish police was very complex and might confuse children into thinking that the police were perpetrators equivalent to the Nazis. He also agreed that children do not have the maturity to understand these issues, or to understand that the behaviour of the police was not identical in all of the ghettos (USHMM.97. 014.23).[28] He ended the memo by advising Morgenstein to explain that this was not a matter that the museum was willing to debate.

In an August 4 letter to Kitzen, putting on record their conversation held earlier that day, Morgenstein confirmed that Kitzen and Kate Waters of Scholastic had agreed to delete the passage (USHMM.2000.061.21).[29] She referred to Weinberg's view on the inappropriateness of the subject, both as a topic that Daniel might discuss and as a topic that the child reader could handle. She also added that Weinberg had instructed that the cover wording, "published in conjunction with the United States Holocaust Memorial Museum" was conditional until this content issue was resolved and requested, for this reason, that Kitzen forward the revised chapter to the museum for review. In response to Waters, who had questioned the pedagogical basis for deleting the chapter about the police, Morgenstein summarized the response of William Parsons, the director of education, who was previously associated with Facing History and Ourselves.[30] Parsons had told her that he believed that no children in the ghetto would have discussed this topic. The same day, in a fax to Matas that began, "the good news is you don't have to do any further work on the manuscript" (CM.A.95-64.4-1), Kitzen told her of the museum's decision regarding "the Jewish police business."

The Voice of Dawid Sierakowiak

There is no further correspondence regarding the Jewish police. In the published novel, not only does the lengthy discussion by Daniel's youth group disappear, but so do all references to Mordechai Chaim Rumkowski. Although the novel refers to "police work" as one of the jobs done in the ghetto (DS 55), the word "Jewish" is never used; for example, a manuscript reference to Jewish police and German guards is replaced by the more generic "policemen and guards" (DS 45), and the proper name Rumkowski is replaced by the less specific reference, "the chairman of the ghetto" (DS 47). In contrast, "Hans Biebow, the German in charge of the ghetto" (DS 68) remains, a naming that is noticeable only because so many other proper names have been deleted. All specific references to Buchenwald forced labour working in factories owned by Krupp, Siemens, and I.G. Farben also disappear— "let's not name companies" [CM.A.95-64.3-17]—and are replaced by the less precise, "Buchenwald was a concentration camp with factories" (DS 112).[31]

The overall impact of these deletions is not only to prevent confusion on the reader's part as to the identity of the real criminals, but also to redirect the reader's attention in "Pictures of Lodz" to the romance between Daniel and Rosa. After the politically specific conversation in the youth group is removed, all that remains as "an act of defiance" (DS 51) is Rosa's smile. In the manuscript and the published novel, Daniel first meets Rosa in Lodz when Erika brings her home and speaks excitedly about the youth group that Rosa has begun. But with the removal of the "intense discussion" of the role of the Jewish police (CM.A.95-64.3-17), the political specificity of Rosa's behaviour is reduced as well. Rosa continues to act politically when she leads a hunger strike at her factory, but the reader is left uncertain regarding the identity of the people she is striking against.[32] "Management [is] furious" (DS 65), but who is management? Similarly Rosa's angry rejection of hope after Erika expresses "the central principle that kept the ghetto going" (DS 65) turns quickly into a moment of flirtation: "I suppose we all hope for certain things, Daniel, but I don't think you should admit what it is *you* hope for" (DS 56). What also disappears from this passage is Daniel's lengthy consideration of how the Nazis took advantage of the victims' hope. He concludes that hope killed the resistance and that in this way the Nazis perversely benefited from the goodness that makes people want to believe in the best. Such troubling thoughts rely, according to the annotations in the manuscript margins, on adult concepts (CM.A.95-64.3-17). The fact that, in the manuscript, Daniel is 17 when he thinks this is irrelevant; the intended reader remains only 8 to 12, and so presumed to be incapable of comprehending such complex ideas.

Despite the pressures on Matas to modify Daniel's voice to better suit the museum's conception of the implied reader, she did not always make the suggested changes. As a result, there are moments in the book when Daniel's tone disrupts the pedagogically reassuring voice desired by the readers of the manuscript, moments when his voice comes close to that of Dawid Sierakowiak, an adolescent who really lived and died in the Lodz Ghetto. Sierakowiak was 15 when the war started and just under 19 when he wrote the last surviving entry in his *Diary* on April 15, 1943. The similarity in age to Matas's Daniel is striking. Daniel is 14 when he is sent to the Lodz Ghetto in October 1941, 17 when he is deported to Auschwitz in August 1944 and narrates his memories of the ghetto. Like Daniel, Dawid is bright, a reader and avid listener to news in the ghetto. Unlike Daniel, he is a Polish Jew who fears the impact of the arrival of German Jews. Certainly there is no happy ending or romance in this *Diary*; the diarist dies as does his entire family. Sierakowiak died in Lodz on August 8, 1943. The official cause of death was tuberculosis; Alan Adelson suggests that he died of "tuberculosis, starvation, and exhaustion, the syndrome known as ghetto disease" (*Diary* 268). The despair of Dawid's final entry, "There is really no way out of this for us" (268), is in stark contrast to the hope that the narrator of a children's book must express. Sierakowiak's anger turns to despair, whereas in keeping with the needs of a children's book, Daniel's anger turns to resistance.

Yet despite the numerous differences between Dawid and Daniel's story, not least of which is Dawid's troubled relationship with his far from perfect father,[33] Sierakowiak's *Diary* demonstrates that objections to Daniel's voice as uncharacteristic of what a child in the ghetto sounds like are misleading, a deliberate turning away from the historical evidence of one child's voice, evidence that at least some of the museum staff would have known. Although *The Diary of Dawid Sierakowiak: Five Notebooks from the Łódź Ghetto* was not published until 1996, the museum did recommend that Matas consult Adelson and Lapides's *Lodz Ghetto: Inside a Community Under Siege*, and that anthology includes already-published excerpts from Sierakowiak's notebooks. Today an excerpt from Sierakowiak is even included as part of a package of post-visit materials for middle school and high school students as a supplement to the voice of the exhibition. In *Teacher Guide: Remember the Children, Daniel's Story*, teachers can decide when and if their students are ready to move from the reassuring fictional voice of Daniel to the more disturbing voices of the diarists, who did not choose their words in order to teach children outside the ghetto a lesson.

But the voice in the novel has to function pedagogically. Thus, in criticizing the moments when Matas's fictional child sounds closest to a real child's voice (in terms of age, Dawid is as much a "child" as Daniel), the museum readers demonstrate the difficulty of merging two contradictory spaces of childhood: the space of the ghetto and the very different space occupied by the implied child reader. How could the voice of Daniel bridge this contradiction except by presenting his experience in simple terms that the listener would comprehend? In the transcript of the "Daniel's Story video-tape," Daniel reaches the contemporary child by asking,

"Have you ever been punished for something you didn't do?" (*Daniel's Story Videotape Teacher Guide* 29).

Counter to Parsons's confident assertion (as paraphrased by Morgenstein in her August 4 letter to Kitzen) that no children in the ghetto would have discussed the actions of the Jewish ghetto administration, Sierakowiak discusses Rumkowski and the Jewish police both frequently and furiously. The references to Rumkowski in the surviving second (April 6 – October 23, 1941) and third (March 18 – May 31, 1942) notebooks are on nearly every page. On June 15, 1941, Sierakowiak calls Rumkowski a "sadist-moron" (102); on August 5, 1941, he writes that "The Germans couldn't find a better man than Rumkowski" (118); on August 30, 1941, he states that "Rumkowski gave a truly 'Führer-like' speech in the afternoon" (124). The museum regarded the intended readers of *Daniel's Story* as literal-minded children incapable of understanding irony, but the irony of the adolescent Sierakowiak is inescapable; for example, in his entry for August 10, 1941, he records that doctors have estimated that nearly everyone in the ghetto is infected with tuberculosis: "The ghetto has become a wonderful scientific experiment. What a pity that our doctors can't present their scientific data to the entire world!" (119).[34] In contrast, Matas was advised continually that Daniel's voice must reassure the reader; for example, he must explain that Nazi doctors are not like the doctors the child reader knows. Her sentence— "And these men called themselves doctors, had sworn with the hippocratic oath to save lives" (CM.A.95-64.3-17)—was criticized for being too adult. In keeping with the constant questioning of Daniel's knowledge, the reader of the manuscript wondered whether Daniel would even know the word, "hippocratic"; in the published book, the sentence is revised to omit the final phrase.

In his Foreword to Sierakowiak's *Diary*, Lawrence L. Langer describes its irony as characteristic of many Holocaust testimonies and memoirs and evidence of how they are so easily misunderstood: "The real criminals virtually disappear, and their prey seem to bear the burden of guilt for their own destruction" (vii). Since Langer's premise is that "a primary task of Holocaust literature is to help us imagine the ordeal of those who struggled to stay alive in ghettos and camps" (vii), and Langer has often criticized the compulsion to find a triumphant lesson in Holocaust literature, he values Sierakowiak's *Diary* over Anne Frank's. Yet the very comparison between Sierakowiak and Frank returns us to the concept of childhood and children's literature underlying the museum readers' critique of Daniel's voice. How could any readers, let alone child readers, be expected to possess the necessary historical awareness to understand the ironies of a Dawid Sierakowiak? The museum's desire to have Daniel take child readers to places not described in Anne Frank's *Diary* conflicts with its pedagogical impulse to have Daniel's voice retain some of the hopefulness we associate with the voice of Anne Frank. That impulse cannot be satisfied by Dawid Sierakowiak who writes on June 14, 1942, "The constant struggle of hope against despair will kill me ultimately" (185).

It was precisely in those passages where Daniel sounds most like Sierakowiak that Matas was told that Daniel does not sound like a child. When Kitzen wrote in the margins of the manuscript that Daniel sounds cynical when he describes the SS family dressed up for their family photograph, Matas responded that Daniel is not cynical, he is bitter (CM.A.95-

64.3-17). Whether Daniel is cynical or bitter, his words are guarded compared to the words of Sierakowiak on March 11, 1943: "Lunatics, perverts, and criminals like Rumkowski rule over us and determine our food allocations, work, and health. No wonder the Germans don't want to interfere in ghetto matters: the Jews will kill one another perfectly well" (257).

It is hard to imagine a Daniel who consistently sounds like Sierakowiak; in saying this, I am considering less the museum's concern that the historically uninformed reader would be confused by the irony, than my own conviction that any reader would be distressed by the overwhelming despair of Sierakowiak's text. Surely it is the purpose of a historical novel to inform the reader (whether child or adult) in order to appreciate the irony. At the end of Adelson's introduction, he suggests that reading Sierakowiak's *Diary* may benefit us by helping us to understand the immensity of the destruction and by encouraging us to better appreciate the richness of the life of which Sierakowiak was deprived. This may be so, but I am not sure that many readers, child or adult, would say that they derive such appreciation from this text.

Matas's strategy was to compromise, to create the positive pedagogical voice that both she and the museum endorsed, but to disrupt that voice so the final result is not quite what the museum had in mind, though it is not as despairing as Sierakowiak's. In contrast to the exhibition instructing the child visitor to listen to Daniel's voice and remember, the final line of *Daniel's Story* suggests that memory is more problematic. The penultimate paragraph provides a communal lesson about the danger of forgetting, which Daniel expresses in the first person plural. However, the final paragraph, which shifts to the first person singular, is far more tentative and personal:

"And for the moment, I am content" (DS 131). Satisfying the requirement of a happy ending, Daniel's final words are themselves signs of a narrative resistance and a refusal of closure.

This ending is in keeping with the voice of the novel. When he leaves Auschwitz, Daniel reminds the reader of the different emotional stages he has experienced: "I remember how confused I was on that first trip, how terrified on the second. Now I am simply a ball of anger and fury and determination" (DS 81). Not only does Daniel waver in his feelings, but Matas often gives him an angry outburst that is immediately followed and balanced by another character's rebuttal. When Daniel calls the human race "a race of monsters" (DS 69) that should be wiped out, Erika yells at him that he is thinking like a Nazi. After seeing the bodies in the burning pit in "Pictures of Auschwitz," Daniel comes close to suicide, until his father stops him by threatening to follow him into the pit. When a friend survives the war only to be mortally injured by Polish antisemites afterwards, Daniel breaks down, screaming "pure anguish, pure anger, pure suffering" (DS 123), and again his father is there to respond. Just as Matas occasionally allows Daniel to express hatred because his words are answered by the way Erika teaches him to choose love, she allows him to despair, because his father teaches him to keep going. Even the scene at the end of the war when Daniel looks in a mirror and does not recognize himself, a scene that obviously alludes to the more distressing mirror scene at the conclusion of Elie Wiesel's *Night*, is framed and softened by the father's presence. Wiesel (a year younger than Daniel when he, too, ends the war in Buchenwald) sees a corpse when he looks in the mirror; Daniel, having been warned by his father of the dangers of overeating, sees only the evidence of starvation, the "gaunt" body of a "stranger" (*DS* 119).

Although she revised many of the passages that Kitzen and the museum readers found too cynical and adult (the words often joined as though to be childlike is to be non-cynical), Matas did not change them all. She toned down some of the passages that readers pinpointed as too violent for children, but the major ones remain, such as the murder of the toddler Anya whose back is broken by an SS soldier. One of the most brutal passages in the text occurs when Daniel is asked by the resistance to take photographs of corpses burning in the pit. When a reader objected that writing "[t]here I saw corpses of every size turning black from heat" was really "too much for our intended audience" (CM.A.95-64.3-17), Matas omitted only the final few words, "writhing almost as if they were alive."

Some of her revisions were quite subtle, a compromise between museum suggestions and her own narrative choices. For example, to deal with objections to Daniel's lack of feeling when he enters an apartment in Lodz and discovers the body of a dead man, Matas added a comment by Daniel that retains his numbness but provides an explanation for it: "In fact, what upset me was that I *wasn't* shocked. Death was familiar now, too familiar" (*DS* 62). In other passages, she simply kept the original version. When Daniel in Auschwitz comforts his weeping father after they see that Erika is still alive, Kitzen observed that the gesture makes him "seem [...] so grown up" (CM.A.95-64.3-17) and suggested that the situation be reversed so that Daniel shows more emotion and his father comforts him. Instead, Matas added a few words indicating that Daniel fights back his tears, but she did not reverse the basic situation in which the child comforts his father. Similarly, she retained the calmness with which Daniel responds to Adam's death after Adam, vowing revenge, shoots an SS guard. Despite suggestions that she cut the passage in which Daniel recalls the soldier who used to "take potshots" at the inhabitants of the ghetto and wonders if he is now "safely at home with his family, the murder of his innocent victims to go unpunished" (DS 126), the passage remains. So too do two sentences that Morgenstein queried in her September 1, 1992 memo to Kitzen (USHMM.2000. 061.22). In this passage, Daniel says that, after Buchenwald was liberated, "We were constantly showered with chocolate, gum, cigarettes. They were wonderful" (DS 120). Even though the context of the passage indicates that it is the American soldiers giving out the cigarettes who are wonderful, Morgenstein, again thinking of her implied child reader, worried that children might mistakenly conclude that it is the cigarettes that Daniel finds so wonderful.

The Voices of Some Child Readers

In discussing the impact of the special exhibition, Morgenstein often quoted a child who wrote to Daniel expressing the sadness the child felt after learning his story (USHMM. 2000.041). She also often mentioned that many child visitors preferred to imagine Daniel as female and wrote to Danielle (USHMM.2000.041). Morgenstein was pleased with this evidence that the exhibition makes Daniel a sympathetic character and that children choose to identify with him/her. But the letters to Danielle may also indicate how adult attempts to give children historically accurate fiction will be subject to the child reader's power to invent and rewrite the story. The letters that children wrote to Matas after the novel's publication reveal some of the ways real children respond to Holocaust fiction. The museum hoped that readers would finish *Daniel's Story* with knowledge of at least a few key events, but the letters tell a different story about how children read and to a great degree ignore the historically precise information that the museum was so insistent that the novel provide. Their questions and comments are directed elsewhere. Child readers who understand that Daniel is invented want to know why. Another child, who recognizes that Daniel is invented, writes a letter in which he imagines Daniel writing about his experiences to the protagonist of Matas's first Holocaust novel, *Lisa*.

Many of the letters assume that since Matas knows so much about the Holocaust, she must have a family relationship to the events. Several demonstrate that child readers enjoy the comic scenes (Daniel in his underwear removing lice when Rosa enters the room) and the romance. Nearly all mention the scenes that the adult readers feared were too graphic, such as the one recounted by Adam about the murder of his baby sister, Anya, whose back is broken by an SS guard. Other letters indicate that some readers understand the cruelty Daniel undergoes at the hands of Mr. Schneider, the schoolteacher, far more than other aspects of the book. One child writes that he likes the book because he learned why the Holocaust happened and then mentions that one reason was because Jews owned all the businesses (CM.A.95-64.7-37). Many of the children offer their own solutions to the Holocaust—detailed accounts of how they would have freed the Jews.

To the extent that children bring to their reading the views that they have formed elsewhere, they read like adults. Many children compare Daniel with Anne Frank. One child speaks of how *Daniel's Story* made her finally understand how awful the Holocaust was. She adds that she knew before, but it was a response on a par with, "Oh well. It's sad. Pass the butter" (CM.A.95-64.7-36). The child who writes that he learned from his great-grandfather that Schindler "freed all the Jews from a living hell on earth that Adolf Hitler made for them" (CM.A.95-64.7-36) may have misunderstood what his great-grandfather said, but no more than the child reader who praises the part "when Daniel killed all of Hitler's soldiers" (CM.A.95-64.7-37).

Perhaps the child response that is most revealing about the prior knowledge that children bring to their reading is contained in another archival file, which includes fan mail and pictures received by Matas in response to *Lisa* (CM.A.95-64.7-39). In contrast to *Daniel's Story*, *Lisa* is a novel about the Danish rescue of the Jews, a novel in which there are no scenes set in either the concentration camps or the killing centres.[35] In response to this novel a child sent Matas a picture titled, "The Jews are getting killed by the Germans" (CM.A.95-64.7-39). It is a simple drawing, one that we might describe as "childlike." On the left is a stick figure of a Nazi guard (swastika on his helmet, gun in his hand). On the right is a mustached figure with the name Hitler written on its chest. The two figures stand outside a rectangular building into which gas is being piped and on the bottom of which three horizontal figures are lying and one is standing. The style of the drawing prevents me calling it graphic, and the drawing certainly does not provide the viewer with many historical facts. In many ways it is not about the plot of *Lisa* at all. Yet to an adult viewer, the drawing is simultaneously comic and terrifying: comic, because it reduces to a simple cartoon all the adult debates over how much we can and should tell children about the Holocaust, and terrifying, because it is so "childlike" and shows one child's response to the Holocaust outside the pedagogical, future-looking framework with which we attempt to narrate this history. The drawing reminds us that whatever we tell children about the Holocaust, we tell them more than we know, and we cannot always know what knowledge they will take from our telling.

NOTES

1. A T. Glendenning Hamilton Research Grant from the University of Manitoba enabled me to work with the Carol Matas papers, University of Manitoba Archives and Special Collections. Funding from the Faculty of Humanities and Vice-President (Research), University of Calgary, supported my research at the United States Holocaust Memorial Museum.

2. Weiss had been following the development of the museum through press reports and through conversations with Susan Morgenstein's son, Leslie, who was one of his employees. In later correspondence, Weiss explained that as a producer he would serve as a liaison between the museum, the publisher, and the writer.

3. Archival material from the United States Holocaust Memorial Museum is cited as USHMM followed by the accession number and box number. Archival material from the Carol Matas papers, Department of Archives and Special Collections, University of Manitoba Libraries, is cited CM, followed by the accession number, box number, and file number. In his initial letter, Weiss calls the travelling exhibition "Remember the Children" and the planned special exhibition to be installed at the Washington site, "Daniel's Story." Early correspondence at the museum normally refers to the special exhibition as "Remember the Children" and the team planning it as the Remember the Children team, but in a July 29, 1992 letter to Susan Kitzen discussing the information that will appear

on the back cover of *Daniel's Story*, Susan Morgenstein says that the special exhibition will be called "Daniel's Story" (USHMM.97.014). On the back cover of the novel the special exhibition is called "Daniel's Story: Remember the Children." I refer to the special exhibition that visitors can still see at the United States Holocaust Memorial Museum as the special exhibition or as "Remember the Children: Daniel's Story," the title that is currently in use at the museum. Although publicity on the travelling exhibition also sometimes calls it the special exhibition (and also Remember the Children: Daniel's Story), I refer to it as either Remember the Children or the travelling exhibition.

4. Morgenstein wrote Sara Bloomfield on February 27, 1994, asking on behalf of Matas and Weiss if there was any museum interest in a sequel. Although Matas's novels *After the War* and *The Garden* could be read as psychological sequels exploring the stories of children who survived the camps, they are neither about Daniel, nor are they sequels written in conjunction with the museum. It is worth noting that Ruth Mendenberg, the central character in both novels, is a survivor of Buchenwald, the camp where Daniel is at the end of the war.

5. I spell Lodz as Łódź only when the work I quote does so.

6. All further references to *Daniel's Story* will be given parenthetically as *DS*.

7. The USHMM Photo Archives dates the photograph that influences the cover image as September 1942, but identifies the photographer as Henryk Ross (Sims).

8. Although Leslie Morgenstein initiated Weiss's interest by encouraging him to see the exhibit, the correspondence and Susan Morgenstein's Weekly Reports that detail the numerous meetings and consultations related to *Daniel's Story* in which she participated between January 20 and September 4, 1992, indicate no further role for her son. The key figure at Daniel Weiss Associates mentioned in both the USHMM archives and the Carol Matas papers is Susan Kitzen.

9. Both exhibitions began as "an exhibition conceived by Mrs. Adeline Yates and originally produced by The Capital Children's Museum, Washington, DC" in 1988; when *Daniel's Story* was published, Morgenstein sent Yates a copy, and Yates's contribution is acknowledged on the inside cover of the *Teacher Guide: Remember the Children, Daniel's Story*.

10. The pages of the diary that the visitor to the USHMM sees in 2000 are in script. Morgenstein's papers indicate that child visitors were offended by the implied childishness of print.

11. In the Visitors Guide brochure that visitors receive in 2000, "Remember the Children: Daniel's Story" is described as a "hands-on exhibition" intended "for visitors 8 years and older." The Permanent Exhibition is "recommended for visitors 11 years and older."

12. The difficulty of writing *Daniel's Story* may be responsible for the ambiguity of the quotation. *Jesper* was published four years before *Daniel's Story*.

13. Not only was Scholastic unknown to Goldfarb, the museum staff did not know Matas's work or seem overly familiar with children's literature in general. When *Daniel's Story* was nominated for a Canadian Governor General's Award, Morgenstein compared it to the equivalent of being nominated for the Caldecott. Although the comparison to the illustrator's award is not invalid, someone more familiar with children's literature would be more likely to compare the nomination to the Newbery.

14. The Carol Matas papers also include a Viewers/Teachers Discussion Guide for the documentary film, *Lodz Ghetto*, and an announcement that the film would be shown on PBS April 22–May 15, 1992 (CM.A.95-64.4-4).

15. The correspondence includes letters clarifying who will write to whom and additional letters that indicate that the agreed-upon process in which Susan Kitzen would review all museum correspondence before deciding whether or not to pass it on to Matas proved unwieldy. It is not always clear how much of the museum correspondence Kitzen forwarded to Matas and how much she simply summarized. Neither is it always clear if handwritten letters in the Carol Matas papers were mailed.

16. Much has been written on the role of the museum as an American institution. See, for example, Linenthal, *Preserving Memory: The Struggle to Create America's Holocaust Museum*.

17. One possible exception is Matas's use of the term "slave labour." The museum preferred the term "forced labour," since they felt that the former would confuse American children. Both terms appear in a March 2001 newspaper advertisement informing survivors that they may be entitled to compensation. The advertisement defines slave labour as "work performed by force in a concentration camp [...] or a ghetto or

another place of confinement under comparable conditions of hardship" ("Were You Forced" 5).

18. The Visitors Guide Brochure is slightly different. It states that the museum has three primary missions; the final is "to encourage its visitors to reflect upon the moral and spiritual questions raised by the events of the Holocaust as well as their own responsibilities as citizens of a democracy."

19. "Canada" was explained in the text, but not in the glossary. Responding to the galleys, Sybil Milton, resident historian at the museum, wanted a far more historically precise and lengthy glossary than Scholastic chose to publish. When Matas's manuscript said only that the prisoners had named the storehouse complex Canada, Milton added a note explaining that Polish prisoners were the first to use the term (USHMM.2000.102). The text was not changed, and Milton's suggestion that Canada should appear in the glossary was similarly not taken up.

20. The USHMM Archives contain a proposal from Peter Weisz to produce a CD-ROM on Remember the Children in which Weisz claimed that the museum's original director of education, Isaiah Kuperstein, named the exhibit after his son, Daniel Kuperstein (2000.061.22). The material on the exhibition forwarded to Matas in March 1992 includes in the exhibit outline, "Erika is beginning to act like a girl" (CM.A.95-64.4-1). In contrast, Daniel's perspective is always characterized as that of "a child."

21. Nechama Tec's memoir, *Dry Tears: The Story of a Lost Childhood*, has a subtitle that is mirrored in countless Holocaust memoirs, such as Yehuda Nir, *The Lost Childhood: A Memoir*. Frequently the memoir of a Holocaust childhood begins by reference to the end of childhood; for example, "I was seven years old and on that day my childhood came to an end" (Defonseca prologue).

22. Like everything else in the book, this information had to be approved by the museum (USHMM.97.014.23).

23. The identity of these two readers is uncertain. The reader's report dated July 6 is by "Ellen"; the report dated July 7 and annotated manuscript are in a file labelled AZ, and so they may be by Alex Zapruder (USHMM.2000.061.22).

24. In comparison, Milton objected that the soap reference is simply not true.

25. The memo sent to Kitzen deleted a statement included in a handwritten draft in which Matas indicated that she too child-tested her manuscripts and valued their responses: "I have given the manuscript to a

nine year old and a ten year old. They both loved it and found it very clear. Only at the beginning of the Lodz section were they confused" (CM.A.95-64.4-2).

26. Morgenstein's papers at the USHMM do not include the July 20 handwritten memo, so Matas may have decided not to send it. On the other hand, Morgenstein's July 20 response addresses issues raised in this memo.

27. The three Holocaust novels that Matas published after *Daniel's Story*—*After the War*, *The Garden*, and *Greater Than Angels*—include either an Author's Note or an Afterword that draws the reader's attention to the difference between history and fiction.

28. On this point, the museum appears either to forget its insistence that the novel be historically specific (Matas is writing about the Lodz ghetto, not all ghettos), or to recognize that this historical specificity may be missed by the child reader.

29. Further evidence that this letter would be the final word on the subject is that Morgenstein sent copies of it to Weinberg, Sara Bloomfield, Ronald Goldfarb, William Parsons, and Kate Waters.

30. Facing History and Ourselves is an educational organization that offers professional development programs for teachers of middle and high school students. Its Website (http://www.facing.org) characterizes the study of history as a moral enterprise in which students learn to make connections between history and the moral choices that they confront in their own lives.

31. In many cases, it appears to be Kitzen who recommended the deletion of specific references to businesses. In comparison, the museum readers objected to passages where Daniel draws on a postwar knowledge of business behaviour, such as when he comments that the businessmen who profit from slave labour will "probably use all that money to buy their way out of trouble when the war ends" (CM.95-64.3-17). This sentence is omitted in the book, but a comparison with the pharaohs in Egypt who employed Jewish slaves remains.

32. On August 30, 1992, Milton provided Morgenstein with a long list of entries for the glossary and chronology. The suggested entry for May 6, 1944 gives details regarding the adolescent leadership of soup strikes in the Lodz ghetto factories (USHMM.2000.102). Many of Milton's recommendations for the glossary and chronology do not appear as formal

entries in the published glossary and chronology, but are similarly incorporated as part of the text.

33. Daniel's father is a model father, constantly teaching Daniel the right way to behave. In contrast, the troubled relationship between Dawid and his father, in which Dawid accuses the father of stealing food, is reflected in the episode in which Rosa and Daniel teach a "horrible and greedy" (DS 59) father to stop stealing his children's rations.

34. Sierakowiak's irony is also evident in the excerpt included in the *Teacher Guide: Remember the Children, Daniel's Story*. The excerpted entry from April 29, 1942 about the difficulties of life in the ghetto concludes, "One thing's for sure: it's not boring."

35. Both Milton and Morgenstein repeatedly suggested that Matas's use of the term, "death camp" is misleading since people died in the concentration camps as well; they preferred the term, killing centre. *Daniel's Story* refers to both. On the back cover, Auschwitz is referred to as a death camp.

PART THREE

◆

The Child in the Picture

6

Like a Fable, Not a Pretty Picture: Holocaust Representation in Roberto Benigni and Anita Lobel

Why, more than 50 years after the end of World War II, are we so fascinated with narratives (memoir, fiction, film) that explore questions of Holocaust survival with child protagonists who are far younger than the adolescent survivors (Elie Wiesel's *Night*) and adolescent victims (Anne Frank, *The Diary of a Young Girl*) whose narratives published closer to the war have become canonical Holocaust texts? Why are we increasingly drawn to stories about much younger survivors even as our historical knowledge about the unlikelihood of such survival makes such narratives less credible? The context for my questions lies in statistics cited by Debórah Dwork's *Children With a Star: Jewish Youth in Nazi Europe*, statistics that tell just how rare young child survival was. Dwork relies on the figures in Jacques Bloch's 1946 report to the Geneva Council of the International Save the Children Union; of the 1.6 million European Jews under age 16 in 1939, only 175,000 survived (Dwork 274). This survival rate of just under 11 per cent is a generalized rate for all the countries that were invaded by the Nazis; thus in some countries, the survival rate was much higher, but in others, much lower. Dwork, for example, refers to a study by Lucjan Dobroszycki that concludes that of the close to one million Polish Jewish children age 14 and under in 1939, approximately 5000 survived, that is, only .5 per cent (275).

In her introduction, Dwork argues that the reluctance of historians to examine child life under the Nazis is partly derived from the different way we respond to the murder of children: "Our unwillingness to accept the murder of children is emotionally different from our incomprehension of the genocide of adults" (xlv). She positions her research as central to an understanding of the Holocaust and insists that it is only by confronting the persecution and murder of children that we will be driven to ask the "right" questions, questions that do not blame the victim and that reveal their unfairness as soon as we apply them to infants and young children.[1] Perhaps our increasing fascination with the narratives of young children surviving demonstrates not only a reluctance to ask the "right" questions, but evidence of a deeper resistance. For we seem unable to confront the murder of young children except by celebrating the exceptional—and sadly the more we know, even more incredible—narratives of very young children surviving not just the European scene of war, but the death and slave labour camps. Again, Dwork's analysis illustrates how our desire for such exceptional narratives conflicts with our awareness that nearly all the "children" who were likely to survive were either adolescents or children pretending to be so. Dwork points out that children who survived the initial selection at Auschwitz were in effect no longer children; they were passing as adults: "There were no young children and there was no child life" (217). For such children, death was a matter of time, but through luck, most often just the temporal accident of when the camps were liberated, some of those adult-like children did survive. Again

Dwork cites figures we need to keep in mind: "180 children under the age of fourteen were found alive at the liberation of Auschwitz, about 500 in Bergen-Belsen, 500 in Ravensbrück and 1,000 in Buchenwald" (309).

If so few survived, and if we remember that at least some of these survivors were barely alive at liberation and died soon after, and many of them have died since, is this sufficient to account for our current fascination with the exceptional young child survivor? Are we more willing to listen now not just because there are so few of these child survivors left, but because those few survivors are now elderly? Do we in effect trust and tolerate their voices because they are no longer children, because their postwar survival and lengthy lives provide the safety of distance as well as the authority granted their present age?[2] Or does our eagerness now to imagine such next-to-impossible stories simply reflect the shift to a culture intrigued by narratives of childhood trauma and more accepting of childhood memory, more willing to believe in what children say?

In acknowledging how unusual her focus on child survivors is in mainstream Holocaust history, Dwork notes specific cultural reasons for ignoring child survivors immediately after the war, when many people, perhaps traumatized by what they learned had occurred in the camps, preferred to forget events that seemed unbelievable, particularly when the survivor was a child. If Holocaust narratives told by adults made us uncomfortable and incredulous, narratives told by children were even more unbearable. It was hard to believe that young children could survive, let alone want or be able to narrate their stories. Narratives of young children hidden outside the camps, or fictional accounts that began once the young child was outside the camp (for example, the excessively vague *I am David*) seemed barely tolerable. Thus for many years, child survivors of the camps who were compelled to narrate seemingly impossible stories were heard mainly by medical professionals interested in the psychological makeup of children who survive extreme situations. The general North American public remained indifferent, content if they thought about Holocaust survivors at all to imagine such survivors only as broken-down adults. In Henry Greenspan's terms, the postwar indifference produced a "stigmatizing discourse" (50) about survivors, whether those survivors were adults or children.

Today the situation is different not only in its attention to child survivors, but in its interest in the trauma of their narratives. There is a prolific literature that reads Holocaust testimonies as trauma narrative and often accepts the premise of a postwar collective trauma. Two titles by Cathy Caruth, *Unclaimed Experience: Trauma, Narrative, and History* and *Trauma: Explorations in Memory*, have been particularly influential in establishing the way Holocaust testimonies are read as trauma narratives. Although one of the essays in the latter, Bessel A. van der Kolk and Onno van der Hart's "The Intrusive Past: The Flexibility of Memory and the Engraving of Trauma," raises important questions about whether traumatic memory can be narrated at all, many readers have turned to Holocaust testimony for what it reveals about trauma. Relatively few, (Peter Novick, Kalí Tal, and Greenspan) have contested the perception of a postwar "conspiracy of silence" (Greenspan 51) produced by a collective trauma.

Attention to the survivor as witness and to the listener who witnesses the survivor's testimony dominates Dori

Laub's "Truth and Testimony: The Process and the Struggle." Laub argues that the Holocaust was an event designed not only to kill, but also to make impossible any understanding of what the survivors had witnessed. According to Laub, "*the event produced no witnesses*" (65) in both a physical and psychological sense. Defining a witness as someone who "is a witness to the truth of what happens during an event" (65), he speaks of his own memories as a child survivor and of his professional work with the Fortunoff Video Archive for Holocaust Testimonies at Yale.[3] In this archive of survivor testimonies, survivors can "bear witness [...] belatedly" (69); that is, they can bridge the "*historical gap*" (69) that prevented their witnessing the truth at the time of the event and prevented others being witness to the truth in their testimony.

Unlike Novick therefore, Laub insists that the recent attention to survivor testimony reveals much about the nature of trauma and its temporal aspect. In *Unclaimed Experience*, Caruth defines trauma not as an event in the past, but as something that "was precisely *not known* in the first instance" (4). Since Laub agrees that for this reason the "listener [...] becomes the Holocaust witness *before* the narrator does" (69), he stresses the moral responsibility of the listener to enable the survivor/witness to repossess his or her story. According to this theory, we listen now to what we could not hear before. Laub ends his essay with the testimony offered by a man who was a four-year-old child in the Krakow ghetto.[4] Sent out of the ghetto with a passport photograph of his mother as a keepsake to which he would secretly pray, the man is doubly traumatized, first by his experiences during the war, and a second time when he is reunited after the war with his parents. When he sees his mother, she no longer resembles "the person in the photograph" (71). Laub uses this testimony to demonstrate that "testimony is inherently a process of facing loss" (74). The mother whom the child longed for stands before him, yet she is not the woman he remembers. In recognizing this, the man who was once the hidden child acknowledges that there is no happy ending even when the parents survive: "There is no healing reunion [...] no recapture or restoration of what has been lost, no resumption of an abruptly interrupted innocent childhood" (73). At most there can be an acknowledgment that there is no happy ending, and that the listener understands this.

With that caution in mind, we might expect little demand for happy endings in the narratives of young survivors. Yet the increasing interest in reading Holocaust testimony as trauma narrative only partially explains what we desire and what we find in these narratives about young survivors. Greenspan has noted the development since the late 1970s of two contradictory discourses about survivors, the "'celebratory' and 'psychiatric'" (49). He argues that the discourses exist separately and often have little to do with the complex way that the individual survivor speaks. Survivors are either "archetypal victims" or "heroic witnesses, tellers of tales, redeemers of the human spirit and of hope" (Greenspan 49). If we expect that the category of traumatized victim would be more appropriate in representations of child survivors, what we find in popular culture is a yearning for stories in which there is some triumph. The child is thus both victim and heroic witness. If in these stories not only the young child survives, but the parents as well, our desire for a happy ending is uppermost and often makes us ignore the ambiguous reunion of parent and child that is recounted in the

testimony Laub provides. We may want trauma, but we also
want a happy ending. At least, we do in Roberto Benigni's *Life
Is Beautiful.*

Like a Fable

Two recent and very different works speak to our increasing
desire for young child survivor narratives. Roberto Benigni's
Life Is Beautiful (1997), a film about a father's determination to
protect his four-year-old son, Giosuè, in a concentration
camp, has received numerous international awards. Anita
Lobel's *No Pretty Pictures: A Child of War* (1998) immediately
made the *New York Times* Notable Book List, and was a final-
ist for such awards as the National Book Award.[5] Because of
her established reputation as a picture-book artist, Lobel's
memoir quickly appeared on recommended children's book-
lists. In contrast, Benigni, because of his audacious willingness to apply comedy to the Holocaust, has created a work
that is highly contentious.

The controversy over *Life Is Beautiful* indicates how problematic we still find the question of aesthetic response to historical atrocity, particularly as such atrocity affects young
children. As the similar controversy over Binjamin Wilkomirski's *Fragments: Memories of a Wartime Childhood* reveals, we
celebrate narratives about the amazing survival of such children only so long as we believe that the stories are true.[6] But
if we keep in mind Dwork's statistics, it is not surprising that
Holocaust stories about young children that give us a happy
ending are nearly always fiction. What "truth" then do we
respond to in *Life Is Beautiful*, a film that is so clearly a fable?

Is there any relationship between Benigni's truth and the truth found in Lobel's memoir? Her title, *No Pretty Pictures*, suggests that she mistrusts aesthetic responses to the Holocaust, and that she is determined to separate her Holocaust memories from the artistic work of her adult life.[7] Whether such separation is possible, Lobel's determination accords with our own desire to protect the child viewer, to construct her as the one who does not know.

But maybe it is adults who do not want to acknowledge what some children already know. Although I hesitate to speak about *Life Is Beautiful*, so excessive and misplaced is the outrage that I have heard since the film's release—it is genocide that should provoke our outrage surely, not the aesthetic question of the limitations of comedy—the outrage cannot be divorced from this question of the viewer's knowledge. Is the film's viewer constructed as a child, the one who does not know and therefore believes that what she sees on screen is the historically real, or is the viewer constructed as the adult, the one who already in some sense knows and can therefore imagine what is not shown? My analysis tends to presume the latter; opponents of the film, I would argue, assume the former. I think that the tension in the film, and over the film, relates to the ambiguity of Benigni's response[8] and to the refusal by critics to acknowledge even the possibilities of a children's literature on the Holocaust and what such a literature might tell us about aesthetic response to atrocity and the related question of the child's knowledge.

Even though Benigni has himself suggested that one significant impulse behind *Life Is Beautiful* is the childhood memory of his father magically transforming war experience into reassuring and comic narrative for his children, reviewers of the film have chosen to disregard both the perspective offered by this particular anecdote and the insights offered if the film is situated in the context of the representational strategies familiar in children's literature. Yet such contexts offer a different way of understanding the limitations and strengths of Benigni's film; that is, it makes a difference to our understanding of how the film works if we situate it not beside *Schindler's List*, but in the context of the representational strategies that it openly asserts that it is using.

In this context, I similarly set aside the claim that Benigni adapts his title, *Life Is Beautiful*, from Trotsky's words just before he was murdered, for I find a different lineage far more provocative and useful.[9] It is one in which the title rewrites a statement that appears in the final chapter of Primo Levi's memoir, *Survival in Auschwitz: The Nazi Assault on Humanity*, a memoir published initially in Italian with the far less hopeful title of *Se questo è un uomo* (*If This Is a Man*). In that chapter, "The Story of Ten Days," Levi describes how, ill with scarlet fever and left behind when the Nazis evacuate Auschwitz in January 1945, he and all the others who have been abandoned to die reach a stage where, despite the armies battling nearby, they are "too tired to be really worried" (149). In this state of exhaustion, Levi makes a surprising statement: "I was thinking that life was beautiful and would be beautiful again, and that it would really be a pity to let ourselves be overcome now" (Levi 149).

The contrast between the English translation's careful use of tenses, "life was beautiful and would be beautiful again," a use that excludes the possibility of beauty in the present time and in the Auschwitz location, and Benigni's insistence on the present tense points to how the practice of a children's literature on the Holocaust is deeply implicated in what is most controversial in the film. Although the second half of Benigni's film ironically repeats incidents from the first half as though to demonstrate how insane and desperate is Guido's attempt to persuade Giosuè that life remains the same even when they are in the camp, Benigni's title insists that the passage of time cannot alter eternal truths. The child who becomes the grown-up narrator of the film may possess a deeper understanding of how his father protected him, but it is one in which the essential loving and trusting relationship to the father remains the same. As in a children's folk tale, life *is* beautiful.

The film thus carefully situates its perspective with the opening voice-over spoken by the grown-up Giosuè in which he twice compares his "simple story"[10] to a fable. At the film's end, still believing in his father's story that the point of their incarceration is to obey the rules, play the game, and win a prize, Giosuè greets the arrival of the American liberators as the evidence that he has indeed won the promised tank. Giosuè's ride in the tank is interrupted by a reunion with his mother, Dora, and immediately afterwards the adult Giosuè in a voice-over provides the fable's requisite and apparently unambiguous lesson, "This is my story. This is the sacrifice my father made for me." This structural dependence on a fable, with its promise of a lesson, like the film's parodic reliance on folk-tale elements, games, and riddles, suggests that much of the success of the film (and its controversy) lies in applying to the Holocaust strategies of representation familiar in children's literature but more problematic in adult Holocaust narratives, particularly films, where we assume that documentary realism alone is appropriate to the subject.[11]

It is striking how similar the film's strategies are to those found in Jane Yolen's young adult novel *Briar Rose*: "I know of no woman who escaped from Chelmno alive" (202) Yolen writes after completing a fairy-tale novel in which she imagines one such survivor. As in a fairy tale, Dora, the heroine of *Life Is Beautiful*, lies in bed like Sleeping Beauty, longing to be rescued by her hero, the man who introduces himself as Prince Guido, and whose last name, Orefice, means goldsmith. Of course parody demands that this prince does not climb up the tower, but meets his *principessa* when she falls out of a barn silo into his arms. Nevertheless, Guido clearly does rescue Dora from the miseries of a wealthy marriage, as they ride away from the engagement banquet on a horse appropriately named Robin Hood.

What Yolen accomplishes through the contrast produced by her concluding Author's Note, Benigni achieves through the visualizing of absence, what the screen does and does not show us. The tension of the film lies in its playing between two registers that always threaten to collapse: a children's fable of rescue, an adult narrative of what cannot be said (at one point a character even says that silence is the greatest cry). Certainly existence in the death camps is governed by rules as ludicrous and insane as those involved in the game Guido invents to protect Giosuè from knowledge of the real nature of the camp, but when Guido tells Giosuè that Schwanz, the other child seen earlier hiding in the sentry box, has been "eliminated," for a second we are not sure which game is being played. Similarly Giosuè tells his father about the other children whose absence no comedy can hide: they took the children to the showers; they make buttons and soap from us. Guido mocks his son's gullibility: What kind of game is that? Who can imagine burning people in ovens? But not even Guido, the one who can answer nearly all of the Nazi doctor's riddles (including one about Snow White), can answer the riddle of Nazi categories, the riddle whose answer we know as the Final Solution.

Cautioned by his uncle to heed the warning when Robin Hood is painted with antisemitic symbols, Guido jokes that he did not even know that the horse was Jewish. Like many Italian Jews, Guido is unwilling to imagine himself as vulnerable and jokes that the worst the Nazis can do is to paint him yellow and white.[12] Whatever they do, he insists that he will still be human. His words are echoed in the unanswered and ultimate riddle that later torments the Nazi doctor and prevents him, a believer in the Final Solution, from seeing Guido as human. The riddle describes something that looks and acts like a duck. But what if the doctor's inability to solve the riddle stems from his mistaken belief that it is a riddle? Maybe if it looks like a duck, it really is a duck. Riddles are often based on faulty categories; as in a riddle, the doctor's loyalty to a Nazi ideology that sees Jews as inhuman vermin in need of extermination prevents him from recognizing that Guido is a man.[13] The Nazi desire for a Final Solution demonstrates not only the horrific consequences of riddles based on faulty categories, but also how genocide can be regarded as merely the solution to a challenging riddle, one which is echoed in Levi's title, *Se questo è un uomo*, as well. Is Levi a man? Is Guido? Yet the film has little interest in philosophical analysis. Guido may think himself indebted to Schopenhauer for his belief in willpower. But when he desperately turns to it as a magic spell to prevent the SS dog from discovering his son's hiding place, few adult viewers are

likely to forget the Nazi fondness for the rhetoric of willpower, a rhetoric inscribed in the title of Leni Riefenstahl's 1936
film, *The Triumph of the Will*, or to accept that Giosuè's subsequent survival is proof of Schopenhauer's theories.

Throughout the film, Benigni draws attention to the difference between what the child sees and what the father/
viewer sees: the contrast between the child's joy and belief in
his father's explanation of the camp rules and the incredulous
faces of the adult prisoners who are never taken in by Guido's
jokes. The sleeping Giosuè does not see the mountain of
skeletal corpses that Guido and the viewer see when Guido
carries the child through the night and fog, a night and fog
that is resonant for the viewer familiar with either Alain
Resnais's documentary, *Night and Fog*, or with the secret order,
Nacht und Nebel (Night and Fog), that "mandated the arrest
of anyone suspected of underground activities against the
Reich" (Epstein and Rosen 205). Most poignant is the contrast between the child's final view of his father as Guido is
marched to execution: in the restricted vision of Giosuè peer-
ing from his secret hiding-place appears a father still confident and clowning for his son, repeating the mocking gesture
he made earlier in the film; in the eyes of the informed adult
viewer is a man fully aware that this time he will not return.[14]

Presumably it is Giosuè's adult voice that makes *Life Is
Beautiful* an adult film. Yet it is worth observing both the
abruptness of the film's happy ending and its dependence on
an adult voice that is remarkably faithful to the presumed
perspective of childhood. Although it is the adult Giosuè
who narrates the film, his adult perspective at the film's conclusion is perfectly consistent with the fable that structures
his childhood memories: "This is my story. This is the

sacrifice my father made for me." Yet this insistence on an unproblematic, coherent narrative is only possible if the film concludes at the moment of liberation, the moment when the fable proves to be both true and impossible to continue. For if the fable is true, and the father saved his life, how does a child live with that knowledge? And does Giosuè really survive because of the father's sacrifice? What then is the sacrifice: Guido's silence about the genocidal purpose of the camps, or Guido's death? Accounting for his survival through the father's sacrificial death seems appropriate to a fairy tale, yet it contradicts the evidence of the film, for it is just as likely that Giosuè might have died because of his ignorance of the camps' purpose and just as likely that Guido might have survived if he had not searched for Dora that final night.

The logic that the father sacrificed himself in order that his son might live does not fit the camp universe where, if any logic applies, it is the logic of death by which any Jews saved for work have only been given a temporary reprieve. And any logic, let alone the patterns of fairy-tale justice and the good luck of being the special child of the prince and princess, always comes up against the role of accident: the accident that the next morning the camp is liberated; the accident that Dora survives; the accident that, riding on the American tank, Giosuè finds his mother. The adult Giosuè's belief in his simple story that begins with his first words as a child, "I lost my tank," and ends with his cry of victory at the film's conclusion, "We won, we won," means that the film must end when it does. It cannot afford to proceed further without confuting its own logic.

A "simple story," *Life Is Beautiful* demonstrates that in speaking of the Holocaust it is not just children who long for consolatory fairy tales. Yet the film also illustrates how questions of intended audience in Holocaust representation often blur the distinction we draw between child and adult. It is evident that the controversy over the appropriateness of telling a fable about the Holocaust seems directly consequent to a binary view of Holocaust representation in which adult representation of the Holocaust, precisely because it is adult, is to be judged only in terms of a presumed full (meaning realistic) representation. In contrast, we expect Holocaust representation in children's literature to work with limits, by employing narrative structures that protect the child reader even as the narrative instructs that reader about the Holocaust and attempts to make meaning of what is too easily dismissed as incomprehensible.

While some might object that these very limits make the idea of any children's literature on the Holocaust itself incomprehensible and trivial, children's books may simply be more honest about their limitations than adult works. The objection to limits of representation in children's books implies that there may be another kind of literature—adult literature— that is somehow free of such limits and can therefore provide the reader with a full knowledge. Such belief in an ideal literature on the Holocaust necessitates setting aside general theoretical objections to the ability of any language to mirror any reality, objections that are further complicated by the oft-cited survivor perspective that whoever was not there cannot know what it was like, that there may well be words to represent this reality, but only survivors speaking to other survivors can possess and understand them. And this survivor perspective has been taken even further, for example by Primo Levi, who says that those who survived, by virtue of their survival, are themselves an exception and cannot tell the stories of the majority who did not survive.

What is even more apparent is that if *Life Is Beautiful* is ultimately and paradoxically an adult film that is dependent upon the techniques of children's literature, it is also a film whose foregrounding of Guido's need to protect the child distracts us from its equally urgent need to protect the adult viewer who wants to believe not only that the power of parental love will persist even in the death camps,[15] but, more wistfully, that the child survivor recognizes and remains ever grateful to the memory of that love. The film provides no space for Laub's child survivor, traumatized by both the war and by the reunion with his parents. Those who object to the film's comic approach do not address the child's memory as central to the film's comic vision, yet I would argue that it is a more wishful aspect of the fable than the arrival of the tank.[16] I do not wish to generalize that all child survivors are not eternally grateful. Certainly most memoirs by children whose parents were murdered are intensely loyal and guilt-ridden at any lapse in that loyalty, as in *Night* when Elie Wiesel confesses his relief at his father's death.[17] But if the parents survive, the relationship described in the memoirs is often far more troubled, particularly so if the child survivor was very young.[18]

The Failures of the Grown-ups

Guido must die therefore, not to save his son, but to save his son's fabulous memory of him and the audience's belief in the integrity of parent-child relationships under all circumstances. Such belief collapses in *No Pretty Pictures* when Lobel recalls her feelings regarding her uncle and aunt the night in January 1945 that she and her young brother arrive in "yet another concentration camp" (108): "They didn't matter to me anymore. First they had pretended to take care of us. And then they had lied. [...] The failures of the grown-ups around us had landed us in this place" (108). Lobel will later learn that her uncle and aunt do die before the end of the war, but that night, having lost trust in all adults, she has just refused their well-intended advice to escape during a forced march from Plaszow to Auschwitz. Lobel's "Epilogue" even considers, then dismisses, the question of how her lack of trust may have contributed to her uncle and aunt's death.[19] That Lobel's parents not only survive (the father in Russia, the mother in hiding) but also avoid imprisonment in a camp, makes her memoir far more complex than Benigni's film in its analysis of child-adult relations in the Holocaust and the possibility of happy endings.

The contrast between Lobel's memoir and Benigni's film lies not in Giosuè's amazing survival, but in the filmic depiction of that survival as the narrative's redemptive ending. Lobel rejects the neatness of Benigni's happy ending, even as she insists in the voice of the American citizen/illustrator/grandmother who writes the memoir that, "My life has been good" (*No Pretty Pictures* 190). The audacity of Guido's hiding Giosuè in the camp barracks seems more credible to those familiar with Lobel's account, which is just as astonishing as Giosuè's, for she and her brother do not have a parent protecting them in the camps even if Lobel does learn years later that the likely reason she was not killed upon arrival in Plaszow was because her uncle pleaded successfully with the

Nazi commandant who still needed his skills as an "architect-engineer" (186).

But no special pleading explains Lobel's survival for several months in the women's camp, Ravensbrück, when no one cared that a ten-year-old girl was accompanied by her eight-year-old brother, a brother no longer disguised as a girl. Although both boys and girls often accompanied their mothers to Ravensbrück, Lobel and her brother were on their own. Their survival is even more remarkable when we consider that, by the end of the war, "no other concentration camp in Germany had such a high percentage of murdered prisoners" (Rittner and Roth 8). Its randomness is even more apparent when we realize that the high percentage of murdered directly relates to the increase in the number of prisoners gassed in the last few months, many of them, like Lobel and her brother, prisoners evacuated from Auschwitz and other "camps in the East" (Rittner and Roth 8).

Unlike the triumphant ending of *Life Is Beautiful*, however, Lobel's liberation from Ravensbrück is a complex moment that represents only one part of her story and one which she misunderstands, not knowing either who her rescuers are or where she is going. Initially "walking in a halo of light" (117), she feels that a miracle has occurred, a miracle she attributes to her wearing of the "holy medals" (117) that her Catholic nanny had given her and that she has managed to retain despite the stripping and shaving that she has been subject to. Yet she also feels shame at being photographed as she steps off the ferry in Sweden wearing the "same layers of rags" (119) that she wore in the camp. Sweden represents a new world; the rags she wears belong to a different world. As a memoirist, Lobel places this photograph of arrival in

Sweden on the cover of her book, as if writing the memoir demands confronting that shame and all the other moments of bodily humiliation that are part of her experience. A reluctant memoirist, she views with suspicion the current fashion for celebrating Holocaust survivors: "it is [...] wearisome as well as dangerous to cloak and sanctify oneself with the pride of victimhood" (xiii).

In an era so fascinated with trauma narratives, in which we look for stories about younger and younger victims, Lobel is ambivalent about her own claim to trauma, and she refuses our expectations that as a child she suffered more than the adults around her. "Mine is only another story" (190) is the final line in the memoir, a line that occurs immediately after she tries and fails to imagine the feelings her grandmother must have experienced when she was transported. This attempt may be Lobel's adult gesture to counter her childhood memory of refusing any recognition to a "large, shapeless woman" (84) thrown in the truck when they are transported. When her brother guesses that the woman is their grandmother, Lobel is terrified that he is right: "'Don't be stupid,' I whispered. [...] I didn't want us to be connected to a Jewish relative" (84).

The ambivalence that the child feels regarding her parents' behaviour (her father's disappearance, her mother's powerlessness) thus produces a memoir in which a child separated from her parents learns to prefer that separation. The parents who find her two years after liberation in a Swedish shelter for Polish refugees embarrass, shame, and anger her. Lobel is outraged when her mother wants immediately to cut her hair, oblivious to how the trauma of having her head shaved would produce a child unwilling to cut her hair ever again. The memoir structurally enacts Lobel's sense of separation: the years in Poland are but one chapter of her life; "Sweden" follows; and then there are her years in the United States, many more, she keeps reminding the reader, than she lived as a child in Poland. If she concludes that hers is a happy story, happiness exists only through her ability to block out a "time from which I have very few pretty pictures to remember" (xiii).

Not a Pretty Picture

This principle of separation seems apparent as well if we turn to Lobel's picture books. For much of her career, the biographical notes on the dust jackets of her books are silent about her Holocaust childhood. Lobel is presented as a decorative artist, capable of pretty pictures, but not much else; typical are the notes to her illustrations of *Three Rolls and One Doughnut: Fables from Russia by Mirra Ginsburg*: "Having lived close to peasant art as a child, Mrs. Lobel has always been interested in the decorative arts. She embroiders clothes whenever she can and designs needlepoint tapestries" (55). What is missing in this description is the political aspect to this aesthetic decision, the politics that makes her not simply a female artist who has time on her hands to do needlepoint, but a child survivor who knows what it is like to live without beauty and who defies that childhood every time she makes a pretty picture. For just as the powerful effect of *Life Is Beautiful* lies in the scenic representation of Giosuè's fabulous survival in the context of the significant absence of the other children, a different story of Lobel's art is told if we position the picture books and what they suppress in the context of the memoir.

Despite the way the title, *No Pretty Pictures*, draws a line between Lobel's later life as an American illustrator and her Polish childhood, the line is not only less solid than Lobel claims, but is itself a marker of the survival strategies she found necessary. What is the relationship, for example, between Niania, the Polish nanny to whose memory Lobel dedicates her memoir, and the many babushka-wearing women who populate her art? The memoirist concludes that Niania was her "demented angel" (189), undoubtedly anti-semitic yet just as clearly devoted, loving, and determined to protect her two charges. Lobel begins her memoir with the memory of her five-year-old self watching the arrival of the German soldiers in September 1939; holding tightly to her nanny's hands, she records how Niania categorizes and identifies the world for her, first saying, "'*Niemcy, Niemcy*' ('Germans, Germans')" (2) and then just as contemptuously muttering whenever she sees the neighbour Hasid "Jews!" (3). In hiding Lobel and her brother, the latter dressed as a girl and, with his curly blond hair, more easily disguised as a Christian than his dark-skinned sister, Niania seems to have regarded the children as somehow not quite as Jewish as the Jews she dislikes. Gradually Lobel too absorbs Niania's attitudes and sees herself as more Catholic than Jewish. She longs for blonde hair, worries that her dark skin betrays her, and shuns association with other Jews. In the Polish village where they first hide, she feels threatened when her own mother comes to visit, yet the Polish countryside is no paradise; exchanging tablecloths for food, Niania and the two children have excrement thrown on them.

Such ambiguous memories of Poland contest the biographical notes in which Lobel admits to only positive images: "As a little girl in Poland, I remember weaving chains of flowers and wreaths for my hair" (*Alison's Zinnia*, n. pag.). Three picture books that span her career—*Sven's Bridge* (1965), *Potatoes, Potatoes* (1967), and *Away from Home* (1994)—further indicate not only that Lobel's separation of her Holocaust childhood from her adult art is less tidy than the memoir claims, but that her need to separate hints at a more complex narrative about child survivors than the one celebrated by the neat happy ending of Benigni's film. Initially the illustrations seem to exist in isolation from Lobel's wartime memories, as though Lobel with her pictures were returning the beauty that was taken away from her by creating a separate utopian world. This is a relationship of replacement, of covering over, like the incident she records in the memoir when the Nazi visit to her parents' apartment is marked by the theft of a beautiful rug. When Lobel later sees her mother crying over the transport of her parents and sister, the first time that she ever sees an adult so vulnerable, she recalls her mother standing "in the middle of the empty spot where the kilim rug had been" (*No Pretty Pictures* 9). What is covered over in Lobel's first picture book, *Sven's Bridge*, what cannot be said in 1965, is the memory of that humiliation. The biographical notes to *Sven's Bridge* carefully avoid any reference to the Holocaust, and we read only that "Anita Lobel was born in Krakow, Poland, where she spent much of her early childhood."

Yet like Benigni's viewer who imagines what is not represented on the screen, the reader of the memoir notices in the utopian world of *Sven's Bridge*, where even kings can be fooled by loyal gatekeepers, that the only colours are yellow and blue, the colours of the Swedish flag and of the pajamas that Lobel and her brother are given in the Swedish sanatorium when they are rescued from Ravensbrück.[20] Surely the book is a tribute to the land where Lobel first learned to do embroidery and watercolours, the land that returned her to a world of life and colour, the land where, when a foolish king blows up a bridge, it is replaced with a more beautiful, ornate design. It is not simply a matter of colours; the narrative itself seems a tribute to Sweden where Lobel could recover from the terror of sneaking out of the Krakow ghetto by crossing a stone bridge that "felt like a tightrope" (51), aware that any moment Nazi soldiers might turn around and discover her. In order to cross the bridge, she forces herself to remember a painting that hung over her bed before the war of a "beautiful angel. [...with] giant wings hovering over, almost enveloping two children crossing a bridge over a ravine" (52), a memory with which she controls her fears of Niania's lack of power. Better a utopia in which Sven, the gatekeeper, protects the wooden bridge and all those who need to cross it; in place of Niania with her string bag to fool onlookers into thinking that she is a "lady" (*No Pretty Pictures* 52) are the men and women whose fishing nets are not disturbed when Sven raises the bridge. In *Sven's Bridge*, bridges are safe places.[21]

In contrast, Poland is the place of death: "In Poland everybody ended up laid out, with noses and feet pointing to the ceiling" (*No Pretty Pictures* 181). This image of death occurs repeatedly in the memoir; Lobel introduces it when she recounts hiding during a Nazi roundup in the Krakow ghetto. Lying beside her mother, she notes her resemblance to

"Mother, Mother, this is our fault!" cried the older son.
"What have we done?" cried the younger son.
"Speak to us! Speak to us!" they begged.

PLATE I

the corpse of an old woman we had known [...]. The
dead woman had been laid out on a table in her
cottage. Her nose, long and thin, reached far away
from her face. And her feet were neatly pointing
straight up. Mother's big nose and pointing feet
looked just like that corpse. (*No Pretty Pictures* 48)

Given the circumstances, it is not surprising that the child
imagines the mother as a corpse, and it is easy to understand
why, when Lobel later acknowledges the contribution of her
wartime memories to her fable *Potatoes, Potatoes*, she gently
belittles reviewers who take the book seriously (Hopkins

158). Although Lobel resists constructing herself as a child survivor, she nevertheless demonstrates the perspective of a survivor who knows too well the difference between fables and the grim historical reality of Holocaust survival where as Primo Levi tells us, "it needs more than potatoes to give back strength to a man" (Levi 153). By ridiculing reviewers who take the book seriously, Lobel maintains her principle of separation and distances herself from the dust jacket reference to the "timeless lesson" hidden in *Potatoes, Potatoes*. Memoir writers rarely offer such clear lessons, and the dust jacket biography remains silent on her wartime experience.

Yet in *Potatoes, Potatoes*, Lobel does draw on her memory of the mother as corpse. (See Plate 1, p. 220). The image of the dead mother becomes the comic turning point of the fable, for the two brothers who left home captivated by the attractive uniforms and swords of the opposing armies have become military leaders battling for the potatoes their mother has hidden behind her walls. When the two armies break through the walls and destroy everything, they discover what appears to be the dead body of the boys' mother, a body that Lobel draws as the image she will describe more than 30 years later in the memoir.[22] Just as Lobel's mother only appeared dead, the brothers' mother is also pretending; a critical difference between the fable and the memoir, however, is that in the world of fables the mother has what all mothers lacked during the Holocaust, the power to teach a lesson and make a difference.[23] The picture-book mother lets everyone cry until the lesson sinks in and then offers the soldiers potatoes only if they "promise to stop all the fighting / and clean up this mess, / and go home to [their] mothers" (n. pag.). Yet a further difference is significant, for the boys' mother is

Craig crawled in Cracow.

PLATE 2

dressed not as the fashionable urban woman who appears in the photographs of Lobel's mother that are included in the memoir, but as Niania, the babushka-wearing nanny whose meals of potatoes come to represent the safety in Polish identity that Lobel longs for and misses as soon as she is separated from her. Niania also resembles the mother in *Potatoes, Potatoes* who learns the impossibility of building "a wall around everything she owned" (n. pag.). For like the "woman who did not bother with the war" (*Potatoes, Potatoes*

n. pag.), Niania learns the futility of advising the children to ignore the fights and hide among the potatoes.

Just before Lobel and her brother are captured by the Nazis in the Benedictine convent where they are hiding, the two children disobey Niania by sneaking out to visit a local carousel. Although having to cross a small bridge to get to the carousel reminds Lobel of the trauma of crossing the ghetto bridge, for a moment she is distracted from the constant anxiety of hiding and is able to see what so rarely appears in her memoir, a pretty picture. It is a picture of Krakow, "the tower of the town square [...] the spire of *kościół Mariaki*" (69). The bridge is hidden. Given the representation of Krakow as a "beautiful painting" (69), perhaps it is not surprising to see how the memory of this picture enables Lobel to risk crossing the bridge between her Holocaust childhood and her pretty pictures. For the memory of "my Kraków" (*No Pretty Pictures* 69) also constitutes the background to the illustration of the letter C in a recent alphabet book, *Away from Home*, and the image shocks, not only because it is so unusual in Lobel's work, but because its aesthetics are so contradictory.

Away from Home is structured (according to the dust jacket) as "a whirlwind tour of some of the world's wonders," in which young boys visit "exotic places in alliterative fashion" (Library of Congress publication data). The dust jacket assures the reader that in the book's pages she can "start with A and go anywhere [she] want[s]!" The travel metaphor works within a theatrical stage set. On each page, Lobel draws a child on a narrow stage and depicts the child performing the action of the letter before an audience of children. Separating the performer and the audience is the line of text. Although the actor, the geographical backdrop, and the words differ on each page, Lobel never alters the children in the audience. Whatever happens on stage, they remain enthusiastic and cheerful, models for the reader on how to respond to the images. The book is also clearly autobiographical; on the dust jacket, Lobel identifies herself as a woman who travels in three different (and presumably equivalent) ways: "I have been a refugee. I have been an immigrant. I have been a tourist." Dedicated to Lobel's son Adam, the dedication page shows the Lobels receiving a letter from him, and the text for the letter A says "Adam arrived in Amsterdam" (n. pag.).[24]

Autobiography is relevant in the letter C as well. (See Plate 2, p. 222). In the background notes for this letter, we learn that "Cracow is the city in Poland where I was born. This is its central square" (n. pag.). What startles me is the illustration's implied narrative, for the letter C shows a child kneeling at stage front, looking at the audience, and caught in the stage lights. The child is obviously Jewish since he wears a Jewish star on his cap and presumably is a partisan since he carries a rifle. When "Craig crawl[s] in Cracow" (n. pag.) and is caught by the stage lights, I cannot help but see a Jewish child caught by other, more terrifying searchlights and even find myself worrying about the intentions of the two men holding the stage set. The image is so haunted by my reading of the memoir that the stage itself starts to look as narrow as a bridge.

While it may be that Lobel can only incorporate the Holocaust into her pretty pictures by repressing her own memories and replacing them with the imagined heroic resistance of a partisan, I am struck by the contradiction between her attempt to allude to the Holocaust in a children's travel

book and her insistence in *No Pretty Pictures* of the stark contrast between two kinds of travel: that of a tourist and that of
"the furtive ride in a hay wagon, the escape from Niania's village on the old train, and the few steps of a frightening walk
across a bridge" (188). Lobel has refused to return to Poland as
a tourist. Her refusal is understandable, far more so than the
aesthetics produced by an alliterative alphabet book in which
the statement, "Craig crawled in Cracow," is no more frightening or meaningful than "Frederick fiddled in Florence," or
"Henry hoped in Hollywood." Lobel ends her biographical
statement on the dust jacket with a very clear pedagogical
impulse: "I hope this theatrical picture-postcard journey is an
invitation to learning more about places far away from home."

But how does the invitation to learning work here?
Making of the Holocaust an alphabetical entry like any other
in a child's tour of the world's wonders, Lobel attempts an
aesthetics that is deeply disturbing, one that makes me question the impossible demands we make upon Holocaust representations for and about young children. What is the point
of a Holocaust image that is so determined to give pleasure
to young children that it is silent about its own implicit terror? Benigni's fable demands an adult viewer whose aesthetic
pleasure is produced and affected by her awareness of a genocide that Benigni refuses to show; thus when Guido is caught
in the searchlights, the viewer knows, even if she does not see,
what happens next. In contrast, Lobel's pretty picture requires
a child reader whose ability to take pleasure in the image of a
Jewish child caught in the searchlights is dependent on an
ignorance of the history that produces it and a refusal to
imagine what happens next.

NOTES

1. For example, asking an infant why she did not resist being taken to the gas chambers.

2. A comparable example of the authority and safety provided by age is operative in Brian Doyle's young adult novel, *Uncle Ronald*. The narrator, Old Mickey, is 112 years old, old enough to tell a narrative of child abuse that is painful, but that he and readers can laugh at because it took place so long ago.

3. Unlike Holocaust deniers, Laub does not deny that "the event" happened. Nevertheless, I continue to be bothered by the language that he uses. Laub's essay first appeared in *American Imago* 48 #1 (Spring 1991). It also appears in Felman and Laub as "An Event Without a Witness: Truth, Testimony and Survival" 75-92.

4. I use the spelling Krakow except where quoting material that uses a different spelling. In Anita Lobel, *No Pretty Pictures: A Child of War*, it is spelled Kraków; in *Away from Home*, it is spelled Cracow.

5. The paperback edition of *No Pretty Pictures* lists eight honours and awards, including ALA Best Books for Young Adults, *Booklist* Editor's Choice, Orbis Pictus Award for Outstanding Honor Book, and Sydney Taylor Award Honor Book.

6. See Chapter Four for a discussion of *Fragments*.

7. Lobel says that her friend and editor, Susan Hirschman, suggested the title (Letter to the author, 21 March 2001).

8. Many critics of the film seem both inconsistent and indifferent to the question of a child's knowledge; they typically condemn the film because they assume that adult viewers are ignorant of the Holocaust and so will naively believe that what they see on the screen is historically accurate. Yet such critics routinely exempt themselves from such ignorance, since they base their objection on their own historical awareness of the Holocaust. They also ignore how the film itself problematizes the child's limited knowledge; that is, Giosuè hears more than what his father tells him. In addition, such critics do not consider how Holocaust representation in children's literature always works within limits. For example, in David Denby's second and highly negative review of the film, he concludes that "Benigni protects the audience as much as Guido protects his son; we are all treated like children" (99). In response, Eric McHenry chastises Denby for treating the film's viewers "like children" when he

ignores how the film "depends upon the audience's remembrance of the Holocaust" (10). My attention to the question of the child's knowledge remains indebted to a colleague who concluded his contemptuous dismissal of *Life Is Beautiful* by asking me if I knew that the concentration camps were dirty and that people vomited in them. My astonishment about his assumptions regarding my knowledge or lack thereof prompted me to think more clearly about the question of knowledge and the construction of the child.

9. Maurizio Viano discusses Benigni's reading of the letter that Trotsky wrote on February 27, 1940 and the filmmaker's decision to abandon his working title, "*Buongiorno Principessa!*" (Good Day, Princess), for Trotsky's words (52). Viano also quotes four sentences from the letter: "Natasha has just come up to the window from the courtyard and opened it wider so that the air may enter more freely into my room. I can see the bright green strip of grass beneath the wall, and the clear blue sky above the wall, and sunlight everywhere. Life is beautiful. Let the future generations cleanse it of all evil, oppression and violence, and enjoy it to the full" (47).

10. Any quotations from *Life Is Beautiful* are from the English version.

11. This faulty assumption has led some reviewers to praise Benigni's film while advising viewers that, if they want the truth of the Holocaust, they should turn to Steven Spielberg. It may also account for how some viewers of Claude Lanzmann's *Shoah* celebrate the documentary's "truth" without considering how Lanzmann pushes his survivor witnesses to communicate only the traumatic truth that he is interested in; Lanzmann is simply not interested in post-Holocaust narratives that tell survivor narratives outside traumatic discourse.

12. See Susan Zuccotti's analysis of Italian Jews' misreading of the Nazi threat.

13. When is a door not a door? When it's ajar.

14. That some adult viewers tell me that they are shocked when Guido is killed (the hero is not supposed to die) indicates how my analysis presumes that the adult viewer is familiar with the history of the death camps and the minimal chances of survival. Like much of the fiction of Aharon Appelfeld, Benigni's ability not to show us atrocities is dependent on our awareness of what is not shown. If the viewer is ignorant of the history of the death camps, then Guido's death works very differently, in

fact more like the educational plot of children's narrative, and the viewer is then responding as adults imagine a child would.

15. I am thinking also of newspaper advertisements for *Life Is Beautiful*, which tell us that the film demonstrates how love and imagination conquer all.

16. When my mother saw *Life Is Beautiful*, the arrival of the tank was the only moment in the film that moved her, since it reminded her of her own liberation and the Italian soldiers singing. In a sense, it was the only moment in which she was willing to accept the fairy-tale conventions of the film.

17. In contrast, in Fern Schumer Chapman's *Motherland: Beyond the Holocaust: A Daughter's Journey to Reclaim the Past*, Chapman realizes that her elderly mother remains psychologically the abandoned child who came to the United States on her own at age 12. The mother is convinced that her parents did not fully understand what they were doing when they sent her away, that it would have been better to stay in Germany with them even if this would have meant dying with them.

18. Although attention to the post-Holocaust trauma of family relations is rare in North American children's literature, the Dutch writer, Ida Vos, examines this issue in *Hide and Seek* and *Anna is Still Here*, both available in translation. The difficulty of post-Holocaust parent-child relations is also addressed in Mark Jonathan Harris's documentary, *Into the Arms of Strangers: Stories of the Kindertransport*.

19. A question that Dwork might say is another example of the wrong kind of question.

20. In discussing *Sven's Bridge*, I am responding to the original edition, not the revised full colour edition published by Greenwillow in 1992. In the revision, the words remain the same. Despite the full colour, the flags are still painted in the original yellow and blue. The new edition is larger than the original; what adds to its size is the white space that now frames the illustrations and becomes the new location for the words. Marketed for parents "who loved it when it first appeared," the new edition restricts its dust jacket authorial information to a listing of Lobel's "well-known" books. Since the dust jacket also asserts that Lobel herself is "well-known" to the purchasers who presumably read *Sven's Bridge* when they were children, there is no need to provide any biographical information. Yet it is worth observing that the original dust jacket identity of an artist "born in Krakow, Poland" has been replaced by the less specific identity of the artist as celebrity.

21. In e-mail correspondence, Maria Nikolajeva has pointed out that the illustrations combine the colours of the Swedish flag and some aspects of Swedish folk art with other details that seem closer to central European art. Lobel has told me that her choice of colours in *Sven's Bridge* was dictated by the production limitations at the time. Since most picture books were done in black and two colours, she used yellow and blue because they allowed her to create a variety of other colours and tones (Letter to the author. 21 March 2001).

22. The relationship of life and art is unclear here. What comes first: the child's memory of the mother as corpse, or the illustration of the picture-book mother as corpse?

23. The most traumatic incident in Lobel's memoir, one that demonstrates the general reality of maternal lack of power, occurs when a woman whose son has just been shot begins to scream and demands from the guards why they have not shot Lobel's brother who is so much younger. Lobel admits that she is more afraid of the woman than of the Nazis and loses her own ability to speak, for fear that the woman's appeal will be heard.

24. Lobel's notes for the letter A tell the reader that in Amsterdam there are "houses that look like these." That Anne Frank lived and hid in such a house only comes to mind because of the problematic inscribing and erasing of Holocaust history in the letter C; the lack of such information is not problematic in the notes to the letter A.

7

Saving the Picture: Holocaust Photographs in Children's Books

"Moralists who love photographs always hope that words will save the picture." (Sontag 96)

Susan Sontag begins *On Photography* by stating that photographs "enlarge our notions of what is worth looking at and what we have a right to observe" (3). As such, photographs are "an ethics of seeing" (3). When we photograph, and when we look at photographs taken by others, we put ourselves "into a certain relation to the world that feels like knowledge" (3). In the awkwardness of that phrasing, its implicit questioning of what knowledge means when it derives from photographic images, lies Sontag's recognition of their deceptive power. A relation that *feels like* knowledge is an imitation, a substitute, something presumably not identical to a relation that might produce real knowledge. As her opening chapter title, "In Plato's Cave," emphasizes, in looking at photographs we are always at a distance from the world we believe that we see in the image. Although Sontag insists that photography "changes the terms of confinement in the cave" (3), there is no doubt that we remain inside. To blame photography for placing us there would be foolish, for we have always been in the cave; what has changed because of photography is our understanding of what we think we can know outside the cave's walls.

Sontag's text remains a foundational and provocative post-Holocaust text on photography, and the epistemological questions she raises remain relevant to a consideration of how photographs function in children's books about the Holocaust. For, if photography gives us a questionable knowledge about the world, it is equally doubtful, given the very power of photography and our belief in its referentiality, how often any viewer pauses to consider if what she derives from the photograph is real knowledge or something less authentic, something that only "feels like knowledge." Isn't the entire point of including photographs, particularly in children's books about the Holocaust, based on our belief that the viewer will learn through a direct confrontation with the photograph that what was "unimaginable" really did take place? Certainly it is not only in children's books about the Holocaust that the knowledge we bring to a photograph, either through prior reading or through the caption that labels the image, controls the possible responses: "We don't know how to react to a photograph [...] until we know what *piece* of the world it is" (Sontag 83-84). But if we understand child readers as those who know less because they bring to the text less experience of the world than adults, then the child's ability to move beyond the implications of the caption is equally diminished. Sontag argues that photographs have multiple meanings; they can never be fully controlled by their captions: "Photographs, which cannot themselves explain anything, are inexhaustible invitations to deduction, speculation, and fantasy" (20).

Sontag is right, but our need to believe that Holocaust photographs give children access to historical truth makes us very anxious to control such speculative invitations. In contrast to the binary critical discourse that has traditionally devalued photographs in opposition to art and the imagination (Shawcross ix-x), in children's books about the Holocaust the photograph acts as a marker of the most privileged site, that of the documentary real. For this reason, the Holocaust picture book that does not in some artistic way reproduce or allude to Holocaust photographs is, with rare exceptions (for example, Eve Bunting's *Terrible Things: An Allegory of the Holocaust*), not the picture book we value. The Alice in Wonderland question—What good is a book without pictures?—may have suited a Victorian culture that celebrated childhood fantasy and imagination. Such words, however, are problematic in the discourse of the Holocaust where fiction has an uneasy place; when picture books introduce children to the Holocaust, photographs keep the pictures grounded in the real. It is as though Alice's question has been transformed: what good is a Holocaust picture book without photographs? What is "curiouser and curiouser" is how photographs produce such knowledge when the child looking at the picture book is not even aware that she is looking at a photograph. What knowledge do photographs validate when the viewer of the picture book does not know that the illustration she looks at is based on a photograph?

Like most questions about the Holocaust, the general question that drives this chapter—what is it we know when we look at Holocaust photographs in children's books?—produces more questions than answers. What are the epistemological assumptions governing photographs in Holocaust memorial discourse, and how do these assumptions affect the narrative framing of photographs in children's books? When children see illustrations that are based on photographs and illustrations that depict photographs, exactly what do we teach them? Do Holocaust photographs in picture books function differently than the Holocaust photographs in other children's books? How does the knowledge we bring to such photographs—not only our ability to recognize the photographic basis to the illustration but also our knowledge that the photographed children were murdered/will be murdered, or that the particular child in the photograph survived—affect our response to the photograph? And finally, why, if we often say that the Holocaust was unspeakable and simultaneously insist that photographs of atrocity do speak, are we so careful in our choice of words beneath the photographs?

By careful, I do not mean historically precise, for the captions in children's books rarely provide the name of the person in the photograph, the location, or the date. I mean the obvious care taken to frame the photograph, to save the picture, with the words we write. The captions underneath the photographs in many children's books are remarkably different from those beneath the same photographs in adult books. By including Holocaust photographs in children's books, we demonstrate our commitment to telling children the truth, but the words that frame these photographs reveal how complicated such truth-telling is when the historical facts are so disturbing. If the photograph-based illustration in the picture book serves to free the illustrator, by allowing her to show more, this is the exact opposite of what I see happening when Holocaust photographs appear in other children's books. The inclusion of photographs in other children's books encourages the writer to say less, to be discrete, a discretion that often produces a narrative in which the writer attributes hopeful and courageous thoughts to the child in the photograph as a strategy to reassure the young viewer. The hope that is thus produced precariously leaps from the child in the photograph, the child who is presumed to be hopeful because she did not know what would happen, to the child viewer in the future who does know. Unable to save the child in the photograph, unwilling to imagine children without hope, we hope to save the photograph with our words.

Questioning the Photograph in Educational and Memorial Discourse

Analysis of the specific epistemological contribution of Holocaust photographs appears rarely in memorial discourse, which has been far more willing to acknowledge the inadequacy of words than to question the expressive power of photographs. Similarly, arguments over the appropriateness of the words that accompany photographs in educational discourse, arguments which usually exhort us to let the photographs speak for themselves, proceed in tension with a refusal to admit that the very images that function as historical truth-markers cannot speak on their own. In contrast, theoretical questions regarding Holocaust photographs appear not only in the critical discourse of Marianne Hirsch, Andrea Liss, and Barbie Zelizer, but equally often in adult novels about the children of survivors, such as in Anne Michaels's *Fugitive Pieces*, where photographs and the child's uncertain response to such photographs are themselves the issue. In *Fugitive Pieces*, Ben, the son of unnamed survivors, recalls the childhood memory of being forced by his father to look at Holocaust photographs, the "horror of those photos"

(Michaels 218), and the "ferocity" with which his father "thrust books" (219) at him. Clearly Ben's terror is not what we wish Holocaust books to convey, and we might conclude that his fear is produced by his familial relation to the Holocaust: the images represent too closely a fate that could have been his. Ben derives a precise cautionary tale from the photographs: "You are not too young. There were hundreds of thousands younger than you" (219). Yet this in itself implies that the photographs are less frightening than the "ferocity" with which his father forces the books upon him. In this case, is it the father or the photographs that speak?

It is also worth considering how the most often quoted passage from Sontag's book, her account of first seeing "the photographs of Bergen-Belsen and Dachau [...] by chance in a bookstore [...] in July 1945" (17), raises questions about how Holocaust photographs speak. The dark epiphany of that moment, "Nothing I have seen—in photographs or in real life—ever cut me as sharply, deeply, instantaneously" (17)—is qualified by her next sentence. In parentheses Sontag mentions that she was 12 when she saw the photographs and then adds: "It was several years before I understood fully what they were about" (17). Was Sontag's lack of understanding determined by her age, the nature of the captions, or the particular historical moment when she saw the photographs? She does not tell us what the captions said, or whether there were captions at all. What she does imply is that her very lack of understanding and the accidental nature of her encounter are essential aspects of what made the episode so transformative for the young girl: "something went dead; something is still crying" (18). If the photographs shocked her because she could not understand them, then the pedagogical decision to protect the child viewer by providing a narrative that explains them may be counter-productive in the sense that it prevents the impact Sontag experienced. But such deadening of response may be inevitable; Sontag's personal account is preceded by her recognition that the horror produced by the first surprised viewing cannot be recaptured: "Photographs shock insofar as they show something novel" (17). Today, Holocaust photographs are no longer novel; even the child who has not seen specific Holocaust photographs lives in a culture in which comparisons to the images depicted in the photographs are commonplace.

The premise of most Holocaust educational and memorial discourse is that such photographs not only continue to shock, but that it is imperative that they continue to shock us and in that way speak to us. That we often refer to the Holocaust itself as "unspeakable" only enforces our need to believe that the photographs do speak. If the photographs do not speak to us, the words beneath them often tell us that we are morally at fault. In addition, because Holocaust representation in educational and memorial discourse is sensitive to the claims of Holocaust deniers, who have themselves not hesitated to question the truth of numerous Holocaust photographs "including the famous shot of a boy in the Warsaw ghetto" (Zelizer 199-200), we hesitate to raise any questions about how knowledge operates in them. To quote Sontag's insight that "there can be no evidence, photographic or otherwise, of an event until the event itself has been named and characterized" (16) seems both risky and offensive when Holocaust photography in educational and memorial discourse justifies its presence as the very giving of evidence, the picturing of the atrocity, the naming of the dead.

Typical of the assumption that Holocaust photographs speak is the foreword to Roman Vishniac's *A Vanished World* in which Elie Wiesel praises Vishniac's "miraculous" ability to make the photographs "speak" (n. pag.). Further demonstrating this assumption is a flyer advertising the observance of *Yom Hashoah*, in Calgary, May 2, 2000. The top of the flyer reads "Memories ... Etched in the Faces of the Past." Below the words is a photograph of three children so young that the two oldest have fingers in their mouths. The children are seated behind some kind of table on which two large books are opened, but none of the children looks at the books. Two look to the side; one faces the photographer. Are the memories really etched in their faces or do such memories reside in the knowledge of the children's deaths that I bring to the picture? The problem of enunciation is that the picture tells me next to nothing, yet I know that the children must have died since their photograph is part of a flyer urging me to observe *Yom Hashoah* (*Shoah* is the Hebrew term for catastrophe; *Yom Hashoah* is the day of remembrance for the *Shoah*). But who are the children? Because of the quality of the flyer's reproduction, I cannot even tell the language of the books the children do not look at, let alone know why they do not look at them. Is it because they cannot read, or because they have been told to look up? Why was the photograph taken? Who took it? Why do the children look so solemn? Are they apprehensive, or do I see them as apprehensive in the same way that Sontag reads the photographs taken by Roman Vishniac in 1938, as "overwhelmingly affected by the knowledge of how soon all these people were to perish" (63)?

In fact the photograph on the flyer is a fuzzy reproduction of a photograph taken by Vishniac. In his *A Vanished*

World, photograph 155 is glossed: "The boy's second day at cheder. He is sitting in the middle. Mukachevko, 1938" (n. pag.). In his notes to the photograph, Vishniac adds, "The next day I visited the boy at school. He was already getting accustomed to his new life" (n. pag.). In not identifying Vishniac as the photographer, the flyer either assumes that we already know his name, or that we do not require it for the photograph to function commemoratively. The careful placing of the photograph between the flyer's reference to Memories and the centred and framed reference to the observance of *Yom Hashoah* tells us how to read the picture. To control this response even further, the flyer positions a familiar quotation from Elie Wiesel, in which he tells us not to forget, immediately below the image and above the words *Yom Hashoah*. It is not surprising that the quotation also is taken from Vishniac, from Wiesel's foreword, in which he follows his imperative, "[n]ot to forget, not to allow oblivion to defeat memory," by commenting that Vishniac has made the victims "live still [...] more alive than we who 'read' without understanding them" (n. pag.). Telling us why we look at the photographs—not to forget—Wiesel refuses to acknowledge the possibility of our understanding. Or do we fail to understand only if we "read" rather than let the photographs speak to us? Of such paradoxes do photographs speak in memorial discourse.

Photographs in Picture Books

Evidence of our conviction that photographs are privileged conveyers of the historical real is manifold. Why else does

Edward T. Sullivan in his Holocaust bibliography, *The Holocaust in Literature for Youth*, praise David Adler's *A Picture Book of Anne Frank* for the "photographic quality" (14) of Karen Ritz's illustrations? Why do picture books about historical Holocaust figures often signal their status as documents of the real by including either simple illustrations of photographs, as in *A Picture Book of Anne Frank*, or the more complexly photograph-inspired illustrations to be found in Adler's *Child of the Warsaw Ghetto*, also illustrated by Ritz? In *A Picture Book of Anne Frank*, the inserted illustrations of photographs imitate the photographs of the Nazis, the Frank family, and their hiding place that children may not have yet seen but will soon come to recognize in other books. In this way, the illustrations introduce children to the truth-bearing function of Holocaust photographs and to the relatively few photographs that circulate to convey that truth.[1] Ritz's illustrations do not assume that children are already familiar with the photographs many adults will recognize. Since *A Picture Book of Anne Frank* is meant to introduce pre-literate children to the story of Anne Frank, Ritz's use of photographs functions differently, not pointing to specific images that children will recognize, but teaching them to regard and value photographic images as the highest proof of the historical real.

A *Picture Book of Anne Frank* is thus different from Ruud van der Rol and Rian Verhoeven's *Anne Frank Beyond the Diary: A Photographic Remembrance*. The latter book is intended for children who already know the diary and want to know more about the diarist's life. But many of the photographs the older child will see in van der Rol and Verhoeven's text—for example, not just the individual photographs of Margot Frank (76) and Miep Gies (41), but also the generic photo-

movable bookcase

PLATE 3

graph of liberation at an unnamed camp (101)—will be familiar to the child who has already looked at *A Picture Book of Anne Frank*. In this way the photographs in *Anne Frank Beyond the Diary* will retroactively confirm the photographic basis and therefore truth of Ritz's illustrations. In progressing from *A Picture Book of Anne Frank* to *Anne Frank Beyond the Diary*, the child will confirm something else about our aesthetic hierarchy regarding Holocaust images. A picture book such as Yona Zeldis McDonough's *Anne Frank*, whatever the symbolic truth of its bright folk art illustrations of a gigantic Anne hovering over the world, has a less secure place than picture books that demonstrate their commitment to historical truth through their artistic depiction of photographs.

PLATE 4

Not only do illustrations confirm that photographs are a privileged site of truth; what is even more paradoxical is how basing an illustration on a photograph gives the illustrator liberty to draw what has not been photographed. Thus, in *A Picture Book of Anne Frank*, superimposed on an illustration of Anne and an adult woman moving the bookcase that stands in front of their hiding place, Ritz inserts a drawing of a photograph of the bookcase with the label, "movable bookcase" (n. pag.), confirming the identity of both illustrations. (See Plate 3, p. 241.) In this way, the drawing of the photograph validates the non-photographic drawing behind it, and confirms the drawing's status as bearer of truth. The drawing of the photographs also allows Ritz to draw other illustrations for which we have no photographs, such as the illustration near the end of the book of Margot and Anne Frank dying in

On May 8, 1945, the war in Europe ended. During the course of the war, six million Jews were murdered by the Nazis. One-and-one-half million of the victims were children. Of the 120,000 Jews who had lived in Holland in 1940, just 14,000 survived. Of the eight who hid in the secret apartment in Amsterdam, only Otto Frank was left. The Nazis murdered millions of others, too, including cripples, the mentally ill, beggars, Russian prisoners of war, Romanies, homosexuals, and communists.

PLATE 5

Bergen-Belsen. (See Plate 4, p. 242.) Even if such photographs existed, we might debate the propriety of including them in a picture book. The use of the earlier photographs thereby helps Ritz avoid the ethical dilemma in showing children real photographs of other young women dying in the camps, photographs that might substitute for the nonexistent photograph of Margot and Anne Frank's dying, photographs that could only have been taken by the perpetrators.[2]

Opposite to her depiction of the dying Frank sisters is an illustration based on an Allied liberation photograph. (See Plate 5, p. 243.) Like van der Rol and Verhoeven who include the same photograph (101), Adler does not identify its location, thereby further reinforcing the symbolic function of the illustration. Representing the triumphant survival of so few, it stands in opposition to prose that tells us how many died in various categories: how many Jews, how many Jewish children, how many Dutch Jews, how many of the people hiding in the secret annex. To understand the significance of this illustration, we need to consider the images Ritz chooses not to illustrate; for example, she might have drawn Otto Frank at Auschwitz being liberated by the Russians in January 1945. Another choice is evident when Ritz focuses on the children in striped clothing, a focus that both depends on, and teaches children to value, one of the iconic images of liberation. Perhaps for this reason Ritz does not include what appears on the far right of the photograph in van der Rol and Verhoeven: two men wearing suit jackets are not how we imagine the survivors dressed (101).

The use of colour also speaks to our expectations regarding Holocaust photographs in picture books. Unlike the other illustrations, Ritz draws the photographs in shades of black and white, as though to colour them would undercut their relation to the real. They are drawings that must be black and white if they are to retain their privileged representational status. That we have come to take for granted that the real in Holocaust photography demands an absence of colour is reinforced as soon as we turn to the colour photographs included in Alan Adelson and Robert Lapides's *Lodz Ghetto: Inside a Community Under Siege*; their colour is so unexpected that the photographs look like stills from a movie. The editors describe the surprise of the Jewish Heritage Project when they received the colour photographs and the limited extent of their knowledge regarding the source. They do not speculate how the viewer might respond to this colour, or to the way the wide postwar circulation of black-and-white photography, accompanied by the frequent references to the absence of colour in the "concentration-camp universe," has naturalized a particular technological practice.

Critical assessments of Holocaust picture books often comment on the appropriateness of colour to express the closeness of the story either physically or temporally to the death camps. Just as Steven Spielberg uses little colour until the end of *Schindler's List*, Sullivan objects *inter alia* to the use of colour by Julie Vivas in Margaret Wild's *Let the Celebrations Begin!* Although Sullivan describes the events in the book as taking place post-liberation, the location, an unidentified camp, makes the use of colour itself problematic: "Vivas's choice to use pastel colors is utterly tasteless" (107). Yet he tends to praise colour when it appears in a book in which the protagonist has survived and/or is recalling the event years later. He is much more positive regarding the "pastel illustrations" (106) of Paula Kurzband Feder's *The Feather-Bed Journey*; the "thoughtful, expressive pastel drawings" (14) of *Child of the Warsaw Ghetto*; and the "bold watercolor" (71) of Adler's *Hiding from the Nazis*. The case of Miriam Nerlove's *Flowers on the Wall* proves an interesting exception to his views on colour. Even though the child protagonist is deported to Treblinka and dies there, Sullivan still praises the "expressive, often poignant, watercolors" (107). Nerlove's book challenges the preference for black and white, for the book is dedicated to the child in the Roman Vishniac photograph, "who stayed in bed all winter because her apartment had no heat. There are flowers painted on the wall behind her bed" (Nerlove n. pag.). Since Vishniac's prewar photograph documents another artist's attempt to provide colour, Sullivan's usual assumptions regarding the place of colour are disrupted.[3]

Not only do we prefer Holocaust picture books that allude to photographs in some manner, we often regard them as signifying differently from other picture books. For example, in *The Holocaust in Literature for Youth*, Sullivan includes *A Picture Book of Anne Frank* and *Child of the Warsaw Ghetto* in his chapter on autobiography and biography, not in his brief chapter on picture books. Explaining his methodology, he says he "chose to restrict this section [on picture books] to fictional works because librarians typically shelve them separately while interfiling nonfiction and biographical picture books" (105). This commonplace practice by librarians, drawing a somewhat problematic distinction between those picture books which are about historically real people and those which are fictional, clearly signals how the presence of photographs in Holocaust picture books serves to confirm the distinction between fiction and non-fiction.[4]

Sullivan similarly lists two other books by Adler, *Hiding from the Nazis* and *The Number on My Grandfather's Arm*, in his nonfiction category. Yet the latter book, consisting of a narrative that glosses photographs depicting a conversation between a reluctant grandfather who is persuaded by his granddaughter to explain the number on his arm, contains a series of photographs presumably staged by the photographer. In the notes to the text, the photographer, Rose Eichenbaum, identifies herself as the daughter of survivors and the child in the photographs as her daughter. However, the identity of the grandfather in the photographs remains ambiguous. Even though the credits distinguish between the three photographs that are provided by Yad Vashem and those that are "Family photographs by Rose Eichenbaum," information that implies that the grandfather must be either the photographer's father or father-in-law, the end note does not identify "Sigfried Halbreich" as Eichenbaum's father. He is identified instead in two ways, as "the grandfather" in the book and as "a Polish-born Holocaust survivor." Is this evidence that we know already and do not need to be reminded that Halbreich is the grandfather of the child in the photograph, or does it suggest that Halbreich is not the child's grandfather? I do not question the psychological truths of the story, that grandparents are often reluctant to speak to their grandchildren about their experiences in the Holocaust, or that a child might overcome that reluctance through her fascination with the number on her grandfather's arm. What interests me is the epistemological status of the photographs and the way they support our conviction that photographs provide a knowledge that illustrations cannot.[5]

Perhaps Sigfried Halbreich is identified as "the grandfather" because his function is iconic; he is representative of all grandfathers who hesitate to tell their grandchildren about the Holocaust. This is similar to how photograph-based drawings function as markers of the truth, even though the photographs have become so removed from their original historical specificity that their truth-telling is more iconic than historically precise. Thus a photograph that has become an icon of Holocaust horror becomes the basis for an illustration of a specific murder. Another Adler picture book illustrated by Ritz, *Hilde and Eli: Children of the Holocaust*, relies on this practice extensively. Although the book is not discussed by Sullivan, its content leads the writers of *Learning About the Holocaust: Literature and Other Resources for Young People* to recommend limiting its circulation to those "primary school children [...] with background already about the

PLATE 6

Holocaust who are prepared for the frightening nature of the death of the children" (Stephens, Brown, and Rubin 39).[6] Their warning is necessary because the text tells us that Hilde was gassed with her mother in a freight car, and Eli was gassed with his father and brother at Auschwitz.

The illustration above the text that tells us how Hilde and her mother die on their way "to the ghetto in Riga, Latvia" (n. pag.) clearly alludes to a photograph labeled more generically in van der Rol and Verhoeven: "People being transported in cattle cars to the camps" (97). (See Plate 6, p. 248.) In both the photograph and the illustration, we see the barbed wire, the bolts on the train car, the women looking out, one woman wearing glasses; the main difference in the illustration is Ritz's addition of a woman wearing a coloured kerchief and looking to the side. Presumably the figure repre-

PLATE 7

sents Hilde, given how the use of colour signals the moment when the illustrator most transgresses the photograph. In the final two pages of *Hilde and Eli*, the left-hand coloured illustration shows the backs of naked men and boys entering "what looked like a large bathhouse" (n. pag.), Ritz's imaginative depiction of Eli, his brother, father, and others entering the gas chamber. The truth of this illustration is reinforced by the black-and-white photographs of Hilde Rosenzweig and Eli Lax superimposed on the succeeding illustration of the train tracks entering Auschwitz-Birkenau on the right. (See Plate 7, p. 249.) The photographs we see on this final page are reproductions of real photographs taken in 1938 when Hilde was 15 and 1940 when Eli was 8. Adler provides this information in his author's note as well as an account of how the two photographs came to the United States. On the

PLATE 8

dust jacket of the book, however, is a variation of these photographs. This time, Ritz has drawn an illustration of Eli's
photograph and an illustration of a photograph of a much
younger girl than the photograph of Hilde that is included
on the final page, but one more appropriate to the subtitle,
"Children of the Holocaust." We are not told whether this
illustration is based on a real photograph.

The most complicated use of photographs in Adler picture books is *Child of the Warsaw Ghetto*. The text tells us that the protagonist, Froim Baum, was liberated at Dachau; above this information Ritz has drawn an illustration obviously derived from the famous photograph taken at Buchenwald in April 1945 by the Signal Corps (Zelizer 103). Although Ritz's illustration crops the photograph, omitting the bottom and top row of men lying on bunks as well as the nearly naked, skeletal male standing on the right, the illustration's allusion to the photograph is unmistakable. It is unlikely that any viewer, seeing this illustration of two rows of gaunt men lying in their bunks, will question how an illustration based on a photograph taken at Buchenwald functions as a depiction of the real liberation from Dachau experienced by Froim Baum.

What is particularly puzzling is the photographic basis to another illustration. (See Plate 8, p. 250.) It depicts a bearded man with a peaked cap holding a child. Given that this illustration stands opposite a page describing how the Warsaw doctor, Janusz Korczak, refused to abandon the orphan children in his care when they were ordered to the trains, surely the identity of the figure is obvious. Yet although the words encourage us to read this illustration as an image of Korczak, Ritz's illustration has an uncanny resemblance to the photograph of an unnamed man holding a child with a kerchief on her head in Gerhard Schoenberner's *The Holocaust: The Nazi Destruction of Europe's Jews* (74). In Schoenberner, the photograph is titled "Before Deportation," and the background figures are blurred, but the central figures of the bearded man and the child are identical to Ritz's illustration. Whoever the man is in the photograph, in Ritz's illustration in *Child of the Warsaw Ghetto* we identify him as Korczak.

But why does Ritz not base her illustration on a photograph of Korczak? For not only do such photographs exist, one is even included in Adler's *We Remember the Holocaust*. Clearly, if we examine the photograph of Korczak that does appear in *We Remember the Holocaust*, we must conclude that it is not the basis for Ritz's illustration in *Child of the Warsaw Ghetto*. Does Korczak's photograph not resemble the way contemporary readers imagine the doctor leading the orphan children to the train? We might wonder even more at the relationship between photographs, illustrations, and the historical real in picture books if we were aware that the photograph of Korczak that I am referring to appears in *We Remember the Holocaust* just above a photograph of Erwin Baum taken several weeks after liberation (88).[7] This juxtaposition matters because after the war, Froim Baum adopted the name Erwin Baum. Not only does Adler first tell Froim Baum's story in *We Remember the Holocaust*, but he includes a real photograph of him. Yet, despite his inclusion of real photographs of Korczak and Baum in *We Remember the Holocaust*, Ritz does not use *either* real photograph as the basis for her illustrations of Korczak and Baum in *Child of the Warsaw Ghetto*. Just as Korczak's photograph does not inspire the illustration of Korczak, Baum's liberation photograph, the only photograph of Baum that appears in *We Remember the Holocaust*, does not factor in the illustrations of Baum that appear in *Child of the Warsaw Ghetto*.

Aesthetic assumptions clearly affect how Holocaust photographs are used in picture books, not just in the reluctance to use atrocity photographs, but even in the choices made regarding which photographs will serve as the basis for the illustrations that depict the historical figures that the books describe. What is even more striking in all photograph-based illustrations is that they validate our adult belief that Holocaust photographs give us privileged access to the real only if we have prior knowledge of the photographs. Without that knowledge, the child (or adult) viewer looks at such illustrations differently, ignorant of what the illustrator knows and what Holocaust picture books teach—the privileged epistemological status of photographs.

Saving the Boy in the Warsaw Ghetto Photograph

Perhaps an additional reason that Ritz does not use the photograph of Froim Baum as the basis for her illustrations of Baum is because we already know what a child in the Warsaw Ghetto looks like. The well-known photograph contained in the report of Jürgen Stroop has become possibly the most famous image of the Holocaust child: it depicts a small boy with his hands up during the liquidation of the Warsaw Ghetto in April-May 1943; he is set apart from the others whose hands are also raised, in front, but not directly in the line of fire of a soldier with a gun. If Anne Frank is the iconic voice of the Holocaust child, the unnamed boy in the photograph is the Holocaust child's vulnerable body. His image appears on the cover of Gerhard Schoenberner's *The Holocaust: The Nazi Destruction of Europe's Jews*, a mild image compared to the photographs contained within the book. Schoenberner emphasizes that these disturbing photographs do not show us the worst atrocities: "The pictures in this book reveal what the murderers considered fit to be photographed" (7). Going on to detail which images he deliberately did not include, he insists, "The reality was that much worse" (7).

In contrast to the disturbing photographs Schoenberner does include and those we dare not imagine, the child with his hands up in the Warsaw Ghetto is an image we have learned to tolerate. It appears in so many texts and lends itself so readily to our symbolic readings. We call the photograph "the child in the Warsaw Ghetto," but the photograph's symbolic resonance has grown far wider. To Geoffrey H. Hartman, the photograph is "sad and eloquent enough" (131), an image that teaches "that no difference was made between children and adults in the Final Solution" (131). To David Roskies, the child represents "the adult made child by the Holocaust that no one can explain to us" (294, 296). Yet he adds that the "meaning [of the photograph] must be supplied by the viewer" (296) for "the soldiers are not particularly malignant [...] the menace is from our reading of the victims' gestures and from our knowledge of the final outcome" (296).

Like the child in the Warsaw Ghetto photograph, the Holocaust photographs that circulate in children's books, a relatively mild subset of the limited number of photographs that circulate in adult books, rarely serve to shock. This is not only because we tend to exclude the photographs that are too horrific, but because we bring to such photographs a prior knowledge. Thus they do not so much give us precise knowledge as they exist within a framework of retrospective knowledge, one that governs our subdued response to their images. We are subdued because we "know" that the child died. But how would we respond to the photograph of the boy in the Warsaw Ghetto if we knew that he survived? According to

Roskies, "there is a man alive today in New Jersey who claims to have been that child" (296). A documentary, *Tsvi Nussbaum: A Boy from Warsaw*, explores this man's claim (Shandler 197-99). However unlikely such survival, even in the context of our knowledge that one-and-a-half million other children did not survive, would we not respond differently if we knew this particular child survived? Even if we conclude that the child died, the photograph does not tell us what happens between the moment it captures and the moment of death.

In Roberto Innocenti's *Rose Blanche*, the photograph of the child in the Warsaw Ghetto influences three illustrations, which cater to fantasies that explore the gap between the moment captured in the photograph and our knowledge of the final outcome. First the child is seen escaping from a truck: the text tells us, "A little boy jumped from the back of the truck and tried to run away" (n. pag.). In the second illustration the child is captured by the mayor and returned to the truck. The illustration of the soldier to whom the mayor hands the boy is clearly based on the soldier in the Stroop photograph, but provides different information since Innocenti draws the soldier turned sideways. Although the child in this illustration most closely resembles the child in the Stroop photograph, the SS insignia that Innocenti places on the soldier's helmet and collar is not evident in the original photograph.[8] As in the photograph, Innocenti positions the soldier's gun ominously yet slightly to the side.[9]

Rose Blanche comes across the attempted escape by accident; until the day she does, "[t]he trucks are fun to watch" (Innocenti n. pag.). However, in the third illustration, when the little boy is forced back into the truck, Rose Blanche covers her mouth and stands still. The episode triggers her quest for knowledge, and makes her sound like a viewer of the original photograph: "I wanted to know where the little boy went" (n. pag.). Yet if the photograph of the little boy in the Warsaw ghetto predetermines how we respond to Innocenti's illustration, our recognition of the photograph does not guarantee any detailed awareness of the history that occasioned it. What happens is the reverse. The photograph that affected us once in a precise way because of its particular history gradually becomes an image freed of that history, available for other uses and meanings.[10] The further we are removed from the historical events of the original photograph, the less we are able to restrict the photograph to the realm of historically specific representation. Describing how all photographs that were once historically specific eventually move into the realm of the aesthetic, Sontag labels even this photograph of the child in the Warsaw Ghetto as inevitably beautiful (97-98). We "learn about the world's horrors mainly through the camera [...]. But the aestheticizing tendency of photography is such that the medium which conveys distress ends by neutralizing it. Cameras [...] transform history into spectacle" (98).

It is difficult to imagine that all photographs can move into the aesthetic. In one of his 1942 notebooks, Oskar Rosenfeld, who was deported from Prague to the Lodz Ghetto in October 1941 and taken to Auschwitz in August 1944, recorded a ghetto resident's account of the abusive power of Nazi photography: "As we sat there answering the call of nature [using the communal latrines], they photographed us, some from below to show us crouched on the bar [...]. What was their purpose: to have 'evidence' of how shameless Jews are, defecating together without distinction as to sex?" (Adelson and Lapides 27). Beside these words, Sontag's comments on beauty seem beside the point.

Does this photograph exist? Given the nature of the Nazi photographs that do exist, there is no reason to believe that it does not. That Adelson and Lapides do not place such a photograph beside Rosenfeld's words in *Lodz Ghetto: Inside a Community Under Siege* could be the result of an editorial decision—what purpose would be served by our looking at such a photograph? The decision to follow Rosenfeld's words with other photographs might remind us that the photographs we look at are always the product of multiple decisions and accidents: not just editorial choices, but also the randomness of survival (which applies to photographs as much as to people). The publishing history of Holocaust photographs would reveal further choices that explain how a few photographs, like the photograph of the child in the Warsaw Ghetto, have taken on an iconic status. But even in Rosenfeld's account, the photograph is something not seen by him, but experienced through the words of another. Its power is verbal, not visual. If the photograph he describes did exist and we looked at it, what knowledge would it give us today? Already in 1942, the testimony by the unnamed ghetto inhabitant challenges the "evidence" such film would provide. Assuming the contemporary viewer's prior knowledge of the extent to which Nazi photography was just one weapon in an arsenal of degradation, Adelson and Lapides present Rosenfeld's words about the photograph as evidence that does not require the inclusion of the photograph itself. If looking at the photograph would produce a questionable knowledge, our willingness to believe the unnamed ghetto inhabitant's testimony acknowledges that photographs are sometimes even more powerful when we do not see them.

Framing the Lodz Ghetto Photographs: The Power of Captions

Sontag says that all photographs are "*memento mori*" (14), that the "link between photography and death haunts all photographs of people" (64). In *Family Frames: Photography, Narrative and Postmemory*, Marianne Hirsch goes further in claiming that "[t]he Holocaust photograph is uniquely able to bring out this particular capacity of photographs to hover between life and death" (20). Hirsch is particularly interested in the role played by such photographs in postmemory. Unlike Andrea Liss who defines postmemories as "the imprints that photographic imagery of the Shoah have created within the post-Auschwitz generation" (86), Hirsch uses the term in the singular and restricts it more to the children of survivors, "those who grow up dominated by narratives that preceded their birth" (22). Thus she distinguishes postmemory "from memory by generational distance and from history by deep personal connection" (22). Postmemory drives the way the child of survivors looks at family photographs of relatives she has never known, the way the child comes to realize that the photographs are themselves survivors.

Hirsch contrasts the disbelief that operates in looking at family photographs with the disbelief operative upon viewing the documentary photographs of mass graves. With the latter, there is an initial response of horror "even before reading the caption or knowing its context" (20). In contrast, family photographs, such as those collected by Yaffa Eliach, provoke horror only when we realize what the location of the images —the Tower of Faces at the United States Holocaust Memorial Museum, or their location through the stories and/or captions that frame them in a book of photographs—tells us. Not only do family photographs tell us nothing—"there is nothing in the pictures themselves that reveals the complicated history of loss and destruction to which they testify" (Hirsch 13)—but Hirsch also argues that the family photographs and images of atrocity are complementary, provoking "a similar sense of disbelief" (21). We need to see both kinds of photographs to understand, or, as Hirsch might insist, to not understand how the person in the family photograph was murdered:

> In both cases, the viewer fills in what the picture leaves out: the horror of looking is not necessarily *in* the image but in the story the viewer provides to fill in what has been omitted. For each image we provide the other complementary one. (Hirsch 21)

The degree to which the photographs of atrocity appear in children's books is limited; ever since their first wide circulation in 1945, access to such photographs of atrocity has been debated in terms of their suitability for children. Sontag's insight that seeing them "does not necessarily strengthen conscience and the ability to be compassionate" (18) and Hirsch's insistence that we need to see the family photographs as well are acknowledged by David Adler in *We Remember the Holocaust* when he includes personal photographs of the people he interviews as a strategy to encourage children to identify with "the witnesses and victims of prejudice and persecution" (ix-x). But the most common photographs in children's books are those taken secretly by Mendel Grossman in the Lodz Ghetto. These photographs stand somewhere in between the family photograph and the atrocity image; they document the effect of ghetto conditions but with an intent other than that of the Nazi photograph, and thus, in the very conditions of their making, they offer children an example of resistance. To Andrea Liss, these "astounding photographs [...] defy the mass of horrific post-memories of the events" (3).

Yet even such photographs do not speak on their own. If Liss reads the Grossman photographs as astounding and defiant, it is because she has seen the horrific photographs she refuses to show her readers and which we are understandably reluctant to show children. What the child viewer knows is only what the narrative and/or the caption tells her. In *The Children We Remember*, Chana Byers Abells's minimal narrative carefully controls the child's response to the photographs. Abells's general dedication "to the children whose lives ended during the Holocaust and to the photographers, known and unknown, who risked their lives to record their story" (n. pag.) immediately informs the reader that the children in the photographs died and that the photographs work within a narrative of heroism. In comparison, her acknowledgments page is more personal, working within the postmemory of the mother who also knows that her children "but for time and space, might have shared the fate of *The Children We Remember*" (Abells n. pag.).

In comparison to the text by Frank Dabba Smith that is included in another collection of Grossman photographs marketed for children, *My Secret Camera: Life in the Lodz Ghetto*, Abells's words seem restrained, eloquent, and factual. If anything, the nature of her attention on children requires her to emphasize how the Nazis "hated the children because they were Jews," and how this hatred led to their murder. The caption to one photograph of a soldier shooting a woman and child, "[s]ometimes they put children to death," does not acknowledge that an adult is also being killed. Yet if we compare the captions that gloss several of the photographs Abells uses with the captions that appear elsewhere, we will see how she respects the facts of history while simultaneously encouraging the reader where possible to see something positive in the image. For example, Abells includes a photograph of a boy facing the camera while holding up the head of a man who is lying on the street. Beneath the photograph the image is glossed, "[t]he children helped the old, the sick" (n. pag.), and the image serves as the second in a series of three demonstrating a narrative about children helping others. The same photograph is the basis for an illustration in Adler's *Child of the Warsaw Ghetto*, but there the text speaks of the death of thousands "each month from starvation, exposure to the cold, and disease" (n. pag.), a demonstration once again how the photograph-based illustration often accompanies text that is more willing to speak about death than the caption through which the writer tries to save the actual photograph. (See Plate 9, p. 262.) In Schoenberner, the same photograph is not only cropped differently, so that we see more people standing in the background, including a child on the far right who appears not to be paying attention to the action occurring on the street, but the caption is radically different. It tells us that what we look at is "Death in the Street" (69).

PLATE 9

The captions for other images are equally contradictory. In Schoenberner, a photograph of two children holding bowls is simply labelled "Soup kitchen" (66); in Abells, the same image stands as the first of three through which she narrates a story of moral choice, of mutual child-focused support: "When the children were hungry, they shared the little food they had" (n. pag.). The third of these photographs, of a boy feeding a girl so young she must be spoon-fed, is like the iconic photo of the child in the Warsaw ghetto, an image that appears in numerous Holocaust texts, perhaps because it is less distressing than so many others. (See Plate 10, p. 263.) The children it photographs do not yet look gaunt from hunger. They do not wear rags; the little girl even has a bow in her hair. Neither child appears aware of the camera as the

PLATE 10

boy concentrates on feeding the child, and the child focuses on eating what is on the spoon. Abells crops the image so that we see only the top half of both children, the dark of their clothing contrasting with the pail of food the boy holds and the light that focuses on the little girl's small hands.

Yet if we turn to the narration and location of this image in other texts, the words that accompany it tell a very different story. In *Lodz Ghetto: Inside a Community Under Siege*—a compilation that followed the publication of *The Chronicle of the Lodz Ghetto*, the making of a documentary film, and, at over 500 pages, intended to bring the "literary and photographic legacy of the Lodz Ghetto" (Adelson and Lapides xix) to a wider and presumably adult audience—the photograph of the boy feeding the girl appears twice. It is first seen on the frontispiece cropped tightly so that the focus on the two figures is even more intense, and the tightness of the image appears to emphasize the child's painful desire for the contents of the spoon. Its second use is as a full-page image captioned "Brother and sister" (123). In it, we see that the boy is sitting in order to feed a very tiny child. We also see the child's bare legs, socks, and sandals, details that increase our response to the vulnerable toddler who is being fed.

Not only does the full-page image reveal more than in Abells's cropped version, our reaction to it is also affected by its location within the text, for the editors insert it within one of the many distressing accounts their compilation includes. The photograph interrupts a report by one of the ghetto residents, Josef Zelkowicz; the numerous questions his report raises make us view the photograph very differently than we do when Abells presents it as an illustration of positive moral choice. The hopeful way that Abells invites us to respond is not possible when Zelkowicz first describes the reaction of people in the ghetto to the news that they will receive an extra 10 kilograms of potatoes, and then explains why two women, presumably as hungry as everyone else in the ghetto, plan to sell the potatoes that they have received. Using coupons that are illegal because they belong to family members whose deaths have not yet been reported to the ghetto administrators, the women tell him that they will sell the potatoes thus obtained to pay for shrouds for their dead sons. Zelkowicz uses the incident to capture the self-deluding psychology of the ghetto: "There must be happy people in this apartment. They've already brought home their potatoes. Beautiful potatoes. Potatoes like apples. Potatoes like fists" (122). Does he wish that the inhabitants had used their fists? Only gradually does his story draw attention to the signs of mourning and the absent men. Once there were five men and two women in the apartment. Now there are only the two women, and Zelkowicz pities those who can be thankful for such circumstances: "God does not abandon. When all hope was lost, God made Rumkowski to distribute potatoes" (122). Lawrence L. Langer might regard this incident as a perfect example of the choiceless choice faced by inhabitants of the ghetto, and Zelkowicz's tone as an appropriate response to the situation, but anger over Mordechai Chaim Rumkowski, the controversial *Judenaltester* (Jewish Elder), and irony at the inhabitants' expense (Zelkowicz's entry is titled "God did not abandon us") has no place in a children's book.[11]

In *My Secret Camera: Life in the Lodz Ghetto*, the words that accompany the same photograph are even more insistent in their need to tell a positive story. Frank Dabba Smith writes an emphatically hopeful narrative to gloss the photograph of the boy and girl that contrasts dramatically with Zelkowicz's story about potatoes: "This young man has so little food, and yet he shares it. In spite of our suffering, we help and care for one another. And this little girl still wears a bow proudly in her hair" (Smith n. pag.). The ambiguity regarding the photographs' ability to speak is evident in the introduction to *My Secret Camera*, in which Howard Jacobson first tells us that Grossman's photographs "can move us to understanding no less than to compassion" (n. pag.), and then, in case we are uncertain what it is these photographs make us understand, he proceeds to tell us.

This need to provide a coherent verbal narrative is evident in the book's structure, for the narrative is presented as a monologue by Mendel Grossman. Giving voice, in this way, to the ghetto photographer who did not survive in order to tell us what story his photographs communicate, Smith begins with a photograph of Grossman, who is aware that he is being photographed (unlike the other people crossing a bridge and seen in the background of the image) and who explains to the reader that he takes photographs to "tell the real story" (Smith n. pag.). After another photograph of Grossman examining his film and another of Nazis, intended to represent the kind of clandestine photographs he took from the top of buildings, Smith as Grossman tells the reader of his heroic determination to take photographs against the advice of his friends: "They worry that the Nazis will catch me. They also know my heart is weak" (n. pag.). And the ability of the photographs to tell the real story is restated: "My pictures will tell the real story, even if I die" (n. pag.).

Although it is misleading to assert that the captions to photographs in all adult books tell "the truth" whereas the captions to photographs in all children's books do not, the captions in this particular children's book repeatedly insist that the truth is there in the image. Hirsch states that a psychological disbelief is a permanent part of one's response to Holocaust photographs, a disbelief not that it did happen, but that it could happen: the "inability 'to take *it* in' is per-haps the distinguishing feature of the Holocaust photograph" (Hirsch 21). In contrast, the captions in *My Secret Camera* make no reference to the viewers' inability to "take *it* in." Instead the narrative voice tells us repeatedly that in the future "the world will know the truth" (n. pag.), but then com-plicates the nature of the truth we will know by using words whose truth does not necessarily accord with what a viewer may see either because of what is in the photograph or because of the knowledge that the viewer brings to the pho-tograph. A photograph in which two men entertain a crowd and where I see at most two people smiling is glossed by Smith: "[i]n spite of everything, we have to laugh once in a while. We laugh at ourselves. We make up funny songs, too. Here Jankele, a tailor from Poland, sings with Karol, a travel-ing salesman from Austria" (n. pag.). A travelling salesman in the Lodz Ghetto?

If Smith's words do not tell us the truth about who Karol is or what brings him from Austria to Poland, what they repeatedly do is imagine ghetto inhabitants resisting hero-ically: a photograph of matzos is glossed, "though we are caged and hungry, we must be brave and remain free in our hearts" (n. pag.). But the most troubling caption is one that does not give us the child's thoughts. Beside a photograph of a boy separated by a wire fence from other children and adult women, we read, "[t]ime and again I witness children left alone, torn from their families. A mother to her son: 'Be strong, my boy'" (n. pag.). I do not object to the words Smith imagines the woman saying to the child, or that Smith's text does not even clarify if it is the mother or the son who is being deported. What disturbs me is the historical knowledge that I bring to this photograph and to the photograph that follows of a girl behind barbed wire, for the same photographs appear in *Lodz Ghetto: Inside a Community Under Siege*. The caption to the first photograph is very precise: "Under the age of ten, this boy was separated from his mother and brothers, who have come to say goodbye" (Adelson and Lapides 357). Smith captions the second photograph, "Will we ever see each other again?" (n. pag.), thereby once again presuming to know what the child is thinking. In contrast, Adelson and Lapides do not presume to tell us what the girl behind barbed wire is thinking; they caption her photograph and another photograph of children, "Captives, awaiting the wagon which will take them to the train" (359).

It is not the captions themselves, but the narrative that precedes them that makes the photographs so distressing. The reference to the child's age is disturbing, because the reader of *Lodz Ghetto: Inside a Community Under Siege* comes to these photographs after a long section recounting the massive deportations from Lodz in September 1942. The photographs appear in a chapter called "Nightmarish Days" after the title of a Yiddish manuscript, *In These Nightmarish Days*, in which Zelkowicz reports the distress caused by Rumkowski when he told the ghetto inhabitants that they had to surrender all children up to the age of 10. The horror of that speech by Rumkowski on September 4, 1942—"Fathers and mothers, give me your children!" (Adelson and Lapides 328)—is augmented by Rumkowski's statement that the Nazis had demanded "24,000 victims," which he had successfully bargained down to "20,000, but only on the condition that these would be children below the age of ten" (328). This is a knowledge that the photographs alone cannot and do not provide.

And the very optimism of the captions that usually accompany photographs in children's books exists in uneasy tension with other words written by Zelkowicz that September: "The logical thinkers and optimists misled us" (326).

Have the optimists misled us? Are the captions used by Smith evidence of resistance to Nazi discourse, the need to prove that logic and optimism were a viable option, or do they simply reveal our unwillingness to tell children certain troubling historical facts? And even if it is psychologically necessary to give children hopeful captions, is it morally right to do so? The precise captions to Yaffa Eliach's *We Were Children Just Like You*, a collection of photographs published in conjunction with an exhibition by the same name, offer a different approach to knowledge in Holocaust photographs. Although the book exists within the framework of memorial discourse—the opening tells us to remember, and the final black page quotes from Joel about the need to tell succeeding generations—Eliach's introduction refuses to pretend that Holocaust photographs speak. Repeatedly Eliach tells us what the photographs cannot show. Describing a photograph of "cheerful children playing in the shadow of trees near their seated mothers" (13), she reminds us "what the photo does not record is the fact that the children and mothers are in Birkenau, awaiting their turn at the crematoria" (13). Her captions do not attempt to imagine what the children are thinking. If Eliach has no information about the photograph, she does not make up a story. Instead, her annotations repeatedly demonstrate our inability to read the photographs accurately. We see what appears to be a photograph of a girl sitting on a park bench; the caption tells us that the child is a boy "who survived the war disguised as a girl, in order to

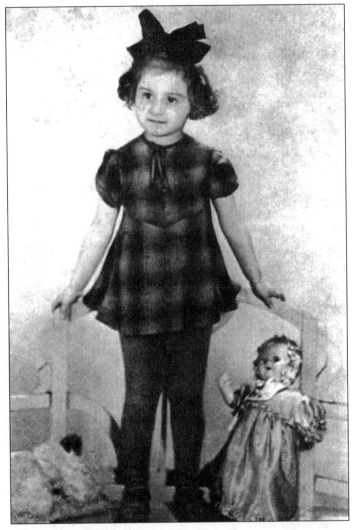

PLATE II

avoid being betrayed by his circumcision" (9). Underneath
the photograph of a baby we learn not only that the child was
Jewish, but that a photographer entered her image in a magazine contest for "the perfect Aryan baby" (31), and she won.
Another photograph of a little girl with a bow in her hair

appears twice. (See Plate 11, p. 270.) Eliach makes no attempt to save the picture other than as the only remaining record of the child's existence. What she tells us of Mala Silverberg contains no hope, beauty, or consolation:

> Mala Silverberg was one of Josef Mengele's victims. In 1944 her family's hiding place was betrayed and she was deported to Auschwitz, the only child in that transport. As Mala, age 4 ½, stood in the selection line, Mengele asked her to sing. Impressed by her beautiful voice, he gave her a candy and then shot her through the head. (80)

Is it fair to demand that the photograph of Mala Silverberg teach us a lesson, or to expect that looking at this photograph will provoke change? What has changed since we began looking at Holocaust photographs? The photographs, which were so shocking in 1945 that editors debated whether children should see them and some newspapers carried them in detachable supplements so that parents could remove them (Zelizer 95), now exist in conjunction with other equally shocking photographs, such as the one taken by Nick Ut in 1972 of Kim Phuc, a naked nine-year-old Vietnamese child burned by napalm, running down a road. Mala Silverberg's photograph is in itself not shocking. Yet because it is a photograph that I have not seen before, and because of the precise documentation that Eliach gives it, I find myself unable to forget her image.

What makes us suddenly respond to a photograph? In Grace Paley's story "Faith in a Tree," a mother does not respond to anti-war posters depicting the burning of a

Vietnamese child until she is prompted by her son's fury over both the image and the adults' passivity. The moment is transformative for Paley's protagonist, driving her out of the playground into anti-war activism. Perhaps our pedagogical faith in the transformative power of pictures requires that we worry less about saving the photograph and more about how to recreate that fictional child's response, a response not of sorrow and protected knowledge, but of anger that such photographs exist, and fury at a world in which adults continue to take such photographs, because such atrocities continue to occur. We might start by looking at Mala Silverberg's photograph and the words that Yaffa Eliach writes.

NOTES

1. Sybil Milton in "Images of the Holocaust—Part II" (195) estimates that there are 1.5 million Holocaust photographs in over 30 archives. The photographs that circulate and influence children's books are a very small subset of this number.

2. See the introduction and opening chapter of Andrea Liss, *Trespassing Through Shadows: Memory, Photography and the Holocaust*, in which Liss explains her refusal to show photographs housed in the Nazi archives. Her decision has nothing to do with the age of her implied readers but with a refusal to "recreate the violence" (xi).

3. Nerlove calls her protagonist Rachel. The Vishniac photograph is #42 in *A Vanished World*. Vishniac calls the child Sara, and in his "Commentary on the Photographs" he writes that "Sara was ten, and the darling of her family. When I returned to the site of her home after the war, the home was no more, and there was no Sara" (Vishniac n. pag.).

4. The difficulty with Sullivan's methodology is that even books that appear on his brief list of picture books allude to the experiences of real Holocaust victims, a reality often confirmed through the book's use of Holocaust photographs, e.g., Nerlove's *Flowers on the Wall*; see also my discussion (pp. 255-56) of the use of the photograph of the Warsaw Ghetto boy in *Rose Blanche*.

5. I witnessed a similar hesitancy on my mother's part when my son asked her to tell him about her experiences during the war. The child's fascination with the number on the grandfather's arm in Adler's text is paralleled by how grade 12 students attending the Holocaust Education Symposium in Calgary, May 2000, were equally interested in seeing the number on the speaker's arm. Seeing the number gave them a knowledge not available through the speaker's narrative.

6. The authors do not include a similar warning for *A Picture Book of Anne Frank* either because they think death from typhus is less frightening than death by gassing, or because even the child being introduced to Anne Frank already is aware of her end.

7. People named in other Adler picture books also appear in *We Remember the Holocaust*; e.g., Julius Rosenzweig had a sister, Hilde, whose story is told in *Hilde and Eli*.

8. For a different reading of this change and Innocenti's use of the photograph to "divest the story of its historical credibility" (99), see Shavit.

9. The position of the gun supports Roskies's observation that "the soldiers are not particularly malignant" (296); the viewer's horror comes from a knowledge outside what is provided by the photograph. Arguments over the angle of the gun are also reminiscent of more recent controversies concerning another photograph. Elian Gonzales, a 6-year-old Cuban child, was rescued off the Florida coast in late 1999, after his mother and stepfather drowned in an attempt to reach the USA. His American relatives refused to return Elian to his father in Cuba. A photograph, taken April 22, 2000, when Elian was forcibly removed from his relatives' home, shows the terrified child facing an armed man. This photograph appeared in newspapers worldwide the next day and immediately provoked arguments over its meaning, often focusing on whether the soldier's hand was on the trigger. That many viewers were convinced of the photograph's similarity to photographs of Nazis terrorizing children may be further evidence of how influential the photograph of the boy in the Warsaw Ghetto has become. Certainly, that photograph frames the way I respond to the photograph of Elian Gonzales.

10. Some photographs are freed of their history very rapidly. The speed with which the photograph of Elian Gonzales was transformed into a satirical editorial cartoon in *The Globe and Mail* is also supportive of Sontag's comment that cameras transform history into spectacle and of

Zelizer's thesis that the way Holocaust photographs have become arche-typal images of atrocity may be counter-productive. Zelizer argues that we become so used to seeing these images that we become numb and suf-fer from what Anthony Lewis calls, "compassion fatigue" (Zelizer 218). The latter phrase also appears in the title of Susan D. Moeller's *Compassion Fatigue: How the Media Sell Disease, Famine, War and Death*. Unable to laugh at real photographs of atrocity, we direct our attention and laugh-ter elsewhere. Elian's photograph, taken on a Saturday, appeared on the front pages of many North American newspapers the next morning. On the following Wednesday, only four days later, even while nearly all Cana-dian newspapers still gave some attention to further developments in the Cuban child's story, *The Globe and Mail* editorial cartoon by Gable adapt-ed Elian's photograph for a satirical cartoon about Microsoft. On the front page of the 26 April 2000 edition were reports regarding the possi-ble breakup of Microsoft. The Gable cartoon shows a terrified Microsoft computer cowering in a closet as an armed representative of the Antitrust Division of the US Department of Justice threatens. This time, the soldier's finger is most definitely on the trigger.

11. Rumkowski was the head of the Lodz *Judenrat*. The leaders of the council were referred to as Elders. For the issues and controversies sur-rounding Rumkowski, see Adelson and Lapides, esp. 49-94. See also my discussion in Chapter Five.

PART FOUR

◆

History and Pedagogy

8

Looking in the Baby Carriage: Representation, Gender, and Choice

"It seems obvious to me that anything written now about the Nazi genocide against the Jews that is not primarily documentary [...] requires special justification" (Lang, *Act and Idea in the Nazi Genocide* xi)

In his preface to *Holocaust Testimonies: The Ruins of Memory*, Lawrence L. Langer explains that he calls the speakers of these testimonies "former victims," not "survivors" (xii). With this language Langer signals his distance from a heroic rhetoric that too easily celebrates survivors by ignoring the fact that the Holocaust is not an event someone simply survives. Contrasting the bleak way that two former victims describe the impact of the Holocaust upon their lives with the radically different language their daughter uses, he concludes: "*She* draws on a vocabulary of chronology and conjunction, while *they* use a lexicon of disruption, absence, and irreversible loss" (xi). The contrast, according to Langer, derives from different levels of meaning in Holocaust testimony: we hear what we want and are able to hear. Quoting one speaker who concludes, "what choice did we have?" (26), Langer insists that most of us have difficulty understanding what the speaker means by that question, for we live in a world in which we continue to believe that people do have choices, a belief that remains central to our understanding of heroic narrative. To Langer, this is the challenge of listening to Holocaust testimony and reading the Holocaust literature that he most values—how can and do we respond to a literature and a testimony that says that choice is impossible?

Any consideration of the narrative choices made by writers and the philosophical meaning of choice in children's historical fiction cannot simply ignore Langer's view. Initially his work appears to discredit the very possibility of a children's fiction on the Holocaust, for how can we imagine children's fiction without choice? John Stephens suggests that "[t]he audience for historical fiction begins at the upper primary years, and probably exists, in so far as it exists at all, most extensively among junior secondary school readers" (202). What would be the justification for giving such young children historical narratives that denied the possibility of choice? Choice is so deeply ingrained in the pedagogic structure that frames children's reading about history that if the narratives permit no choice, the need to choose will be transposed outside them. Reading a story in which the characters no longer have legitimate choices, the readers will be encouraged to exercise choices so that this terrible story never happens again. When adults approve Holocaust stories about choice (and surely *Schindler's List* is about choice), when Anne Frank's *Diary* is celebrated as a story about a girl who chose to believe that people are really good at heart, it is unlikely that children's historical fiction will abandon this pattern.[1]

Langer first calls the dilemma faced by victims of the Nazis a "choiceless choice" (72) in *Versions of Survival: The Holocaust and the Human Spirit*, and he uses the phrase in his chapter, "Auschwitz: The Death of Choice." The very impossibility of choice within Auschwitz and the other death camps partially explains why, with a few rare exceptions, children's historical fiction stays outside the camps.[2] Carol Matas's *Daniel's Story* does have a section set in Auschwitz, but that setting is unusual for her Holocaust fiction, one that she develops because it is inherent in the book's function as companion to an established children's exhibit at the United States Holocaust Memorial Museum. If children's fiction postulates possibilities of choice and locates these possibilities only outside the camps, this is clearly different from writing narratives of coherent choice within the camps. References to choice within the camps are misleading only if they are presented as no different than the choices readers make every day.

But if a statement about how choice has helped the character to survive is then challenged by a later statement, the situation operates differently. In Matas's *After the War*, the protagonist, Ruth Mendenberg, recalls how lying about her age helped her pass a selection. Her belief that lying was essential to survival is soon followed by questions about how she knew enough to lie and uncertainty about how much agency was involved in her survival. Ruth does not really know why or how she survived; all she knows is that it keeps happening: "somehow I've survived again" (17). When she later remembers being found alive on a heap of dead bodies piled in Buchenwald, she further questions the consequences of her choices: "I fought so hard to survive and now I'm dead anyway" (69). What was the point to the choices that she made? Ruth, like others, did not choose to die, but in a psychological sense the opening line of the novel—"I thought you were all dead"—is accurate.

Comparing the work of Langer and Tzvetan Todorov's *Facing the Extreme: Moral Life in the Concentration Camps*, Michael Rothberg argues that Langer, like Todorov, "exclude[s ...] evidence that does not fit his thesis" (120). Todorov's belief in the possibility of moral choice appears closer to the patterns of children's fiction than Langer's preference for speaking about former victims and his critique of attempts to contain the complexity of Holocaust survival by writing about "the survivor." Yet attention to the title of Langer's earlier work, *Versions of Survival*, indicates his recognition that there are many ways of being a survivor and narrating that survival. So, too, children's fiction need not restrict itself to the predictable, and misleadingly cheerful, version of survival. Some children's fiction even examines the possibility of choice in ways that respect Langer's notion of choiceless choice and still satisfy the requirements of children's pedagogy.

Raul Hilberg argues that "survival was not altogether random" (*Perpetrators* 188). Finding a place for luck in survival, he says of one particular group of survivors, "[t]hey were lucky *after* they had tried to save themselves" (188). Hilberg's reference to both luck and choice is a paradox that best describes what happens in the children's fiction of Carol Matas. In her work, characters never speak of choice outside the context of luck and are even willing to admit that good luck can itself bring misfortune. When Ruth in *After the War* fears that she may be the only one of an extended family of 80 to survive, she not only wonders why she survived, but whether her survival is her "punishment for being the bad child of the family" (7). While it may seem that luck implies the absence of choice—my mother survived because she was lucky—

Hilberg's statement also makes me consider the place of choice in my mother's lucky survival, in particular, the choices made by my aunts. Magda and Marta switched lines during what they did not know would be a key selection, an act followed by their luck in not getting caught; surely this choice also contributed to the luck of the three sisters and their mother surviving. Just as clearly, the choice to switch lines could have been disastrous; they did not know if the line that my mother and grandmother were in was better. They made a choice, and they were lucky. And undoubtedly my grandmother survived because she was lucky, but she also survived because she lied about her age, and her daughters chose to protect her in whatever way they could. Like Matas's Ruth, "somehow" they survived.

Unlike Langer, the literary scholar, who questions narratives of choice, and Hilberg, the historian, who states that narratives of luck and choice are feasible for at least some survivors; the philosopher, Berel Lang, raises a different issue, one emphasized in the quotation that begins this chapter. Lang insists that non-documentary writing on the Holocaust requires "special justification," that the human agency that "shapes literary plot" (*Act and Idea* 147) is simply not descriptive of the Nazi genocide. Special justification in children's historical fiction is complicated by the need for this fiction to serve as a pedagogical tool that teaches children that they do have agency. For this reason, the question—what choice did I have?—resonates somewhat differently in children's historical fiction than in Langer's reading of Holocaust testimony. This chapter examines the implications of that resonance and the representational problems raised by the choices made in children's historical fiction. A focus on questions of choice helps clarify not just the different kinds of choice operating in the historical fiction of Christa Laird, Carol Matas, and Ida Fink, but also the pedagogical values of their fiction.

A focus on the different choices that shape this fiction reveals a contradictory conceptual border between the Holocaust fiction written specifically for children (the work of Laird and Matas) and the Holocaust fiction not originally marketed for children (the work of Fink), which nevertheless has made its way on to children's reading lists. Fink's two collections of stories—*A Scrap of Time and Other Stories* (winner of the first Anne Frank Prize for Literature) and *Traces: Stories*—as well as her novel, *The Journey*, all appear in Edward T. Sullivan's Holocaust bibliography. Hazel Rochman and Darlene Z. McCampbell include Fink's "Splinter" in their collection, *Bearing Witness: Stories of the Holocaust*. Not only is the determination of Laird and Matas to write narratives of choice absent from Fink's work, but Fink is a writer whom Langer has consistently praised and to whom he is indebted for the subtitle to *Holocaust Testimonies*. It may well be that the inclusion of Fink's work in children's Holocaust anthologies and bibliographies teaches adolescent readers how to move away from "the vocabulary of chronology and conjunction" (*Holocaust Testimonies* xi) that so disturbs Langer when he first hears it.[3] Fink is one of the few female writers whose work consistently appears in anthologies of Holocaust literature intended for adults, a canonical status that may explain why Sullivan includes her.[4] Yet Sullivan also makes choices in excluding other well-known adult books. What is it about Fink's work that enables it to cross the boundary between the work that Langer approves and children's reading lists in a way that other works, such as Tadeusz Borowski's *This Way for the Gas, Ladies and Gentlemen*, do not?

Baby Carriages, Imagination, and Choice in Christa Laird's Beyond the Wall

In Nechama Tec's memoir, *Dry Tears: The Story of a Lost Childhood*, the writer recounts an action that took place in Majdan Tatarski, a ghetto "on the outskirts of Lublin close to Majdanek" (17). Eight years old when the Nazis occupied Poland in 1939, Tec is 11 in 1942 when her mother wakes her because of advance warning "that there was going to be a partial liquidation of the ghetto" (27). At first, the mother and daughter can find no hiding place; as they run from house to house, Tec notices "a few baby carriages in full view, babies inside" (28). They have been left outside, she concludes, because the people in hiding fear that the babies will cry and give away the hiding places. After the action, Tec reports that all the babies were shot; she learns this not through the words of others, but by looking into a baby carriage as soon as she is allowed to emerge from the cellar: "I saw an unrecognizable bloody mass, that seemed strangely alive" (29).

As her title indicates, Tec's memoir goes beyond the simple consolations of childhood tears; even more significant is her insistence in telling the reader exactly what she sees. The babies are "unrecognizable"; in this one word she forces the reader to recognize the essence of her memory. The difference from what the babies were a few hours before overwhelms her: "I began to run, trying to avoid the bloodstained baby carriages and the bodies scattered in every direction on the ground" (29). She has seen enough, and so has the reader. Eventually she permits herself tears, but not until she is back in hiding and reunited with her mother. If she feels "numb with guilt" (29), it is not for looking in the carriage but for making her mother worry about whether she has survived.

Like Yaffa Eliach's words beneath Mala Silverberg's photograph (discussed in Chapter Seven, page 271-72), Tec's description of the babies in the carriages is powerful in its brevity. Perhaps for this reason, I recognize its similarities to a passage in a children's historical novel published several years later. Christa Laird's *Beyond the Wall* (also published under the title, *But Can the Phoenix Sing?*) is a sequel to her *Shadow of the Wall*. Both books concern a fictional protagonist, Misha Edelman. In the first book, Misha is 14 when he escapes the Warsaw Ghetto. In the sequel, he describes his subsequent adventures as a partisan in letters written nearly 30 years later to his troubled 17-year-old stepson, Richard. *Beyond the Wall* presents the Holocaust as a history that Richard knows nothing about. Typical of the children's adventure story, it also functions as a way of teaching a lesson by also providing the child reader with some clear historical information. This premise allows Laird to ascribe Richard's earlier tolerance for antisemitic behaviour to sheer ignorance, for after Richard has heard Misha's story, he confesses that he laughed when his friends defaced property with painted swastikas because he did not really understand what a swastika represented. Explaining himself, Misha explains history and alters the behaviour of his stepson. Telling his story not only helps their relationship, but leads to Richard writing a friend that he plans to look up Babi Yar and wishes that he "*was doing the Second World War for A level*" (64).

Laird's acknowledgments make no reference to her possible reliance on Tec's memoir. It is not surprising that in wanting to be truthful to the Holocaust a novelist might rely on details from a memoir.[5] In *Act and Idea in the Nazi Genocide*, Lang argues that figurative discourse on the Holocaust proves its inferiority to historical discourse through the novelists' attempt to mimic historical documents by using narrative forms such as the memoir, diary, or chronicle, and through the frequent and often problematic inclusion of eyewitness accounts. Both Lang and James E. Young cite the controversy regarding the use of the eyewitness account in D.M. Thomas's *The White Hotel*. In "Holocaust Documentary Fiction: The Novelist as Eyewitness," Young observes that writers are driven to use witness accounts because of the conviction that only the eyewitness can tell the truth. Mistrusting their own ability to tell the truth, novelists rely on an eyewitness, even if they then use the eyewitness account to tell a very different story.

It may well be that the passage about the baby carriages in Tec's memoir owes a debt to descriptions in other memoirs that I have not read. Even if this is so, and the relationship between Laird's account and Tec's is not what it appears to be, what is pertinent to my analysis are the moments where Laird's fictional account, which is so strikingly similar to Tec's, diverges from it, and what that divergence tells us about children's historical fiction and the choices that shape it. Misha hears about the action in Majdan Tatarski from Eva, a 19-year-old partisan, who begins her report by saying, "I thought I'd seen it all before" (Laird 67). In *Beyond the Wall*, a protective distance of time and focalization blurs the matter-of-fact reporting of the child's voice. In *Dry Tears*, the memoirist describes what she saw as an 11-year-old. Tec's adult voice clearly mediates a child's view that is no longer her own; in neither text is there an immediate child's voice. However, the result of the mediation is very different in each case. Like Tec who writes her memoir years after the event, Misha tells the story nearly 30 years later, but even in 1942, the 14-year-old Misha did not see the atrocity directly. Now the child reader hears Misha mediate Eva's account as he writes to Richard. And even in this doubly distanced account, Laird emphasizes Eva's hesitancy and traumatized silence. She is reluctant to speak and has to be encouraged.

Richard cannot hear Eva's words. The "whole grisly account" (67) is neither whole nor grisly, because it is mediated through Misha's summary, which in turn relies on Tec's account, presumably used for its historical accuracy. Tec's reference to a warning about "a partial liquidation of the ghetto" (27) becomes Laird's "someone told Eva there was a rumour that the ghetto was about to be partially liquidated" (68). Tec describes how she and her mother run to "friends who had a special hiding place, a skillfully camouflaged cellar" (27), but are denied a place: "They were crowded, sitting virtually on top of each other" (27-28). They keep running until Tec's mother leaves her "squeezed into a cramped cellar where I almost had to sit on someone's head" (28). In Laird, Eva joins a family who do the same thing until they finally find a place "in a cellar which was already so crowded that people were quite literally sitting on top of each other" (68). Laird even mentions that Eva sits "beside two children aged about eleven" (68), the age that Tec was when she witnessed the consequences of the action. In *Dry Tears*, Tec explains that one reason she later passes as a Christian is because of her appearance (35). In contrast, Eva notices that the two children beside her are endangered by their "Jewish" appearance (Laird 70). Yet in a detail that echoes Tec's title, we are told that after the action, neither child "shed[s] a tear" (Laird 70).

In the next paragraph, Laird continues to paraphrase Tec. Tec writes that "loudspeakers blared that all Jews were to come out of their houses and into the square" (28), and a voice says "that farmers were needed in recently reclaimed lands, and that those selected would work the land and lead good lives" (28). This speech is followed by a "thorough search of every house" (28). In Laird, "[g]uards with loudspeakers [...] shout [...] for all the Jews to come out of their houses and assemble in the square" (68). In the next sentence, they say "that farmers were needed in recently 'reclaimed' lands and those people who were selected would be able to work the land and live rewarding lives" (68). But following the reference to "a house to house search" (68), Laird avoids the precision of Tec's eyewitness description of a mother whose son is shot and who is pushed into the lineup for deportation holding her dead child. Instead she shifts into a less shocking discourse of what is heard, but not seen: "people screaming, dogs barking, doors banging" (69).

Laird's anxiety about how much she should tell her child reader is further demonstrated when Eva emerges from the cellar, and Misha suddenly switches from describing the Nazi action to a comment about the gardens in Majdan Tatarski, a comment that appears to be influenced by a brief description of one such garden earlier in Tec's memoir (26). Laird presents this description to illustrate the destruction wreaked by the action, but its main narrative function is to delay the account of what is inside the baby carriages. The delay is puzzling; surely as a novelist Laird is free not to tell her readers about the baby carriages at all. But the narrative seems compelled to complete its indebtedness to the memoir. When Laird finally turns to the baby carriages, what she writes is in stark contrast to Tec's brief but precise description of the "unrecognizable bloody mass." Tec's description could, in fact, have been far more detailed, but Laird chooses not to include it at all.

Instead Misha summarizes and invites Richard to imagine what Misha is unwilling to say: "It was what she saw in the first pram [...] that made Eva cry for the first time in the whole bloody operation. I leave the rest to your imagination" (69-70). Shifting the adjective so that "bloody" vaguely modifies the "operation" rather than the bodies of babies, Laird keeps her style within the conventions of proper discourse in children's fiction. She chooses not to report what the child in *Dry Tears* sees, but Tec's three words have a far more powerful effect upon my imagination than Laird's vague gesture at the imagination's power. That Tec's words remain with me when I read Laird's account is evidence to that effect. Even when writing about the choiceless choices of the Holocaust, writers make choices; Laird's reluctance to tell her readers directly that the babies were "bloody" puzzles me. Does it speak to her belief that Tec's words are not strong enough, that she would use stronger language? But then why doesn't she? Do only women (19-year-old Eva) and girls (11-year-old Tec) speak about bloody babies?

Gender and Choice in Carol Matas's Fiction

The incident with the baby carriages is a small part of *Beyond the Wall*. By the end of the novel, Misha has told his story and begun to reconcile with his stepson; the conflict at the beginning has been resolved. In contrast, *Dry Tears* has two endings and no real resolution. In an epilogue added for the 1984 paperback edition, Tec addresses the unsatisfactory nature of her memoir's first ending and includes more details of her postwar life that "compromise between a new intellectual willingness to recall what happened after liberation and a continued emotional reluctance to face it" (218). If the narrative choices that Laird makes—her refusal to describe what Eva sees in the baby carriages, her move towards the possibility of a happy ending—are characteristic of most children's Holocaust fiction, these requirements are far less evident in the novels of Carol Matas.

In Matas's work, the child reader is rarely protected from graphic details. In *Daniel's Story*, Adam gives a vivid account of the murder of his sister, Anya, and Daniel recalls seeing corpses in the burning pit. In *After the War*, Ruth resists communicating the horrors that she has seen—"Telling it won't change what happened" (59)—but the stories she hears from the other children are so disturbing that they trigger her nightmare fragments of memory. A 10-year-old tells her of living in the sewers for 18 months. Another child, Jonathan, recalls being eight years old and witnessing a mass shooting of naked Jews. Jonathan describes how a slightly older boy emerged from the pit. The bullets missed him only because his mother pushed him into the pit. The boy in this maternal narrative of choiceless choice is Zvi, whose traumatic memory of surviving the shooting only to nearly suffocate under the dead and dying reappears in the conclusion to *The Garden*. Matas recognizes that the child reader may well be disturbed by these details; Jonathan is hysterical after he tells his story, but he does tell it. Matas provides the graphic details based on her conviction that children require this information if they are to understand the history to which her characters respond. The child characters are encouraged to speak because it might help; the child readers are given the graphic details because such details might teach. Without the details, the novels' lessons pose no challenge.

Nor is Matas's reader always granted the consolation of the happy ending. Particularly in the four Holocaust novels published after *Daniel's Story*, the conclusions are far from closed and often imply a story that is just beginning. The final line of *Daniel's Story*, "And for the moment, I am content" (131) is paradigmatic of the temporal fragility of these endings. In the ending of *Greater Than Angels*, the heroine, Anna Hirsch, escapes to Switzerland. In the penultimate paragraph, she thinks "for this moment at least, we are free" (131), but in the concluding paragraph she is already thinking about sneaking back and getting revenge for the murder of her family by joining the resistance. *After the War* ends with Ruth's arrival in Palestine; the concluding words are "Welcome home" (115). Although this sentence indicates the narrative closure that we expect in children's books, the sequel, *The Garden*, undercuts the certainty of that ending. By its conclusion, set in "May 1948," Ruth has decided that the newly declared state will be her home, but equally is aware that the war to defend her new home is only just beginning. The garden of the title is a kibbutz garden assigned to her as a form of post-Holocaust therapy; its image returns in the final paragraph as Ruth vows to continue planting her garden over and over again.

Several characteristics distinguish Matas's body of Holocaust fiction. The first is her prolific output. Not only is she Canada's premier writer of Holocaust fiction for young readers, but in Sullivan's chapter on fiction, a chapter that includes 143 works (from chapter books to short story collections, novels, and novellas), there are six titles by Matas, a number equalled only by James Forman.[6] Sullivan lists *Lisa's War* 1989 (published in Canada in 1987 as *Lisa*), *Code Name Kris* 1990 (published in Canada in 1989 as *Jesper*), *Daniel's Story* 1993, *After the War* 1996, *The Garden* 1997, and *Greater Than Angels* 1998.[7] Since the publication of Sullivan's bibliography, Matas has published another Holocaust novel, *In My Enemy's House* 1999. This prodigious output has also been matched throughout the 1990s by her publication of other kinds of children's fiction. These novels are not Holocaust texts, but they clarify the shape of her fiction and the representational consequences when she moves from exploring issues of gender and choice in non-Holocaust texts to Holocaust fiction. In the incident with the baby carriages, gender and choice are irrelevant whether we read Nechama Tec or Christa Laird; in Matas's work, gender and choice are nearly always an issue.

The non-Holocaust fiction includes *The Race* 1991, *Sworn Enemies* 1993, *The Burning Time* 1994, *The Primrose Path* 1995, *The Freak* 1997, *Telling* 1998, and *Cloning Miranda* 1999. Two of the novels (*Sworn Enemies* and *The Burning Time*) are historical fiction; four of the others are contemporary novels with a Canadian setting; *Cloning Miranda* is a fantasy that takes place in an unnamed locale with a climate warm enough for lemon trees. The historical novels focus on problems of persecution and survival. *The Burning Time's* narrative about women falsely accused as witches in seventeenth-century France has clear parallels to Matas's understanding of anti-semitism. *Sworn Enemies*, which examines the ethical dilemmas faced by Jewish conscripts in nineteenth-century Russia, tells a story about characters who must come to terms with the choices that they make in order to survive.

Matas's non-Holocaust fiction is relentless in its examination of complicated choices, and increasingly attentive to issues of gender, often in a Jewish context. *The Race* gives a teenage daughter's perspective on what happens when her mother runs for leadership of the Canadian Liberal Party. The plot focuses on opposition to the mother's candidacy because of the "[d]ouble whammy" (57) of her being both female and Jewish. Her daughter, Ali, learns the difficulty of making choices—is it ethical to lie to another candidate who is encouraging his people to tell lies about Ali's mother? Whether lying is the best choice and how choosing to lie can paradoxically serve ethical ends are philosophical issues that the reader must address, for Ali does choose to lie. The mother wins the leadership race, and the novel ends with Ali contemplating a lesson about the difficulty and significance of choice: "one person can make a difference" (155).

The Primrose Path examines sexual abuse of children and ends with an afterword providing readers with the Kids Help Phone number—implicitly demonstrating how reading a Matas novel should teach the reader that she does have the power to make a difference. Its adolescent narrator, Debbie Mazer, is puzzled when her mother, "this major feminist"

(22), begins to attend Orthodox services and enrols Debbie in a Hebrew school. The novel's interest in the relationship between feminism and Jewish orthodoxy is linked to a consideration of how choice operates within Judaism. Debbie is told by Rabbi Werner that "free choice and good deeds" (78) not only exist within a framework of orthodox Judaism, but that they are central to it. The rabbi tells the children: "It is not enough to follow the rules. We must do good. And to do good we must always be aware of choice" (78). Debbie is so confused by a rabbi who speaks eloquently about choice, yet sexually abuses her and other young women, that she comes close to committing suicide.

Ultimately, *The Primrose Path* endorses the value of choice and emphasizes that feminists can be orthodox Jews—a subject that Matas returns to in the Holocaust novel *In My Enemy's House*—but the story that Debbie tells is ambiguous about the consequences of choosing to tell the truth. Daring to speak publicly about the abuse, in a scene that parallels the mistrust of women's voices in *The Burning Time*, Debbie is discredited and abandoned by many of her school friends. The majority of the school-board supports Rabbi Werner and extends his contract, driving 30 families (including Debbie's) to quit the synagogue and start their own minyan. In a pattern that Matas returns to in *In My Enemy's House*, the voice of authority and trust is masculine. Debbie's father tells her to remember that she must distinguish between the values of orthodoxy and a particular rabbi's behaviour. He tells his wife that she has fallen under Rabbi Werner's spell in the same way that people are drawn to cults, a speech that his wife interrupts with a comment about his confidence: "You've got all the answers, don't you?" (127).

After Debbie's mother is shunned and called Amalek,[8] one woman defends Rabbi Werner by saying that "[e]ven if he'd raped those women" (125), the community should not question his word. Such details encourage a reading of the text as a reworking of *The Burning Time*, particularly when Debbie concludes that her story is not really about an abusive rabbi, but about what happens when women "tr[y] to stand up for [them]selves" (144). Roberta Trites describes *The Burning Time* as coming close to "male bashing" (82). In contrast, in most of Matas's fiction, and particularly in the novels that explore feminist issues in an orthodox Jewish context, when girls learn to stand up for themselves any initial conflict with the father is resolved, and the father's voice is ultimately confirmed in his authority. Like Debbie, Marisa Ginsberg in *In My Enemy's House* learns the value of listening to her father's voice.

Holocaust analogies and references appear frequently in all of Matas's work. Jade, the psychic heroine of *The Freak*, is encouraged by a fortuneteller to "look beneath the surface" (Matas 106); looking not very far beneath the surface, the reader sees that Matas often alludes to the Holocaust when she imagines alternate futures. This is apparent in some of her earliest fiction, the three novels that make up the Time Tracks Series. In *Zanu* (1986), the second in the series, guards mock the naïveté of people who persist in believing that they will be taken care of even as they are thrown into a "disintegrator" (132). The parallel between the disintegrator and the gas chambers is even more explicit in the final book, *Me, Myself, and I* (1987), when Jonathon dreams of police pushing "men, women, even little children" (72) into the booth from which no one emerges. *Me, Myself, and I* also demonstrates

how Matas's interest in speculative fiction as a way of exploring alternate futures always focuses attention on the impact
of specific actions taken by individuals. The best illustration
occurs when Jonathon, a character in one future, reads that
Rebecca Lepidus (the central character of the Time Tracks
Series) was one of four children to lead a demonstration, "the
first in a series which was to train young people in ways of
effecting change" (53).[9]

Speculative fiction readily provides a more optimistic
space to examine choice than Holocaust history and in *The
Freak* (discussed in Chapter 9, page 353-58), Matas most
clearly relies on fantasy to develop Holocaust issues of choice.
It is as though Matas herself is constantly looking for the best
choice she can make to present these issues to children. For
instance, the plot of *Telling* foregrounds the narrative choices
storytellers make. In one narrative strand, the subject of *The
Burning Time*—witch-burning—returns as the topic for a
performance at a summer fair. When the narrator wants the
performance to be historically accurate, she is told that
tourists visiting the fair do not care what happened to women
several hundred years ago: "this isn't a university credit. This
is fun" (59). Does Matas suspect that her child readers are
equally indifferent to historical accuracy?

Anxiety about the impact of her historical fiction may
also underlie the intertextual reference to *The Freak* that
appears in *Cloning Miranda*. Certainly the book that Miranda
reads sounds like the plot of *The Freak*, "a really neat story
about a girl who suddenly develops psychic powers" (87).
Miranda tells her reader that the book is far more enjoyable
"than all those depressing books [... that have] won every
award in the world" (87). What makes the Holocaust fiction

so "depressing" is not just what is inside the baby carriages, but that its overall history cannot be changed whatever choices the protagonists can make. The survival of the protagonists in the four Holocaust novels written after *Daniel's Story* is always framed by the murder of their families and the erasure of their communities. The discovery that her brother, Simon, has survived surprises and delights Ruth in *After the War*, but she still wakes up the next morning with a flashback to American soldiers liberating Buchenwald and finding her barely alive on a heap of dead bodies. Whatever triumph there is in survival, Matas increasingly draws attention to the ambiguous meaning of that survival in view of the immense number who did not survive.

When protagonists make choices in Matas's work, whether in the serious historical fiction or the lighter fantasies, they tend to do so in response to an impassioned speech made by another character. In effect, they hear and act upon the lesson that Matas intends the child reader to receive. In *Cloning Miranda*, Miranda discovers that she is a product of genetic engineering, an improved version made from the DNA of her dead sister. Recognizing that she is programmed to behave in a certain way, Miranda despairs at her lack of choice until her friend, Emma, giving the speech about choice that appears throughout Matas's work, reminds her that she still has choice and that this is precisely what makes her human: "we can learn to be different. Maybe that's what being human *is*" (123). Miranda is so impressed that she then chooses to repeat the same speech to her sister clone. Since all humans have DNA specific to them, she decides that the question of choice for clones is really not that different for anyone. In nearly every Matas novel, the central character comes to believe that she has no choice. Asking a version of the question, "What choice do I have?" (*Cloning Miranda* 111), or "What choice have I got?" (*The Freak* 72), the protagonist learns through the words of another the answer to her question.

Questions and speeches about choice also appear in Matas's Holocaust fiction, but the central protagonists have far more difficulty believing that they do have options. In *After the War*, Zvi, while repressing his own traumatic experiences, has clearly chosen to believe in good. He is angry when Ruth does not recognize that this belief is a choice that he has made in defiance of what he has seen and experienced. When other child survivors debate the existence of God, Zvi gives the standard speech: "God gave us free will" (80). His words silence Ruth, but do not satisfy her: "Why am I the only one who doesn't have an answer?" (80). Unlike Anne Frank, who believes in spite of everything and often appears to have the answers, Ruth is uncertain. She shares with Anna Hirsch, the narrator of *Greater Than Angels*, a deep suspicion about choice. Although Anna is dismayed that her mother is willing to kill her own mother—"We have no choice" (17)—she is soon using the same language to justify her own behaviour. The victim told by the Nazi to go to the left or right has no choice; the gender of the character makes no difference once the order to go to the gas chambers has been given.

Is God Female?

Matas's Holocaust fiction clearly delineates her interest in Jewish female protagonists. (The only exceptions are *Jesper*, which is a sequel to the female-focused narrative of *Lisa*, and

Daniel's Story, where the book's relationship to an already-existing children's exhibit at the United States Holocaust Memorial Museum predetermined the gender of the protagonist.) This is unusual in Sullivan's bibliography of Holocaust fiction. Although Sullivan includes more female than male authors in the fiction chapter, many of the female authors choose to write about male protagonists. I am not always sure that I can identify gender based on the author's name, but, based on the many names that I can identify, a pattern emerges in which far more female novelists write about male protagonists than male novelists write about female protagonists. The latter includes Aharon Appelfeld's *Tzili: The Story of a Life*. The former includes Fran Arrick, *Chernowitz!*; Barbara Cohen, *Benny*; Malka Drucker, *Jacob's Rescue: A Holocaust Story*; Anne Holm, *North to Freedom*; Christa Laird's two novels about Misha, *But Can the Phoenix Sing?* and *Shadow of the Wall*; Elizabeth Mace, *Brother Enemy*; Donna Jo Napoli, *Stones in Water*; Karen Ray, *To Cross a Line*; Gertrude Samuels, *Mottele: A Partisan Odyssey*; Sarah M. Schleimer, *Far from the Place We Called Home*; Martha Bennett Stiles, *Darkness Over the Land*; and Cynthia Voigt, *David and Jonathan*.

In light of what is obviously a strong preference for male protagonists in children's fiction, Matas's interest in female protagonists is itself unusual. This preference for female protagonists cannot be separated from her interest in using children's fiction to explore feminist issues. But while feminist issues clearly affect Holocaust representations—why do writers prefer male protagonists to female?—the subject of gender and the Holocaust remains controversial, and the motivation for interest in reading gender in Holocaust narratives is equally contentious. Obviously women and female children are victims of the Holocaust, and their stories should be heard. Yet it appears far easier to talk about how gender affects Holocaust representations—why do so many women authors write about male characters?—than to write a gendered analysis that avoids obscuring the historical reality that when the babies in the carriages are killed, their gender is irrelevant.

Although circumcision means that Jewish boys in hiding had specific fears that Jewish girls did not have, while the latter possibly faced more sexual abuse than the former, statistics about childhood survival rarely distinguish between male and female survival.[10] While Mengele may have saved Elli Friedmann's life because he was struck by her golden hair, Elli was 13 when he tells her "remember, from now on you're sixteen" (Bitton-Jackson, *I Have Lived* 73). The golden hair on a four-year-old child might have helped save her life if she was passing as a Christian, but once she was standing on the ramps at Auschwitz, it made no difference. The beautiful voice of Mala Silverberg did not stop Mengele from shooting her through the head. Whether he shot her to save her being gassed is irrelevant; she was murdered because of her age. If I respond to her image for personal reasons—I too was photographed with just such a ribbon in my hair—my sympathy does not clarify how a gendered response helps me to understand mass murder other than to see how little gender mattered. Did Mala Silverberg have brothers? What happened to them?

Scholars who examine gender often acknowledge the difficulty of a "gender-sensitive approach" (Baumel 20) in the context of mass murder and quote the phrase that titles

Myrna Goldenberg's essay, "Different Horrors, Same Hell" (Goldenberg 337, footnote 2) to clarify their intent. Baumel cautions that gender should matter, not because women or men suffered more, but because in certain ways they suffered differently (50). Yet she ends *Double Jeopardy: Women and the Holocaust* with an acknowledgment that gender often played a minor role "when challenged by religious hatred or racial antisemitism" (260). Raul Hilberg insists that "the road to annihilation was marked by events that specifically affected men as men and women as women" (*Perpetrators* 126). Comparative statistics for male/female survival can never be complete, but Hilberg still concludes that "women were most probably more than half of the dead, but men died more rapidly" (*Perpetrators* 127). Like Hilberg, Joan Ringelheim in "Women and the Holocaust: A Reconsideration of Research," cites records demonstrating that more women than men were deported from the ghettos (392). Hilberg attributes this statistic to the phenomenon of men dying first (shot first in the mass shootings; dying sooner from malnutrition in the ghettos).

But what do we do with this information? If women's survival in the ghettos only meant that once the deportations began, more women were considered as surplus labour (Hilberg, *Perpetrators* 129), if the greater likelihood of women surviving the ghetto only meant that upon arrival in the death camps, particularly if they were mothers with small children, they were immediately selected for gassing, what does this prove beyond recognition of the "different horrors, same hell"? Hilberg concludes, "Possibly a third of the Jews who survived Auschwitz were women" (*Perpetrators* 130). Ringelheim cites UNRRA (United Nations Relief and Rehabilitation

Agency) figures that indicate that in January 1946 the displaced person's camps were 39.5 per cent female and 60.5 per cent male ("Women and the Holocaust" 394).

In my mother's story, one possible reason for her survival was the support of her sisters and her mother. In contrast, her father was on his own, and when he mistakenly concluded that his wife and three daughters were dead, he lost the ability to live. Ringelheim addresses the way that women often attribute their survival to the support of their biological sisters or to the non-biological families that they formed within the camps. Insisting that women's experiences in the Holocaust deserve study, Ringelheim does not deny that women helped each other, but she critiques her earlier work as an example of cultural feminism, a safe feminism that believes in the "values of individuality, autonomy, and self-determination" (386). Calling this feminism a "reactionary politics of personal [...] change" (386), in which it is too easy to forget that inspiring stories "are not at the center of the Holocaust" (387), she argues that to look for evidence that women survived better because they knew how to form bonds or came to the camps with domestic skills that even there proved useful is to valorize oppression: "Oppression does not make people better; oppression makes people oppressed" (387). One of the new questions that Ringelheim offers is "[w]hat is at stake for us?" (390) when we look for narratives that celebrate female friendship and relationships.

If Ringelheim's cautionary words make me question my attentiveness to women's Holocaust stories and how I understand my mother's story, a reading of gender in children's Holocaust fiction is also complicated by the Nazi policy of killing all children (generally defined as those under the age of 14 or 15), regardless of gender. The scholars who examine gender in the Holocaust focus on the experience of adult women and quote statistics that often divide into only three categories: men, women, and children. Hilberg's discussion of "Men and Women" is separate from his chapter on "Children." Like Langer in *Art from the Ashes*, but for somewhat different reasons, Carol Rittner and John K. Roth exclude Anne Frank from their anthology, *Different Voices: Women and the Holocaust*. Their reasons may differ from Langer's, but their decision "to concentrate on writings by and about adult women" (xii) has the same result. In contrast to Baumel who begins her historiographical overview with the words, "In the beginning there was Anne Frank" (39), and concludes her book with a brief chapter on using the *Diary* for Holocaust pedagogy, Rittner and Roth exclude Frank's "youthful voice" (xii). Yet this tendency to treat Frank as a youthful voice may explain why Matas prefers female protagonists. Aware that Anne Frank dominates children's Holocaust representations, Matas uses female narrators who do not sound at all like her. With her preference for female narrators, Matas can examine why gender matters while simultaneously teaching her readers that the values represented by Anne Frank's voice are not gendered.

Matas makes several narrative choices in order to make gender matter in her Holocaust fiction. The first is to make all of her protagonists adolescent, so that even if her plots do not include selections, the protagonists are just old enough that we can imagine their survival. Like the male protagonists of *Jesper* and *Daniel's Story*, her female protagonists exist on the border between childhood and adulthood as defined by the Nazis. In *Lisa*, the heroine is 12 at the beginning, but 15 when she escapes Denmark. In *After the War*, Ruth is 15, which is also the age she said she was when she lied and passed the selection. Anna Hirsch in *Greater Than Angels* and Marisa Ginsberg in *In My Enemy's House* are both 15 at the beginnings of their stories.

Matas's second choice is to offer her readers an adolescent heterosexual romance. Baumel observes that Holocaust heroines tend to be young, beautiful, and sexual (149); this pattern is obvious in Matas, where the heterosexual romance plot functions as a carrot to keep her readers going. Repeatedly we read about kisses, for example, the "real kiss" (*Lisa* 106) that Jesper gives Lisa just before she leaves for Denmark, that Zvi gives Ruth in the final chapter of *After the War*, and that Rudi gives Anna in *Greater Than Angels*. Since Marisa, the protagonist of *In My Enemy's House*, is reprimanded by her orthodox father when he sees her touch the hand of Shmuel and subsequently feels responsible for her father's murder because of the accidental consequences of this act, the romance is more subdued. But if Marisa does not gush like Anna Hirsch about Rudi—"what eyes!" (*Greater* 108)—Matas still structures the novel as a recollection by Marisa after she learns that Shmuel has also survived, and she is waiting for transportation to his camp.

At first, gender matters in Matas's Holocaust fiction because adolescent males can join the resistance, and adolescent females cannot. The Danish heroine of *Lisa* initially can only look on as her brother, Stefan, and his friend, Jesper, distribute anti-Nazi leaflets—"he said I'm too young and I'm a girl" (18); by the end of the novel, she is helping the resistance and shoots a Nazi. When her father objects to her staying behind until the last boat leaves for Sweden, her mother defends her choice: "Let her decide, David. She's not a little girl anymore" (92). After *Daniel's Story*, gender matters differently. With Daniel as the male narrator, his sister Erika takes on the voice of Anne Frank, the voice that urges Daniel to choose goodness and love. Several times in the novel, Daniel questions not only why he should survive, but why any humans should live. He is convinced to think otherwise through the moral voice of his younger sister, Erika, who tells him to defy Nazi ideology by living justly and dying, if necessary, with dignity. It is Erika who instructs Daniel to live and to remember those who do not. When she tells Daniel that choice still matters, she sounds like Anne Frank, and she represents a point of view that the central narrative voice can only struggle towards. Matas makes Erika the same age as Frank (the first time that Daniel mentions Erika, he says that she is 12 in 1941), and gives her similar physical characteristics (brown hair, brown eyes). Daniel's final meeting with Erika through the barbed-wire fence of Auschwitz echoes Lies Goosens's encounter with the dying Frank at Bergen-Belsen (Lindwer 27-28). Frank dies just before the end of the war; Erika holds on slightly longer in Gross-Rosen.

Since the speech about choice in Matas's fiction is always spoken by a character other than the narrator, and since Matas's fiction emphasizes heterosexual romance plots, if the narrator is male, the likelihood that the speech will be attributed to a female voice increases. When Erika dies, her death is reported by Daniel's love-interest, Rosa, who takes over the Anne Frank voice and speaks the words about choice, hope, and the future that Daniel is unable to say on his own. By switching to female narrator/protagonists, Matas demonstrates not only that such speeches are not gender-specific, but that the way to the female heart is through the power of the male's speech about choice. We find this pattern in each of the Holocaust novels after *Daniel's Story*. In *Greater Than Angels*, a novel that celebrates the citizens of Le Chambon-sur-Lignon who chose to rescue Jews, the heroine, Anna Hirsch, learns to believe in choice and falls in love at the same time. A performer who always has a joke to distract her fellow deportees, Anna loves the theatre. When she arrives in the French internment camp at Gurs, she motivates the other girls by mocking clichés about gender and romance: "Pretend we're in a horror film and we all have the lead part of the spunky heroine" (25). Yet even if Anna's reference to "demented Nazi[s]" hiding behind every building is a cliché that doesn't really suit her circumstances—let alone her willingness later to climb into the cattle car in order to tell her mother one last joke—Anna's reference to rescue by "a very tall, *very* handsome young man with green eyes" (25) proves to be true when she falls in love with Rudi and realizes that he is indeed "incredibly handsome" (123). Rudi, a 17-year-old German Jew, does not rescue her from the Nazis—she must cross the Swiss border on her own—but he rescues Anna spiritually and psychologically by teaching her to believe in choice.

Anna starts to revise her view of Rudi when she joins a Torah study group in Gurs. The teacher, a former professor of religion and philosophy at a German university, has his lecture on Genesis interrupted by a young man, Peter, who blames Eve for the imperfection of the world. Anna, angry that women are always blamed, defends Eve by saying that if "God knows everything" (44) he must have known what Eve would do and wanted her to act the way she did. When Rudi suggests that *Tikkun Olam* explains the role of choice in an imperfect world, Anna is not only surprised, but impressed: "That was a really interesting way to think about things" (45).[11] Challenged to identify what choices exist under their present circumstances, Rudi says, "Love or hate" (46). In a later debate with Peter, he argues that the possible absence of God only makes "moral choices" (65) more necessary, and Anna backs him up.

In *In My Enemy's House* Shmuel gives the same speech, when he tells Marisa that they can choose to "have love in our hearts, not hate" (63). Matas alludes to this speech when she ends the novel with an otherwise inexplicable lesson. Not only does Marisa remember Shmuel's voice throughout the war, she vows in the end to "never forget the most important lesson I have learned" (167), the lesson that "My scholarship must never take second place to my heart, because only there does God truly reside" (167). This lesson has nothing to do with the details of the story—what happens to Marisa when she passes as a Polish-Christian labourer in Germany—but much to do with the narrative difficulties produced by Matas's attempt to examine gender in a Holocaust novel.

Disrupting our assumptions regarding the gender of the voice of choice and hope, Matas also increasingly introduces gender into adolescent discussions of religion. Readers often resist the latter, most likely because they have their own assumptions about whether adolescents during and immediately after the Holocaust would have engaged in such discussions. Readers may well respond to debates over whether God is female with bewilderment.[12] Whether or not adolescents did engage in such debates, Matas's interest in them may speak to the pedagogical impulse of her texts and to her reluctance to explore other, more obvious aspects of how gender creates different horrors in the Holocaust. The child who reports in *After the War* that Russian soldiers raped her mother uses language that is both naïve and obscure. She says only that the soldiers "did bad things. [...] I don't know what" (82). Just as Laird awkwardly shifts when she is unwilling to look inside the baby carriages and talks about gardens instead, I am tempted to conclude that when Matas is unwilling to represent sexual horrors, she talks instead about the gender of God. This conclusion may not be persuasive, but neither is the textual evidence for why debates over the gender of God appear in both *Greater Than Angels* and in *After the War*.

Matas examines gender somewhat differently in *In My Enemy's House*. There is a brief mention of Marisa's relief at the paradoxical situation in which an abusive German employer locks her in and thereby protects her from the sexual advances of one of the Polish labourers; however, most of the attention to gender is directed elsewhere. Nazi discourse on gender is first addressed when Marisa accompanies Charlotte, the daughter of her second employer, the Nazi Herr Reymann, to a lecture on the "role [of] women in the Third Reich" (97); the conflict between this discourse and the language of sisterhood is emphasized later in the novel when Charlotte admits that she loves Marisa "like a sister" (161). The consequences to this confession are both striking and problematic. Charlotte is puzzled because she believes that Marisa is a Catholic Pole, and she has been taught to believe that Poles are inferior. In contrast, Marisa is terrified of what Charlotte would think if she knew that the person she calls Maria is actually a Jewish girl called Marisa, let alone knew that Marisa had revealed to her father Charlotte's romance with a boy opposed to Hitler. Although Marisa is delighted at seeing some evidence that not all Germans support Hitler, her fear that, if Charlotte's relationship with the boy were exposed, the investigation might lead to the revelation of her own identity leads her to inform Herr Reymann of his daughter's behaviour. Her betrayal of Charlotte's confidence is followed by Frau Reymann praising Marisa for "making a difficult choice" (125) that proved her friendship for Charlotte.

If Charlotte's reference to sisterhood confuses Marisa, the same can be said for the reader who observes what happens when Charlotte cries that she does not want "to have babies for the Reich" (162). Her crying moves Marisa, as though for a moment gender overrides the categories of Nazi racial theory, in which Aryan women must have nothing to do with non-Aryan women. Matas acknowledges the dilemma that this poses for her protagonist. Embracing Charlotte, "feeling almost like I was embracing a land mine" (162), Marisa is further terrified as she feels "the huge chunk of ice in my heart start [...] to melt away" (162). What makes the passage problematic is not only the lesson that Marisa draws from it, but the way that this scene contributes to the resolution of the religious crisis that she experiences during the Holocaust.

As with her speeches about choice, Matas uses the female narrator to remind her readers that during the Holocaust not just male adolescents—as in Elie Wiesel's *Night*—struggle with their faith. Marisa, the most orthodox and studious of Matas's Holocaust heroines, confronts questions about faith in the absence of a father to whom she had never admitted her desire to be a scholar: "Papa would never have approved of a woman having ideas like that, so I never told him" (32). In a narrative strategy that not only imitates the structure of the gendered speech about choice, but also parallels the voice of the father in *The Primrose Path*, Marisa's dead father speaks to her during her crises of faith, reveals that he always knew about her secret studying of the Torah, and repeatedly reminds her of Shmuel's words to keep love in her heart. If Marisa believed that her father while alive opposed Shmuel because he was not a sufficiently observant Jew, she now wishes that her father were alive so he could hear how "Shmuel reasoned like a scholar" (66). The dead father obviously approves of Shmuel's words and restates them in his own terms. He tells Marisa that love is another word for God, and when he refers to God, the pronoun is masculine. The exploration of gender grows increasingly murky because the father's words about love not only affect Marisa's desire to be a scholar, but are consistent with the lesson she draws from the episode with Charlotte and the books that she reads in Herr Reymann's library.

Matas does not tell her readers that the only books in a Nazi home would be books that supported Nazi claims, that books by the intellectuals who opposed Hitler would not be available in Herr Reymann's library. Although the conditions of the war change gender roles so that the timid Marisa increasingly learns to look after herself, her observations regarding how the intellectual elite of German society accepted the Nazis confuse her and lead to her offering the readers an equally confusing lesson. Reading that intellectuals generally supported Hitler, she concludes that heart is more important than intellect. However, it is the personal lesson that Marisa draws from this reading that particularly disturbs me: she concludes that her "problems [...] stemmed from the same place—[her] intellect was big, but [her] heart was empty" (105). A character who passes as a Christian in Germany, works in the family of a high-ranking Nazi, and nearly passes out when she realizes that the clothing that the League of German Maidens is sorting came from murdered women—possibly her own family, forced to strip before they were killed—says that the emptiness of her heart is the source of all her problems. Even if there were real young women who after the Holocaust concluded, as does Marisa, that the most important lesson is the lesson about the heart, this is an astonishing lesson with which to conclude a children's novel about the Holocaust. What if my heart tells me that I want to become a Nazi?

Gender and Choice in Ida Fink's Fiction

There are no debates about the gender of God in Ida Fink's writing. Noting that the Library of Congress classifies Fink's work as fiction, Sara R. Horowitz adds that Fink insists that the events "really happened" (8). Born in 1921 in Poland, confined to a ghetto in 1942, in hiding for much of the war, Fink writes stories not only about what she saw, but about what others saw, often in a way that makes the gender of the narrative voice impossible or difficult to determine. Fink must imagine the stories because many of the people they describe are unable to tell them; for example, in "A Spring Morning" she gives us the thoughts of a man as he marches to his death, carrying his murdered child. In the story "Traces," the character testifies "because only she can leave that trace, because she alone survived" (137). The stories are themselves recorded as scraps: "'Just by chance' ... 'not until decade later'—these phrases keep coming back" ("Sabina Under the Sacks" 106).

Fink's narrator is sometimes, but not always, female. Even when I hazard the guess that the narrator is female, as in "A Second Scrap of Time," I do so only because of my stereo-typical assumption that, when the narrative voice refers to serving tea to guests, this is something that women would do. When the narrative subject is the second SS operation, and the knowledge that this was not a roundup but an *Aktion*, gender does not really matter. The narrative voice begins as first person plural; during an *Aktion* "[a]ll of us, young and old alike" (55) are terrified, running for cover. After the nar-rator learns that because of her youth and health she is safe for the moment—and she can no longer remember how she learned this—the narrative voice switches back to first per-son singular. The narrator does not remember what hap-pened between hiding and finding herself sitting beside a kitchen window, through which she glimpses an old woman once ridiculed by the town as crazy and silent, now "scream-ing that she didn't want to be dragged off to be executed" (57). "A Second Scrap of Time" ends with the narrator out-side the next morning, listening to two young women console their trembling mother. The next day, reports emerge that the train went to Belzec, a death camp in eastern Poland from which only one person successfully escaped (Epstein and Rosen 27). I do not know if the person who escaped was male or female, just as the narrator, returning to first person plural in the final paragraph, observes that when they first heard the name Belzec, it meant only a popular song about the town of Belz. The question about how gender operates in this story is as perplexing as any attempt to draw from it the kind of lesson we expect to find in children's historical fiction. When Matas uses female narrators, they challenge the reader's gendered assumptions about the values represented by Anne Frank's voice; when Fink uses narrators, they challenge our ability to draw any general conclusions about gender.

The first person plural narrative voice of "*****" has no gender. Neither do we know how much the "we" who narrate this story about hiding and watching the old men in the town square comprehend what is taking place. The narrative voice does not tell us where the town is or who is watching. Normal markers of identity have been erased in the way that the title has itself been erased. Knowledge exists not in the time of the story but in the moment that comes after. In a children's Holocaust novel, knowledge normally comes with the reading of the text. We end the story knowing more than we did before. In "*****," the narrative voice assumes our post-Holocaust knowledge, the only way that we now can understand what the truck "with shovels in the back" (24) means. In a similar manner, again without reference to a narrative of explanation that would accompany the episode in a children's Holocaust novel, we read about the young woman with the "huge pregnant belly" (24) who emerges from one of the houses to wish her father well. The narrative voice tells us that the daughter shouts, *Zei gezint, Tate!* (24) and an asterisk directs the reader to the English translation. How does gender matter in this story in which "all of us" (24) repeat her words, "bidding farewell [...] to our loved ones who were walking to their deaths" (24)? When will it be the turn of the young woman? If her huge pregnant belly means that she will be killed sooner, rather than later, the asterisks of the title imply that it is an entire Yiddish world that is now hidden from us.

If we learn from Fink's stories that women experience specific horrors, we also learn that even when gender appears to be at the centre of the story, to read only gender tells us too little. In "Aryan Papers" a 16-year-old girl sells herself in exchange for identity papers. When the story ends with a debate over whether a virgin can be a whore, gender may seem to be the key issue, but despite the girl's silent nausea, and the men's mocking language, the Holocaust context is inseparable from its gendered horror. To think that gender has anything to do with children's chances for survival is a naïveté that Fink also explores. The parents in "Description of a Morning" are hiding in a barn attic; that the father once greeted the birth of his daughter with relief that she was not a boy is now background to the mother's guilt about her daughter's murder by the Nazis. The husband reminds her that when they were ordered to identify themselves and did not, their daughter was already dead, that choosing "to step forward" (95) would not have made any difference. The mother feels endless guilt, but she also tells herself that she and her husband could not have escaped if the daughter had survived. Whether the mother believes this is left open. Certainly the male narrator of "Crazy" cannot forget the sight of his three beautiful daughters rounded up, and how the seven-year-old silenced the three-year-old so that the father could escape being deported with them. In this reversal of the choices made in *Life Is Beautiful*, as in much of Fink's work, we seem closer to Langer's language than to the language of children's historical fiction.

In Fink's world of choiceless choice, those who think that gender matters soon learn otherwise. Although Fink knows what is inside the baby carriages, she chooses not to focus on those details. Giving her readers a radically different style compared to those who choose to write within the demands of Holocaust pedagogy, she presents a fiction in which the readers learn only that there are too many horrors for words to describe and survivors remember "meaningless bits" ("Julia" 195), that children are killed quickly and casually, and that people do not find each other after the war. If they do, the reunions bear little resemblance to those depicted in most children's fiction. Fink's novel *The Journey*, about two sisters who pass as non-Jews and take on various identities as Polish labourers in Germany, has a plot with some resemblance to *In My Enemy's House*. When the war is over, the two sisters return to their father who has survived through hiding. The narrator of *The Journey* draws attention to the problem of writing an ending to such a story: "Oh, don't get melodramatic. What's the matter with you? They left at dusk because of the danger and returned at dawn because that was when their train arrived. Please, no symbols, no sentimentality" (240).

It is likely that Fink's quiet tone and refusal to concentrate on graphic details account for her inclusion in Sullivan's bibliography, which does not include Tadeusz Borowski's *This Way for the Gas, Ladies and Gentlemen*, perhaps because its Auschwitz setting and darkly ironic tone are regarded as pedagogically questionable. Yet Fink's powerful stories are as bleak as anything in Borowski. In "Night of Surrender" the 17-year-old female narrator meets an American, Mike. Her knowledge of the world, she says, is limited to what she has learned through the war: "I knew death, terror, cunning, how to lie and trick" (94). When Mike asks for her life story, she tells him a lie: "it moved him as it was meant to" (95). In contrast, his own story sounds to her "like a fairy tale [...] for well-brought-up children" (96). As Mike woos her (the title refers to both the end of the war and her sexual surrender), he encourages her to tell him more of her story. Sounding very much like Zvi in *After the War* but without Zvi's painful awareness of the complexity of his advice, Mike tells her that she needs to believe in the goodness of people.

The end of the story shows how pointless Mike's advice is. When the narrator breaks her silence about the past by revealing to him her real name and the fact that she is Jewish, the significance of her revelation escapes him. Not listening to her, as so often Fink's characters do not listen, Mike tells her that it would be best for her to forget her past suffering and her Jewish identity. But that is a choice that Fink's narrators cannot make. If the conventions of children's historical fiction presume that readers need both knowledge and hope, Fink's fiction works totally outside that pattern. Seeing the flies on the foot of her murdered husband, the narrator of "Henryk's Sister" concludes, "They made me understand, destroyed my hope" (140). Unlike Christa Laird and Carol Matas, the knowledge that Fink offers does not easily translate into Holocaust pedagogy or lessons about the future. But the knowledge that she offers is Holocaust fiction at its best, neither "primarily documentary" nor requiring "special justification" (Lang, *Act and Idea* xi).

NOTES

1. Even as I write, I sign a permission form that is required by my son's high school before he will be allowed to watch *Schindler's List*. Not only do I choose whether Nicholas can see it, but when he is disturbed during the screening, the teachers commend his courage in choosing to view the entire film.

2. One of the rare exceptions in which the protagonist dies in the death camp is Gudrun Pausewang's *The Final Journey*. In time-travel novels, characters return from their journey to the past, which often involves an episode in a death camp, transformed by what they have learned and determined to apply that new knowledge in the choices they make in the present.

3. Although I continue to be perplexed by age recommendations, I refer to adolescent readers for Fink on the basis of my own reading and Sullivan's categories. Sullivan recommends grades 7 to 12 for Laird's novels and one of Matas's novels, *The Garden*. He recommends grades 5 to 10 for four other Matas novels and grades 6 to 10 for another. Although I cannot comprehend the difference between those works by Matas that can be read by grade 5 students and those that require one more year's maturity, it is clear that Sullivan recognizes that Fink's work is suitable for an older audience. All of Fink's work is recommended for grades 9 to 12.

4. See, for example, Table of Contents for *When Night Fell: An Anthology of Holocaust Short Stories*, ed. Linda Schermer Raphael and Marc Lee Raphael. Five of the 26 stories are by women.

5. In her acknowledgments to *Beyond the Wall*, Laird merely refers to "the generous help of a wide variety of people" and adds that "they are too numerous to mention by name" (304).

6. Sullivan includes a recommended list for "Building a Core Holocaust Collection in Your School Library." He includes two of Matas's novels, but nothing by either Forman or Laird. Fink only appears through the one story that is included in Rochman and McCampbell's anthology.

7. *The Garden* is actually about the months leading up to the creation of Israel. Many of its characters, including the chief protagonist, are Holocaust survivors whose stories are first explored in *After the War*. On Matas's Website, all the works that Sullivan lists as Holocaust fiction are categorized as World War II stories. See Arnow on scholars who

challenge the problematic redemptive ethics implicit in narratives that base the creation of Israel on the Holocaust.

8. After the nation of Amalek attacked the Israelites in the desert (Deuteronomy 25:18), God ordered the Israelites to show no sympathy towards them and to never forget that the Amalekites must be destroyed. When Saul later defeated the Amalekites in battle, but did not slay their ruler, he was viewed as disobeying God, and therefore lost the kingship to David. Calling Debbie's mother Amalek is equivalent to saying that she is the ultimate enemy.

9. Matas's daughter is named Rebecca. The name Lepidus reappears in *After the War* as the family name of the heroine's mother.

10. See Ringelheim, "The Split Between Gender and the Holocaust," for an analysis of possible implications of gender upon the hiding of children as well as Ringelheim's reading of why Holocaust scholars have been reluctant to examine gender. For stories of hidden children, see Marks, Rosenberg, and Stein.

11. According to Rabbi Luria, when the world was created, the divine light shattered the vessels that had been prepared to receive it. God's light was dispersed; creation will not be complete until the sparks of light are reunited. *Tikkun Olam* teaches that repairing the world is dependent upon human actions; the phrase is usually understood as repairing the world or perfection of the world. The requirement to "'perfect the world under the rule of God,' is reiterated three times a day in the *Aleinu* prayer" (Telushkin 549).

12. See Gann's review of *Greater Than Angels*.

9

Future Tense: The Anxious Pedagogy of Young Adult Fiction

In December 2000, a 16-year-old male from Cornwall, Ontario, was jailed for 34 days before being granted bail. Under the Young Offenders Act the newspapers could not identify him, but they did report that he was accused of four counts of uttering death threats against his classmates. What made the story newsworthy was that one of the threats came from his writing and then reading a story to his drama class, a story about a boy who carried out a violent fantasy of revenge, a story whose details occasionally mimicked the real events of the mass shooting that took place in Littleton, Colorado, in April 1999.[1] In a post-Columbine society, the case became a "cause célèbre" (Honey R6). Although the information regarding the circumstances of the alleged death threats was vague, it was reported that the writer, like the protagonist in his story, had been bullied. It was also reported that Stephen King was one of his literary heroes.

In response to the furor raised by the case, King was interviewed and expressed his belief in the rights of the imagination. On January 28, 2001, several distinguished Canadian writers attended a free speech rally at the National Arts Centre in Ottawa. In a front page article in *The Globe and Mail* the next morning, Margaret Atwood was quoted as saying that childhood "can be hell"; Michael Ondaatje was paraphrased as saying that "writing about strong feelings can be therapeutic" (Sallot A1). In contrast, Tim Wynne-Jones, despite his initial criticism of the Crown Attorney "for saying that the typical student does not dwell on death and violence" (Honey R2), received further media attention for his decision not to read at the rally. Claiming that such attention was not in the young man's interest, Wynne-Jones described the school and police response to the youth's behaviour as symptomatic of "acute Columbinitis" (Honey R1). On CBC Radio on the day of the rally, he also condemned "acute Columbinitis" for its characteristically Canadian obsession with things American, yet lack of interest in Canadian culture. Other articles, however, pointed out that Canada had several events that parallel Columbine, including the fatal shooting in Taber, Alberta, only eight days after the events in Columbine.

Two aspects of the newspaper coverage interest me. The first is the contrast between the views of the writers who organized the rally and those expressed by Wynne-Jones; that is, between those who see in this a threat to freedom of speech, and a writer who, in his own work, tests the conventions of young adult fiction and therefore is very aware of what can and cannot be said in this genre. Yes, childhood may be hell, but how we represent that hell in children's literature is very different from how we might represent it in adult texts. However, the aspect that most intrigues me is the symbolic role played by Stephen King, not just as inspiration for the adolescent now facing criminal charges and as spokesman for the rights of the imagination, but also in his adversarial position in relation to official education. The episode indicates how King's fiction, even though it is likely read (and seen in its many film adaptations) by far more adolescents than those who read the books that schools regard as pedagogically useful, has an uneasy relationship to the young adult fiction that librarians and educators normally recommend.

Explaining the rationale behind his Holocaust bibliography, Edward T. Sullivan indicates that librarians define "young adult" as ages 12-18, but adds that "the literature published in the category of young adult is typically for the age range 10-14" (9). If his comment suggests, ironically, that young adult literature is what young adults do not read, Sullivan also states that he has "included numerous adult titles that [he] believe[s] will be of some interest to [older teens]" (9). Not surprisingly, he includes no titles by Stephen King. In this chapter, I do not wish to argue that King's novella "Apt Pupil" should be included in bibliographies of Holocaust literature for young adults, but I want to consider precisely why we exclude it and what that exclusion reveals about the anxieties shaping Holocaust representation in contemporary young adult fiction. The exclusion is puzzling because, in many ways, "Apt Pupil" has much in common with what happens to Holocaust representation once we move outside the genre demands of children's historical fiction and into the more open and questioning discourse of young adult fiction.

Despite two critical differences—the characterization of King's young adult protagonist and his use of the Holocaust to explore homophobic anxieties—"Apt Pupil" shares with young adult fiction such as Todd Strasser's *The Wave*, Fran Arrick's *Chernowitz!*, Mary Reeves Bell's *The Secret of the Mezuzah*, and Carol Matas's *The Freak* a questioning of the possibilities both of Holocaust knowledge and of choice in a post-Holocaust world, as well as a deep suspicion of the efficacy of Holocaust pedagogy. In all of these works, a school's well-intentioned efforts at Holocaust pedagogy prove to be so dangerous or inadequate that the texts become counter-narratives that problematize the very act of reading about the past that they seemingly encourage. Published in the 1980s and 1990s and set in a contemporary post-Holocaust world, they all also rely on familiar genre conventions —the horror story, the school story, the detective story, and speculative fiction—to ask questions about Holocaust pedagogy that distance them from the optimistic narratives of children's Holocaust historical fiction.

The genre conventions that these young adult texts adapt are highly problematic when used in children's historical fiction. Writers of children's historical fiction about the Holocaust face a dilemma shared by well-informed readers of any Holocaust literature—that is, the burden of the facts that we know now. Such knowledge makes horror stories gratuitous and any story that ends triumphantly, such as the adventure/spy/detective story, misleading. Michael André Bernstein uses the term "backshadowing" to describe the process by which we judge the behaviour of characters set in the past as though they should have known what we know now. He demonstrates that backshadowing is philosophically problematic, for it implies a fatalistic view of history; but even if a writer avoids backshadowing, it is difficult for the knowing reader to read without it, whether we read Holocaust diaries or Holocaust fiction. When Anne Frank tells herself that hiding from the Nazis is "an interesting adventure" (Frank 276), when she imagines publishing a novel about the Secret Annex and delights in how readers will mistakenly assume that a book with such a title is a detective story, the impossibility of reading victim diaries outside the perspective of our post-Holocaust knowledge is highlighted. For we know, if we know anything at all about the Holocaust, that it was not a great adventure and that the rules governing detective stories did not apply. We also know, if we read the definitive edition of the *Diary* and not just the one uplifting line that is emphasized in the Goodrich and Hackett play, that the diarist herself did not always believe that "people are really good at heart" and that in the history of the Holocaust, let alone the end of Frank's own history in Bergen-Belsen, to focus on the good at heart is a distortion of the facts.

Yet the child reader who gains knowledge through the books she is given will only learn what the narrative is willing to tell her. While a careful reading of the *Diary* will teach the child reader more about the Holocaust than its critics often assert, the temptation to read the Holocaust as an interesting adventure is even more apparent when we turn to children's historical fiction. As I have argued throughout this book, with a few rare exceptions, North American children's historical fiction is desperate to find some optimism, some way of writing about the Holocaust as an adventure; the result is a literature that focuses on the exceptional: the survivor story, the rescuer story. The more we know about the brutal facts of Holocaust history, the more problematic become our attempts to reconcile it with our understanding of the requirements of children's reading. In this regard, Steven Spielberg's *Schindler's List* is not so different from the children's films that first established his reputation.

A further narrative problem is that children's historical fiction is often constructed as a series of events in which the protagonist (and the reader) learn the value of responsible choice. This is not surprising given how North American culture celebrates choice, a cliché that Bryan Singer ironically foregrounds in his film, *Apt Pupil*,[2] when the protagonist refers in his graduation speech to the myth of Icarus and then links this myth to "the responsibility of choice."[3] Aware of the limitations upon choice in the Holocaust world, the best writers of Holocaust historical fiction, such as Carol Matas, walk a fine line between their commitment to the possibility of choice and historical facts. But others, such as Kenneth Roseman in *Escape from the Holocaust* (part of his Do-It-Yourself Jewish Adventure series), set remarkably few limitations upon choice. Structuring his book as a series of choices in which the reader plays the role of a Jewish medical student who manages to survive the Holocaust through the clever choices he makes, Roseman creates a falsely reassuring and inappropriately adventurous narrative. To jump from the factual "some European Jews did survive" (1) to a fantasy in which nearly all plots end in survival is to leap from the general to the exceptional. Even Roseman's two plots that end in death during the Holocaust are emphatically cheerful, despite the fact that in one of them the protagonist dies from carbon monoxide pumped into a sealed truck. Fully aware of what is happening, the protagonist, Roseman tells us, "smile[s], recalling the happy events of [his] life before the great tragedy befell Europe's Jews" (Roseman 83). All the other narrative choices lead to a happy ending, or at least, a postwar death.

Roseman warns that despite the way his book will "give [the reader] a sense of excitement, of adventure, and of triumph" (1), it is not intended to make the reader think that the Holocaust was a game. Yet how can we avoid this conclusion given the focus on survival, control, and making the right choices? Is the reader supposed to conclude that the murdered victims died because they made the wrong choices, or that they died even though they made the right choices? To reach either conclusion only emphasizes how inappropriate narratives of choice are in representing Holocaust victim stories. Repeatedly, Roseman's book teaches the power and significance of choice; in one plot when the character after the war chooses Communism and too late realizes the error of his ways, the narrator announces, "you must accept the consequences of your decision" (80). Usually, however, Roseman's character ends up content, knowing that he has made the right decision; the plot line that ends the book as a whole declares, "You are sure that you have done the right thing" (169). In contrast to the luck and lack of control that dominates the memoirs and fiction not marketed for children, choice is a formative generic feature in Roseman's text, an extreme example of what happens in much Holocaust historical fiction intended for North American children.

Not only does the valorization of choice in children's historical fiction oppose Lawrence L. Langer's description of the Holocaust in terms of choiceless choice, but it also contradicts Sue Vice's observation that the historical reality of the Holocaust "entails the loss of such novelistic staples as suspense, choosing one's ending, constructing characters with the power to alter their fate, allowing good to triumph over evil, or even the clear identification of such moral categories"

(3). If the truth of the numbers killed makes historical fiction for children problematic, young adult fiction with a contemporary setting appears initially to provide a less traumatic space for Holocaust representation. In it, the writer, ironically freed of the need to reassure the reader in the face of such overwhelming historical horror since it is too late for such reassurance, can proceed to explore questions of knowledge and choice.[4] What does knowing about the Holocaust mean? Why are we drawn to this knowledge and what do we do with it? What choices exist within young adult fiction?

The answers provided to such questions are far from hopeful. Challenging the construction of knowledge in children's historical fiction, contemporary young adult texts also assume that many readers are not interested in historical fiction. Like Becca's friends in Jane Yolen's *Briar Rose* who do not want to listen to Gemma's fairy tale, young adult readers are also assumed to be resistant to Holocaust stories. One of the marketing features of these texts is that they barely, if at all, mention the Holocaust on their paperback covers, but often draw the readers in with tantalizing reference to spies, thrilling adventures, and the possibility of fighting back. In effect, they promise the reader exciting narratives of choice. In their reticence about any Holocaust content, they resemble the cover of Stephen King's *Different Seasons*, the collection of four novellas of which "Apt Pupil" is the second story. The back cover of my paperback copy clearly advertises the three movies inspired by King's novellas, but is silent on the Nazi identity of Kurt Dussander, the character who will torment the protagonist. There are references to Dussander's "dark past" and "the seductive lure of evil," but no mention of Nazis.[5] Similarly, although a swastika is included on the back cover of *Chernowitz!* and figures prominently as part of the front cover design of *The Secret of the Mezuzah*, the back cover of the latter speaks only of international espionage: "In fact, one out of every ten adults living in Vienna is a spy!" (Bell). The front cover of *The Wave* describes the book as "the classroom experiment that went too far" (Strasser); the back cover is somewhat more precise in linking the novel to "Hitler and the Nazis." The cover of *The Freak* makes no reference to the Holocaust; instead it promises the reader "A thrilling adventure story" (Matas). The problem of drawing the young adult reader to the subject of the Holocaust is there in the packaging; as in "Apt Pupil," Holocaust knowledge becomes a shameful, hidden secret. A quest for knowledge drives all of these stories, but the relation between that quest and the Holocaust is itself obscured.

Grooving on All That Concentration Camp Stuff in "Apt Pupil"

The opening paragraphs of "Apt Pupil" repeatedly insist that the protagonist, Todd Bowden, looks like and is an "all-American kid" (111). Sharing the eagerness of *The Secret of the Mezuzah* to type a character through physical description and then undercut it—who looks like a Nazi? who looks like a spy?—the rest of the novella is similarly willing to evoke characters through descriptions that soon prove to be both correct and inadequate. Does the elderly Arthur Denker look like the Nazi Kurt Dussander, whose photographs Todd has studied, or like some other old man, a weird mixture of Albert Einstein and Boris Karloff? Even before Denker admits that he is Dussander, Todd has decided that who Denker really looks like is one of the winos, whose murders by both Todd and Dussander later in the novella indicate one of the many ways that the all-American kid and the elderly Nazi come to resemble each other. Dussander eventually tells Todd that there are six winos buried in his cellar; the novella hints that Todd may have killed even more.

Just prior to the first murder that he commits, we are told that Todd and the narrator have difficulty distinguishing between one wino and another. Looking the same, the winos rarely have names, and the text refers to them interchangeably as winos or stewbums. The only exception is Hap, the one who happens to recognize Todd's grin in a newspaper photograph celebrating his naming to the Southern Cal All-Stars and thereby helps to link him to the unsolved murders. Being recognized through a photograph is another way in which Todd is linked with Dussander, for Todd has initially unveiled Dussander's disguise by comparing his present appearance to the grainy images in 30-year-old magazines. Dussander never calls Todd by his name; in killing the no-name winos, Todd enacts a fantasy in which he becomes Dussander and exerts the same power over others, the ultimate power of anonymous death. The nightmares in which a dead wino turns into Dussander disappear as soon as Todd kills again. Killing the winos substitutes for the prohibited and dangerous desire to kill Dussander and becomes a way for Todd to prove that he is not like the Holocaust victims, winos, and boys who, despite their surface differences, share the humiliating vulnerability and anonymity of the power-less. Todd is both repelled and aroused by their humiliation. What he fears, however, is being identified, not as a Nazi, whether by others or by himself, but as homosexual. He has no guilt about the murders that he commits, only anxiety about being exposed. Wanting to break up with Betty Trask, he worries about the effect upon his reputation. When Betty questions his sexual identity, he wants to kill her. In the "all-American" success story he imagines for his life, there is no place for forbidden desire.

Repeatedly King tells us what characters look like and what other characters think other characters look like, but he keeps undercutting the value of these descriptions. When Dussander is recognized by Morris Heisel, a Holocaust survivor, it is the tone of voice, not his appearance, that gives him away. Todd's father, Dick Bowden, mistakenly believes that he can "read his son like a book" (140). Todd later blames his impotence with Betty on the way her family only pretends to be white. Yet the reader never knows if the Trask family is secretly Jewish, or if this is just Todd's self-justifying fantasy to mask his sexual anxiety.

At the end of the novella, Todd kills Edward French, the only victim whose name we know for sure. French is also characterized by a physical description that draws attention to its contradictions and produces its own comic alias. A guidance counsellor who wants to look young and believes that wearing Keds sneakers will do the trick, French does not know that his habit of wearing rubbers over his sneakers means that the junior high students he wants to bond with secretly refer to him as Rubber Ed French. When Dussander poses as Todd's grandfather in a school interview that French has requested to discuss Todd's failing grades, French is totally taken in.[6] He has trouble placing the accent, but is certain that Dussander looks exactly like an elderly Lord

Peter Wimsey, straight out of a Dorothy Sayers novel. Yet when Dussander is finally identified as the Nazi, French's wife looks at the photograph in the newspaper and doesn't see any resemblance to Wimsey.

If the name Rubber Ed French hints at a sexualized mocking of the counsellor, the film is equally insistent in addressing both Holocaust and sexual anxieties. However, there are major differences in the film that serve to simplify and separate the two. While the Holocaust discourse still serves as a screen for sexual anxieties, the film is careful to make Todd's sexual anxieties a temporary consequence of listening to Dussander's stories. In the film, his girlfriend mocks Todd's sexual performance—"Maybe you just don't like girls"—but as soon as he stops visiting Dussander, he is reinscribed as a heterosexual.[7] In a major plot change, neither Todd, nor French, dies. Instead the film ends with Todd threatening to expose French for changing Todd's grades in exchange for possible sexual favours. In the novella, French is happily married and dies with his daughter's name on his lips. But in the film, he tells Todd about his messy divorce, and Todd asks if his preference for boys explains why his wife left him. Quoting lines that Dussander has said to him— "The things I'll say, they'll never go away"; "You have no idea what I can do"—Todd takes advantage of the homophobic anxiety that pervades American culture, in a scene whose language implies that the scandal of associating with Nazis is equivalent to the scandal of homosexual misconduct.

Although the film's point of view on this homophobia is not clear, there are further changes in the plot that foreground homophobic anxieties. In the novella, Dussander's compulsion to wear the Nazi uniform is explained as an

indulgence that allows him to escape the nightmares provoked by his past. In the film, the uniform functions differently in that Archie, a man picking through Dussander's
garbage, sees him in the uniform and concludes that the elderly man dressed up as a Nazi indulges in sexual fantasy
games with the adolescent boy who visits him.[8] When
Dussander kills Archie, not as one of a sequence of anonymous murders, but as the only murder that the audience sees
him commit, the context encourages the audience to believe
that Archie has approached Dussander, eager to profit from
the sexual secret he thinks he has observed. Given that we
already know that the Nazi uniform Dussander wears is a
costume, we are encouraged to fantasize as well, imagining
that Dussander murders Archie not simply for the sadistic
reenactment of the Nazi pleasure of murder, but in order to
avoid being exposed as a homosexual. Archie says to Dussander, "I know something about you. I know you're a nice
guy. I'm nice too, just like the boy. I will do anything you say."
Although the film encourages us to hear two different meanings when he tells Dussander, "I've done this before," and
Dussander replies, "That's all right, so have I," it is not at all
clear what meaning is implied when Dussander tells Todd
after the murder, "It was self-defence."

In a film in which homosexual desire is a secret that is
equal, if not more dangerous, than a Nazi past, only the
Holocaust survivor stands, as he does in the novella, outside
the homophobic circle. Ben Kramer (called Morris Heisel in
the novella) represents the Holocaust victim's reality, a reality in which horror is not at all sexualized. The nightmare in
which he recognizes Dussander does not bring him to
orgasm. In contrast, in the novella, killing the winos, or just

thinking about killing them, arouses Todd. The first time that he thinks of killing, he has an erection. When he takes his rifle and imagines shooting several people, he goes home to masturbate. When he has trouble getting erect, he imagines Betty as a Holocaust victim about to be electrocuted even as she is raped. The novella is full of derogatory language linking homosexual desire, female vulnerability, and Holocaust victims. In Dussander's dreams, he is consoled by the "winey smell" (206) of the crematorium. Heisel refers to himself as Morris the cat; this is a comic version of Dussander listening to the howling of a burning cat and being reminded of the cries of a "young boy" (159). Dussander tells Todd that the difference between American naïveté and Nazi awareness is symbolized by how Americans love newspaper "photographs of firemen rescuing kittens" (204). In a novella where pussy and faggot are the ultimate insults, where cats, winos, Jews, and women are equivalent victims, to be a Nazi is to be powerful, masculine, and in control of sexual discourse. As victimized object, the wino, like the Holocaust victim, is denied a sexual response. In both film and novella, Dussander tells Todd, "My boy [...] we are fucking each other—didn't you know that?" (197).

If the novella's insistence that Todd looks like an all-American kid raises the anxiety-provoking possibility that homosexuals also look like all-American kids, this is a knowledge that Todd never fully realizes and a possibility so disturbing that the film refuses to develop it.[9] There is at most a partial acknowledgement in the novella; in this way, the exploration of sexual anxiety hides behind the surface exploration of Holocaust anxiety. In contrast to contemporary young adult fiction where the Holocaust is the secret the narrative probes, in "Apt Pupil" the nature of the secret keeps shifting, moving uneasily between sexual anxiety and Nazi discourse. What is Todd? With blond hair and blue eyes, the 13-year-old who bicycles up to Dussander's hideaway at 963 Claremont in summer 1974 could be a poster boy for the Hitler Youth. Less a Nazi in disguise than a boy getting in over his head, Todd brings to his Nazi hunting a precarious and American innocence. The only Nazis he knows are the cartoon figures he sees on television; when Todd first hears Dussander speak without his false teeth, he thinks that the Nazi on *Hogan's Heroes* sounds more authentic.

We are pointedly told that Todd doesn't even have adolescent acne yet; he fantasizes being a private detective, but has a vocabulary that is childishly limited. In *Different Seasons*, "Apt Pupil" appears under the heading Summer of Corruption; in "The Body," the novella that immediately follows, under the heading Fall From Innocence, we are told that 12 is the age at which boys lose their innocence.[10] When Todd first meets Dussander, he is still like Teddy in "The Body," the boy who loves to hear gruesome stories—"the gooshy part" (297). By the end of "Apt Pupil," Todd's knowledge of the gooshy parts has taken him too far; the only way to stop the nightmares is to die, presumably in a violent shootout fueled by the 400 rounds he takes with him to the hill overlooking the freeway. In a rare moment of discretion, King does not give us the final shootout; to dwell on it would be to return to the pleasures of the "gooshy." Instead, the final shootout is preceded by a speech in the adult voice of the Nazi hunter, Weiskopf, who explains what Todd is never able to explain. Even as Todd is last seen, smiling as he goes off to shoot as many people as he can, the question of what he looks like returns. Is he still the all-American boy? A boy going off to war? Are Americans at their most childlike when they kill others?

What Todd does have from the start is precocious insight, the honesty of the child's voice in adult fiction, the one who sees through the rhetoric of Holocaust pedagogy. Like King, who in his "Afterword" appears far more interested in details of horror than political analysis, Todd is not at all interested in politics. He admits to Dussander that he "really groove[s] on all that concentration camp stuff" (119). Having read in *Men's Action* magazine about Kurt Dussander, formerly of Bergen-Belsen and Auschwitz, and *Unterkommandant* of the death camp Patin, Todd cannot believe his good luck in discovering a real live Nazi who can tell him the uncensored truth, a desire tied up with his fantasies about Ilse Koch, lampshades made of human skin, and details of sexual torture. The first questions that Todd asks Dussander make clear the sexual sadistic nature of his interest, for what he really wants to know is whether Dussander spanked any of his female victims and whether he removed their clothes.

Inverting the paradigm of Holocaust education, in which survivors tell young people about their horrific experience and the young people, moved by the survivors' narrative, suitably vow, Never Again, Todd tells Dussander that what he wants are stories, the voice of the perpetrator who can tell him what being a Nazi was really like. When Dussander later begins to quote Santayana—"He who will not learn from the past" (201)—Todd tells him to shut up. His interest in atrocity stories dates back to the day he accidentally discovered the stories of concentration camps in a pile of pulp magazines in a friend's garage. The director, Bryan Singer, omits this scene in the film. Making Todd 16 when he con-

fronts Dussander and setting the film in 1984, Singer provides a brief opening sequence suggesting that Todd's interest
in the Nazis derives from high school instruction on the
topic.[11] In contrast, in the novella the initiation scene parodies
Susan Sontag's description of the first time that she saw
photographs from the death camps, as well as the rhetoric of
public school hope in a better future. King presents Todd's
discovery of the images as a grotesque fulfillment of his
fifth-grade teacher's promise that one day the children will
discover their "GREAT INTEREST" (119).

What Todd sees in the magazines challenges his former
sense of knowing anything at all about World War II. Seeing
the photographs of Dachau, he realizes that until now he
has understood nothing. He is stunned by the number,
6,000,000, but it is not the number that repels and excites
him so much as the sexually sadistic image of a woman about
to be tortured by a grinning "guy in a Nazi uniform" (121).
This becomes the image that, with slight modifications,
occurs repeatedly in his dreams, and gives him his first wet
dream. When Hap recognizes Todd, it is the grin on his face
that he recalls.

Todd has no interest in the hopeful lessons that justify
representing the Holocaust in children's literature. What
King emphasizes is Todd's distance from the conventional
lessons of Holocaust pedagogy and his ability to recognize
the contradiction between the surface morality of a culture
that condemns Nazi behaviour and the magazine ads that in
1970s America continue to cater to Nazi fantasies. The
encounter with the photographs in the pulp magazines gives
Todd a desire for knowledge far outside the parameters of
what his school would teach him. He wants to know every-

thing that happened in the camps; only then can he learn for himself what is the real truth.

Although the episode of discovering the magazines in Foxy's garage does not appear in the film, the opening of the film is even more pointed in positioning its narrative in opposition to official Holocaust pedagogy. The film begins with a teacher's hand erasing a pie chart of groups murdered in the Holocaust, and a teacher's voice telling the class that this concludes their one week's study of the Holocaust, but if they want to know more, they should go to the library and find out. Only Todd goes to the library; only Todd finds out more and is destroyed by what he learns. In the film, he specifically tells Dussander he wants to hear everything that they are afraid to show them in school.[12] In the novella, the dream that occasions Todd's first wet dream is framed in the language of forbidden knowledge, his sense that in the dream he goes beyond what even the magazines are willing to show.

In both film and novella, libraries are dangerous places, and American adults are naïve for not recognizing this danger. This is knowledge that the adult figures in Todd's life— his father, who thinks that children should learn about life; his mother, who agrees with her husband that children need to learn through experiment; his guidance counsellor and the school librarian—do not know how to handle. Using Todd's naïve voice, King asks what is behind the American fascination with the Holocaust. The answer is framed in the language of desire, as Todd tells Dussander of his amazement at the number of books in the library about the concentration camps: "[a] *lot* of people must like to read about that stuff" (122). Not only does Todd trick the librarian into letting him read books in the adult section by telling her that it is for a school project, he also gets an A+ for the research paper he writes. Again, he confides to Dussander that he had to write in a certain style. He then mocks the world of Holocaust pedagogy: "All those library books, they read a certain way. Like the guys who wrote them got puking sick over what they were writing about. [...] How we've got to be careful so nothing like that ever happens again" (123). For Todd, the only lesson he derives from the "gooshy" stuff is the simple one of excess. The Nazis, he tells Dussander in their first meeting, went "overboard" (122). Whether that excess had anything to do with antisemitic ideology, or any other history, is irrelevant. In the film, Todd tells a friend concerned about his falling grades, "I don't need a lesson ok?"

Although King describes "Apt Pupil" in his "Afterword" in psychological and apolitical terms, the Holocaust echoes extend far beyond the surface plot with its "gooshy" details. Turning the Holocaust into a screen for a psychological horror story, the novella also mocks the conventional language of Holocaust discourse. Weiskopf, the Nazi hunter, confesses that his attempts at understanding have failed, but his words apply to Todd's actions, not the "unbelievable" Holocaust. Morris Heisel, the Holocaust survivor, announces that God does not exist, but he loses his faith merely by falling off a ladder. After he identifies Dussander, Heisel believes in God again. Edward French asks Todd to explain how he became involved with Dussander, and Todd's response mimics the functionalist explanation of the Final Solution, "Oh, one thing just followed another" (289).

To a reader familiar with German and Hebrew, the novella's Holocaust excess extends to the names that King invents. German for death is *tod*; does the German meaning of Todd's name have any bearing on Dussander's refusal to say it? Does the German homonym, *boden*, with its meaning of ground or base, cast further light on the hidden desires of the all-American kid? Is it simply accident that 963, the street number of the house where Dussander has been living in disguise, adds up to 18, *chai* or life in Hebrew? Dussander's alias, Denker, suggests the German verb, *denken* (to think), exactly what Dussander tells Todd he is incapable of. The character of Weiskopf, the Israeli special operative who tracks down Nazis when he is not teaching literature and writing novels, most clearly fits "Apt Pupil" into Holocaust pedagogy. As befits a man whose name merges *weis* (wise) and *kopf* (head), he suspects that Todd's interest in Dussander has led to his involvement in the unsolved murders. And it is Weiskopf who revises French's question and asks, not "how" it happened, but "why."

Although Weiskopf admits that knowing what happened in the camps can still sicken him (the nausea that Todd mocked in his first meeting with Dussander), he rightly suspects that the Nazi atrocities are exactly what drew Todd to Dussander. Although Weiskopf is not American, he offers an explanation straight out of American Holocaust pedagogy: the fascination that evil has, the "secret knowledge that under the right—or wrong—set of circumstances" (283) we would do the same thing. And his answer returns the narrative to the language of desire, secret knowledge, and the question of what Todd looks like. Dussander is still tormented in 1974 by the hanging in 1962 of Adolf Eichmann. In Hannah Arendt's analysis of his trial, *Eichmann in Jerusalem: A Report on the Banality of Evil*, she described Eichmann as looking banal, more like an anonymous bureaucrat than the monsters we want to believe that the Nazis were; surely her words are echoed in Weiskopf's description of the perpetrators: "I think most of them would look like ordinary accountants" (283). What does Todd Bowden look like?

Only once does Todd see the atrocity photographs as grounded in the facts of history, not just images "staged like a scene in a horror film" (144). This occurs when he forces Dussander to put on the Nazi costume. Yet, even if this momentary realization and Weiskopf's words indicate that "Apt Pupil" is intended as more than exploitation of the Holocaust, whether readers are likely to see beyond the horror scenes is uncertain. The episode is recreated in the film, a film which won the 1999 Saturn Award for Best Horror Film. And the very horror strategies King uses, while successfully reminding us that the Holocaust is "a creepy subject" (King 283), also encourages us to adopt a psychological analysis that takes us further and further from history, and caters to other fantasies regarding the Holocaust's evil inexplicability. Such a retreat from history and from complex explanations, which may include psychological components but do not stop there, is heard in the unanswered questions that open the film. In a series of rhetorical questions asked by the teacher—"Was it economic? Was it social? Was it cultural? Or was it simply human nature?"—the film, like the novella, implies that the answer is simply human nature.

This answer is exactly what we find in contemporary young adult fiction. Certainly the homophobic anxiety of "Apt Pupil" distinguishes it from much contemporary young adult fiction, where texts tend to explore such anxiety apart from their analysis of the Holocaust. However, the novella's homophobic anxiety and fondness for the "gooshy" should not distract us from recognizing how much "Apt Pupil" shares with the Holocaust representation found in young adult fiction. Two similarities are striking: a shared preference for psychological analysis over historical explanation and a deep skepticism about the effectiveness of American Holocaust pedagogy upon sheltered students to whom the Holocaust is just another horror movie.

It is not just that Todd's "gooshy" language sounds remarkably similar to the words Philip Gourevitch hears grade-eight students use during a school visit to the United States Holocaust Memorial Museum (Gourevitch, "What They Saw" 44). What young adult fiction shares with "Apt Pupil" is a deep suspicion of adults and official pedagogy, as well as an anxiety regarding the possibility of learning about the past through the act of reading. The protagonists in young adult fiction may not all be as "apt" as Todd Bowden, but reading about the Holocaust or watching documentary films that depict its horrors do not necessarily teach what we want them to teach. Like the counter-story "Apt Pupil" offers to the hopeful Americanization of the Holocaust, young adult novels have little faith and less hope in the effectiveness of saying, Never Again.

Watching Documentaries
in The Wave and Chernowitz!

Both Todd Strasser's The Wave and Fran Arrick's Chernowitz!, two young adult novels published in 1981, foreshadow King's view that the educational system is baffled by the challenge of Holocaust pedagogy. The Wave "is based on a true incident

that occurred in a high school history class [...] in 1969"
(Strasser 5), and was first told in a short story by Ron Jones,
the teacher involved in the real event. The novel tells the story
of a well-meaning high school history teacher, Ben Ross, who
invents an experiment to teach his high school seniors why
the majority of Germans, even though they did not belong to
the Nazi party, did not protest Nazi behaviour. Unlike Todd
in "Apt Pupil," who is obsessed with the secret of what it feels
like to be a Nazi, the mystery that perplexes Ross's students
is the behaviour of the non-Nazi Germans. The novel begins
with the teacher showing his students "a documentary
depicting the atrocities" (15). Some students are moved; others either fall asleep, or wait impatiently for the film to be
over so that they can go to lunch. Characterizing his students
as "surprisingly naïve and sheltered" (17), Ross is careful to be
selective about the facts he gives them. He not only refrains
from explaining what is in the smoke rising from the camp
chimneys, he is also occasionally and unintentionally inaccu-
rate. Ignoring the difference between slave labour camps and
killing centres, he tells the students that the victims were
gassed once they could not work, but does not tell them that
many victims were gassed immediately. Such historical impre-
cision characterizes contemporary young adult fiction, where
historical accuracy matters less than psychological response.

Strasser characterizes Ross as young, naïve, and idealistic.
In a detail possibly intended to identify him as a child of the
1960s, the heterodiegetic narrator tells us that the older
teachers dislike "the way he never wore a suit and tie" (11).[13]
These teachers also disapprove of Ross's experiment, but the
novel takes for granted that teaching history presents special
pedagogical difficulties. If history is a story about other

people who are remote in time and place, and we only learn from personal experience, how can we possibly learn anything authentic about them? Thinking about his inability to answer his students' questions, Ross concludes that the answer about German tolerance of Nazi behaviour will not be found in any textbook; it can only be experienced through a partial staging of the original situation. He designs an experiment in compulsory conformity that he calls The Wave, and it proves to be too successful.

The central character who resists the appeal of The Wave is the class star, Laurie Saunders. In a major deviation from "Apt Pupil," the one who has most to gain is the "class loser" (12), Robert Billings. With the exception of Laurie's friend, Amy, who is relieved that The Wave means that they no longer have to compete, key female characters (Laurie, Laurie's mother, and Ross's wife Christy) are suspicious. Implying that Nazi collective behaviour automatically holds more appeal for men, a suggestion reinforced after a student introduces The Wave as a strategy to help the losing football team, Strasser also stresses how much the "class loser" has invested in the experiment by emphasizing the transformative effect of The Wave on Robert Billings's behaviour and appearance. Robert is initially depicted as a "heavy boy with shirttails perpetually hanging out and his hair always a mess" (13), but he is soon tucking in his shirt, brushing his hair, and volunteering to be the teacher's bodyguard.

If the experiment ultimately teaches students how willingly they too might have endorsed the Nazis, and in that sense is successful in teaching the psychological dynamics of group behaviour, Ross nevertheless concludes that this is a lesson he dares not repeat (Never Again). He has learned the headiness of power, as well as how easily the experiment gets away from him, as students invent refinements to it that he never imagined. (Are we meant to be reminded of the historical debate over whether there was an order from Hitler for the final solution?) Having learned his own lesson, Ross assembles the students in the auditorium and echoes the opening episode by showing them a gigantic image of Hitler that was part of the original documentary footage. He tells them that Hitler would have been their ideal leader and that their future appears in the faces of the adolescents who once followed him: "Take a look at your future!" (139). He reminds them of their earlier confidence regarding the past: "You say it could never happen again, but look how close you came" (139). Apologizing for what he has done, he uses the word "lesson" repeatedly, and continuing the rhetoric of "Never Again," he concludes, "If we're smart, we won't dare forget it" (140).

It is worth noting that, as in "Apt Pupil," neither Ross, nor any of the central characters, is Jewish, for this raises the central issue of what exactly they will not forget. Although one student jokes that the room where Laurie goes to avoid participating in the mass rally is "Anne Frank's attic" (95), this questionable parallel between a bystander and a victim is not developed any further. Similarly, although Laurie's father reports secondhand that a Jewish boy has been beaten up for refusing to join the experiment, the unnamed boy plays only a minor role. Hesitant to blame The Wave for provoking antisemitic acts, Strasser quickly raises other possible reasons that the boy has been called a "dirty Jew" (103). Despite a passing and gratuitous reference to the boy's rabbi having been in Auschwitz for two years and therefore, according to the principal, not "giv[ing] a damn about [the] experiment"

(127), *The Wave* shows little interest in antisemitism, the experience of the victims, or the Holocaust as a genocide whose primary victims were Jewish. Its focus is the attraction of conformity, indicated through comparisons between The Wave and cult behaviour, as well as through the group mottoes that Ross invents: Strength Through Discipline, Strength Through Community, Strength Through Action. The lesson is psychological: "Fascism isn't something those other people did, it is right here, in all of us" (140). The problem is not the psychological focus, but that the psychology and its universal lesson can only be achieved through a detachment from historical specificity. As the work of Saul Friedländer and Dominick LaCapra demonstrates, the insights of history and psychology can be combined.

Whereas King deconstructs the all-American boy by presenting him as a bright individual who does not appear particularly concerned whether or not he has any friends, in *The Wave* friendship is all-important, and the unproblematized American values of individualism and legitimate questioning of authority are the answers to the dangers of fascism.[14] These values are expressed by Ben Ross in the conclusion: "If people were destined to be led [...] this was something he must make sure they learned: to question thoroughly, never to put your faith in anyone's hands blindly. Otherwise ..." (138). Such values are also expressed by Laurie's anti-Wave editorial: "It condemned The Wave as a dangerous and mindless movement that suppressed freedom of speech and thought and ran against everything the country was founded on" (104).

In contrast to the heterodiegetic narration of *The Wave*, which permits a variable focalization, *Chernowitz!* presents a Jewish perspective through the homodiegetic narrator and

15-year-old protagonist, Bobby Cherno. Suffering the anti-semitic taunts and acts of Emmett Sundback, Bobby intro-duces his *"true story [... of] how people are with each other"* (Arrick vii) through an anecdote about his family that demonstrates the persistence of antisemitism in America while simultaneously insisting that his story is universal: "I'm Jewish, but if I were black or gay [...] it would have been the same" (viii). For years Bobby endures Emmett's racial slurs (including his referring to Bobby as Chernowitz; Bobby con-fides to the reader that his great-grandparents did change their name, but it was originally Chanyakov, not Chernowitz). Even so, Bobby is never sure if Emmett hates him because he is Jewish or for some other reason.

In "Apt Pupil," intelligence does not preclude an attrac-tion to Nazi discourse; in contrast, in *Chernowitz!*, intelligence belongs to the narrator/victim. Emmett is a far more stereo-typical construction of the antisemite in young adult fiction: he is characterized as a "stupid slob" (15), who has trouble in school, lives in a broken home, and uses antisemitic taunts to help him endure the abuse he suffers at the hands of his alcoholic father. A "loser" like *The Wave*'s Robert Billings, Emmett "probably flunked history" (106), but still knows about swastikas. Yet Bobby's historical sophistication is not much better when he metaphorically links Emmett and Hitler: "Six million Jews died under that sign because an insane bully had an insane idea" (105-06). As in "Apt Pupil," the more complex analyses of politics and history are reject-ed in favour of dramatic psychological displays. In "Apt Pupil," Dussander burns cats in his oven; Emmett tries to kill the Cherno family cat by running it over with his motorcycle.

After Bobby plays detective and gets revenge by planting a radio in Emmett's locker and framing him for stealing it, he realizes that there is no satisfaction in punishing the bully for a crime he did not commit when the true crime of anti-semitism goes unpunished. When Emmett is suspended for the wrong reasons, and Bobby's confession to him resolves nothing, Bobby finally confides in his parents. He tells them not only about the theft but also about the series of antisemitic events Emmett has participated in, including tossing a burning cross on their lawn and painting a swastika on the family car.

Since Bobby's parents are also teachers, they respond both personally and pedagogically to their son's revelations. They are shocked to learn the truth about Emmett and the other adolescents who participated in the incidents. Nevertheless, Mrs. Cherno advises her son that revenge is futile: "You can't take revenge against prejudice, it doesn't make an anti-Semite stop hating Jews" (167). The mother's response, which Bobby eventually adopts, also reveals the psychological focus of the text and the way that focus blurs historical comparisons. Mrs. Cherno tells Bobby that hatred will always exist and adds that the only response to hatred lies in ensuring that others are made aware of the pain produced by it. For this reason, she had insisted earlier that the local newspaper photograph the swastika on the car. But her advice (and her earlier action) takes for granted that the others who are made aware of the pain do not also hate, or will not learn to hate. This may be true in contemporary America, but was it true in Germany in the 1930s? The historical reality of the difference between the depth of antisemitism in 1930s Germany and contemporary America is obscured when Mrs. Cherno compares her refusal to hide the swastika on the car to what happened in Nazi Germany: "nobody said anything, everybody swept it all under the rug, *it can't happen here*, remember?" (115). We can argue about how many Germans were aware of the gas chambers, but to assert that Germans in the 1930s did not see the pain produced by Nazi hatred assumes a psychological dimension to seeing that is true, but also inadequate. It can't happen here not because Mrs. Cherno can get the incident reported in the newspaper, but because the contemporary American community responds to those newspaper reports differently than the German community did in the 1930s.

Mrs. Cherno's refusal to hide the evidence also contrasts with the behaviour of Bobby's teacher, who responds to a note with the swastika on it by crumpling it and then tells the class to take out their copy of *The Merchant of Venice*.[15] The school would prefer not to deal with such incidents, and when they finally do, the results are ambiguous. After the principal, Mrs. Wardwell, announces that there will be a special assembly and that Bobby's father will participate, Bobby is appalled and not at all reassured by her suggestion that the assembly will provide "A lesson for everybody" (175). Mrs. Wardwell opens the assembly by telling the students she wants them to be shocked, "to be so upset by what will be shown [...] that [they] will never forget it throughout [their] lives" (176). And she concludes her introduction by saying that she wants it "to be one of the most important school lessons [they] ever have" (176). What she shows are documentary films comparable to those that initiate the action in *The Wave*. Bobby summarizes what he sees in the first film: images that move from the inanimate (heaps of clothing, piles of bodies) to the barely animate (the survivors). In the second film, the images are of deformed victims of Nazi experiments. Because many of the students cry or get sick, the third film is never shown.

Unable to listen to everything that the narrator of the films says, Bobby proves even less able to listen to his father's speech on prejudice and bigotry. Escaping the auditorium, "hyperventilating" (181) because of his father's participation, and still shocked by what he has seen in the documentaries—"No matter what you hear or read, you can't believe it" (182)—Bobby has a final confrontation with Emmett. Whatever lesson he learns and *Chernowitz!* offers takes place through this confrontation, not through the films.

When Emmett taunts Bobby about the films—"Was that for me, Chernowitz?" (182),—Bobby realizes that no Holocaust atrocity film will ever change Emmett's views or the views of other antisemites: "There was nothing I could do to him that would make him change except kill him. And even if I could do that it wouldn't kill his ideas" (182). If Bobby is consoled by the memory of how many students were moved by the films, the novel's ending diminishes any easy faith in the transformative power of graphic Holocaust imagery. Unlike Todd Bowden who, King tells us, is fascinated by what he sees in Holocaust photographs, Arrick does not tell us what Emmett thinks as he views the films. We only know what Bobby concludes: "But nothing happened to Emmett's insides, nothing" (182).

Disturbing the Happy Ending in
The Secret of the Mezuzah *and* The Freak

At the end of Mary Reeves Bell's *The Secret of the Mezuzah*, the mother of the narrator/protagonist tells her son, Con, not to look for happy endings in the Holocaust. Published in the mid-1990s, both *The Secret of the Mezuzah* and Carol Matas's *The Freak* situate their narratives of Holocaust education outside the schools and rely on the conventions of the detective story to attract their readers. In Matas's case, these conventions exist within the framework of speculative fiction, which so obscures the Holocaust content that I feel accused when Matas's detective heroine, Jade, confides, "I hate it in English when the teacher starts to talk about interpretation" (43). Yet this obscurity draws attention to the difficulty of making the Holocaust the subject of young adult fiction and to the peculiar way that such fiction makes Holocaust history itself the secret. In both books, the 15-year-old narrator/protagonists Con and Jade, solve one specific Holocaust-related crime, but whatever lessons the books offer, they do not provide the confidence in a well-ordered world that is often found in the neat endings of detective fiction. In both books, the schools offer predictable and ineffective responses to antisemitic acts, forcing the protagonists to solve the crimes on their own; in both cases, the detective story proves inadequate to the subject and the lesson. One crime might be solved, one Nazi recognized, one neo-Nazi caught, but in both books there are others who still remain at large. Both books present protagonists who move from a naïve perception that they live in very dull places—the Christian Con believing that "nothing exciting had happened [in Vienna] for hundreds of years" (15), the Jewish Jade thinking that "Winnipeg used to be a really safe place" (52)—to an anxious recognition that such beliefs are part of the childhood they must now leave behind.[16] Learning to mistrust appearances, they realize that the Holocaust is no longer simply a word in a history book, but this knowledge only raises more questions. If in historical fiction such as *Stones in Water* the need to escape the Nazis and the adventure plot allow the narrator to say, "now was the time for action; unanswerable questions couldn't matter" (Napoli 137-38), in contemporary detective stories concerning the Holocaust, the protagonist finds time for both.

The first book in a series called Passport to Danger, *The Secret of the Mezuzah* is the more conventional adventure story. Initially the protagonist, Con, born in the United States but living in Austria for most of his life, takes his world for grant- ed, blind to the antisemitism that still prevails, and slightly bemused by his mother's explanation for living in Vienna. The mother tells her son that they live there so that she can study Hebrew at the university; he decides that this only proves how eccentric his mother is.[17] The novel begins, and Con's life changes, the day that he delays going home because he is worried about a note that his history teacher has writ- ten. Bored with school and particularly with the study of world history—"The information you pick up at school is rarely important" (24-25)—he notices a swastika-tattooed skinhead leaving the bakery. When this skinhead in his red Jaguar nearly runs him over, Con, who is more perceptive when observing cars than people, immediately decides that the baker, Branko Loveric, must be a spy, particularly after Branko tells him "there are spies amongst us" (19). Branko is teasing; he later tells Con that spying is not a game. But Con is totally enchanted; he wishes that Branko were his history teacher.

Bell assumes that her reader will share Con's interest in fast cars and Clint Eastwood movies and will respond with the same lack of interest that Con displays to the swastikas and xenophobic graffiti that disfigure his school. Having never been discriminated against, Con is sure that the principal's concern is excessive and that the graffiti means very little. His Jewish friend, Hannah Goldberg, tells him that his indifference is directly related to the blond hair and blue eyes that make him look exactly like an Austrian. Only now does Con, who is naïve enough not to recognize that Hannah has a stereotypical Jewish name and does not look like "the Aryan heroine" (33), start to notice how several of the adult Austrians he knows treat her.[18] When a school friend, Gregor Müller, invites Con to play a Nazi computer game—the goal is to kill Jews; the game is called KL Manager—Con reluctantly starts the process of learning and making choices that culminates in his identifying with Hannah. Recognized by one of the neo-Nazi terrorists who plants a bomb in Simon Wiesenthal's office, a man he has noticed only because of his supposed resemblance to Dirty Harry, Con and Hannah are kidnapped and interrogated by the neo-Nazis. When "Dirty Harry" threatens Hannah, "I'll send you where we sent the rest of your relatives" (169), Con says that he is Jewish too. In the final chapter, he confirms the symbolism of this choice by putting the mezuzah on the doorframe of his room.

Unlike Stephen King, Bell never complicates her narrative with any ambiguity about the difference between "all-American" kids and Nazis. Several of the Austrian characters are clearly neo-Nazi or at least nostalgic for the past; Gregor's mother is "sick of foreigners who don't understand telling us to remember" (41); Gregor's father installs the Nazi computer game; there are numerous references to Austria's abysmal record in prosecuting war criminals. In contrast to Gregor's enthusiasm, Con feels no attraction to the images of torture in the game. The difference between Nazis and non-Nazis remains clear, as Bell takes for granted that her reader will be equally repulsed by these images. Gregor challenges Con: "Why are you so uptight about a game? Besides, you fight Nazis in your games. Killing Nazis, killing Jews—what's the difference?" (47). Con does not have to answer; he knows that there is a difference. What he does not know is that this knowledge is not enough: "I didn't play, but I didn't leave, either" (47).

What Con must learn is that he has to choose so that the history of indifference does not repeat itself. Choosing to say "*Ich bin Jude*" (170) so astonishes the neo-Nazis that the chief kidnapper refuses to believe that Con can really speak German. With these words, Con rejects the role of naïve American bystander, a choice for which Hannah's father later commends him: "You did what the majority of people failed to do during the Holocaust: You stood with the victim of that kind of irrational hatred" (89). What proves more difficult is accepting that his childhood friend, Herr Donner, is an unrepentant Nazi. "[N]ot a good reader at the best of times" (145), Con blames himself for this blindness. When he does so, his mother tells him, "There is no connection between you, what you are, and a man who was once kind to you and what he is" (142).

The novel's title arises from a gold mezuzah that Donner mistakenly gives Con and then tries to retrieve. Through her ability to read Hebrew, Con's mother is able to read the scroll inside the mezuzah; in her role as an undercover agent who helps Simon Wiesenthal hunt Nazis, she recognizes that the mezuzah is just the piece of evidence Wiesenthal needs to bring Donner to justice. Con, who is as stunned to learn that his mother is an undercover agent as he is disbelieving that Donner is a Nazi, learns from his mother that Raoul Levi, a Jewish child deported in November 1944, secretly inscribed in the mezuzah a record of Donner's acts. Although the message added to the mezuzah scroll helps Con accept that Donner was once a member of the SS, he resists this knowledge: "I don't want to know. I liked him" (143).

Although the plot of *The Secret of the Mezuzah* relies on an elaborate and cumbersome series of events, the novel abandons the confident ending of the detective story, one in which the guilty are exposed and punished. Con reports that the police arrest the neo-Nazis who kidnapped him and Hannah, but the capture of Donner is left uncertain. The lesson that Con draws from his adventure concerns his own guilt, the guilt of the adolescent who thinks world history is a bore.

In contrast to Con's initial belief that the Holocaust is a closed episode that has nothing to do with him, Jade, the Jewish narrator in *The Freak*, is not quite as obtuse about her personal connection to this history. Yet her story of waking up with the freakish psychic power of hearing what people are thinking and anticipating future catastrophes is not that different from *The Secret of the Mezuzah*, for the choice that Jade faces between being a zombie (drugged so that she can ignore her psychic powers) or being a freak (different and therefore viewed with suspicion by those around her) is essentially identical to Con's choice. Neither book explores King's interest in the adolescent drawn to the perpetrator's perspective; both focus on the protagonist's move from indifferent bystander to active opponent.

Jade is not like Todd Bowden; she finds Nazis repulsive and she is clearly heterosexual. The mystery she unravels accompanies a heterosexual romance. Like Yolen in *Briar Rose*, Matas offers her reader romantic kisses; when Jade first sees Jon, the East Indian Canadian who will become her boyfriend, she says that he is "movie-star stunning, beautiful, incredible, words cannot describe, drop-dead gorgeous" (43). But within the romantic framework, Matas also makes Jade an active heroine, capable of saving Jon's father from a car bombing and then an entire synagogue from another bomb. She is also careful to make Jade a role model for ambitious, middle-class adolescent girls. Jade prefers math to English, is aware of female eating disorders, and has "tried drinking and doing weed" (23), but does so only occasionally since she intends to get a scholarship to an Ivy League college. She even confides that she could have sex, but is in no rush: "Guys will have sex with a watermelon if they're desperate enough" (24). Until Jade becomes a freak, she describes herself as "so straight I don't have secrets" (23).

Her mathematical proclivities represent more than an easy way for Matas to contrast Jade with traditional heroines such as Anne of Green Gables, who are incapable of doing math. Jade has always believed that logic can explain everything, "and if one just stayed focused life could be controlled" (10). At first she tries to explain her new insights logically, but as such explanations prove inadequate, she turns to her grandmother, Baba, who is the only adult in Jade's family not surprised by her new abilities or her belief that her dead grandfather spoke to her. Baba does not believe that logic can explain everything. She tells Jade that her psychic powers run in the family; they usually skip a generation; she has them, as did Jade's great-great-grandmother. Baba tells Jade that there are multiple futures, "depending on what choices we make" (106). This view may not be conventional or logical, but given how often we say that the Holocaust was "unbelievable," that human beings could not act this way to other human beings, examining Holocaust issues outside the realm of the logical becomes tempting.

Baba becomes the instrument through whom Matas turns a fantasy about an adolescent who does not want to appear different into an exploration of post-Holocaust questions. Matas has always been interested in narratives of choice and difference; in the post-Holocaust speculations of *The Freak* she creates a less restrictive space for such narratives than that provided by her historical fiction. Backshadowing, according to Bernstein, encourages Holocaust novelists to blame characters for not knowing what the future would hold; with Jade's psychic powers, Matas writes a narrative in which a Jewish girl does know what might happen. Jade has the choice to prevent a "catastrophe" (106); by preventing a small-scale catastrophe, the terrorist bombing of a synagogue on Yom Kippur, she can act on knowledge that the victims of the *Shoah* (catastrophe) did not have. Through the fantasy context, Matas makes backshadowing feasible and avoids the problem of seeing history as inevitable. Yet the fantasy context, its speculation about preventing future catastrophes through choices informed by psychic powers, is hardly reassuring. At the end of the novel, Jade is horrified when she thinks of how many children might have died had the synagogue blown up; that their lives were saved only through the freak accident of her powers is equally disturbing. Are we meant to think that God gave her meningitis so that she could prevent the bombing? Where was God during the Holocaust?

Baba tells Jade that God has nothing to do with the Holocaust: "I say that God didn't make the Holocaust. Hitler and those that collaborated with him made it happen. *They* made those choices" (100). If the victims of the Holocaust had very few choices precisely because of those made by Hitler and his collaborators, Jade now does have a choice. Baba describes God as the "*Ein Sof*, the unknowable" (100)—an example of how the Judaism of *The Freak* combines traditional Judaic concepts with the New Age Judaism of Jade's Aunt Janeen. According to *Tikkun Olam*, the world is a broken vessel in need of repair. Jade tells Jon that her favourite Leonard Cohen song is about the crack in the world that lets the light in. As in the song, *Tikkun Olam* teaches that the human task is to mend the world, a concept that clearly insists on the responsibility of human choices. This is linked to Janeen's idiosyncratic conception of reincarnation, a belief not only alien to traditional Judaism, but also distinct from the Hindu concept of karma. Janeen tells Jade that people are not punished for their past lives, but are meant to learn from them and use that knowledge in choosing their next life. When Jade and Jon spy on the neo-Nazis, who include Klaus Schmidt, the former Austrian chief of police "responsible for the murder of an entire town of Jews" (44), Jon suggests that Jade must have fought in the resistance in her former life. Jade does not totally dismiss the possibility; she even jokes, "Maybe our friend Klaus has already murdered me" (95).

In contrast to the Austrian setting of *The Secret of the Mezuzah*, the Canadian setting of *The Freak* allows Matas to blur the line between Jews and non-Jews, Canadians and Nazis. On the surface, the world of Jade's family is comfortably multicultural; the difference of being Jewish is not an issue. Baba is not upset to learn from the fortune teller that not all her grandchildren will marry Jews; her daughter, Janeen, dates a Hindu, Sahjit; and Jade, who quickly falls for one of Sahjit's sons when she meets him at a Rosh Hashanah dinner, is only surprised that the sons do not have East Indian names. By making Sahjit an immigration lawyer working with B'nai Brith to have Schmidt extradited to Austria, Matas constructs a plot in which Jade soon realizes that Jews and people of colour are equally despised by the neo-Nazis. After antisemitic hate literature appears in the school lockers, the school responds in a predictable manner. The principal announces that she will find survivors to address the students as part of a Holocaust Awareness week. She also directs every class to read at least one Holocaust book. As Jade's class discusses *The Diary of Anne Frank*, Jade has a vision that connects Anne Frank and Sahjit, a vision that enables her to save Sahjit's life. What proves equally disturbing is that her powers also allow her to sense that some of the students are not opposed to the hate literature.

The only student specifically associated with the "gloating" (56) Jade senses is a skinhead, Roger, whose face she first sees in one of her dreams. There may be others, but Matas never describes them. The difference between the "all-American" appearance of King's apt pupil and Roger could not be broader. Roger, "no neck, all bulging muscles, shaved head, and a tattoo on his arm" (67), threatens Jade as a "Yid" (68), but then runs away when she tells him she is a witch. Jade categorizes Roger as the stereotypical "geeky kid who couldn't fit in" (78), one who has trouble in school and is now under the bad influence of his uncle, Klaus Schmidt. What is even more obvious is that Roger, like Emmett in *Chernowitz!*, is not affected by the Holocaust education the school offers. Surely Roger, in grade 12 for the second time, is also assigned a Holocaust book. Can he not read? Or is he simply demonstrating that he too has a choice, the more troubling choice of refusing the lessons such books are meant to provide? Is Roger another version of a freak, one who is not gifted with special powers, but regarded as an outsider, a freak, by his fellow classmates? Post-Columbine, do we read Roger differently?

The day that Jade prevents the bombing of the synagogue, the police arrest Roger, Schmidt, and ten others. As in *The Secret of the Mezuzah*, we are told that there may be others who were not caught. When a "catastrophe" can only be prevented through extrasensory powers, when a novel celebrates choice but demonstrates that making the right choice is difficult even if one is freakishly gifted, we can only conclude, once again, that reading about the past is of limited value because "Knowing it is different from experiencing it" (59). Holocaust pedagogy in young adult fiction remains inherently anxious, questioning its own effectiveness even as it returns incessantly to looking for the right way to tell a history that has no happy ending.

NOTES

1. On April 20, 1999, two students at Columbine High School in Littleton, Colorado, murdered one teacher and 12 classmates and then killed themselves.

2. Throughout this chapter, I refer to the novella as "Apt Pupil" and the film as *Apt Pupil*.

3. This quotation from the film appears as a Memorable Quote on the Internet Movie Data Base Website (http://www.imdb.com). All other quotations from the film are based on my viewing.

4. This chapter does not examine young adult fiction that primarily explores Holocaust denial; such works often use time travel/fantasy to take the denier back to the past. In such texts, the character often takes on a Holocaust victim's identity; e.g., Han Nolan, *If I Should Die Before I Wake*, and Bruce H. Siegel, "Jewboy." Although the protagonist in "Jewboy" shares with the protagonist of "Apt Pupil" a love of reading that initiates his antisemitic crimes, he is transformed in a positive way by what he sees during his time travel. Such time travel fantasies thus have much in common with the hope found in historical fiction. The character in the story does exactly what the reader of historical fiction is supposed to do, identify with the protagonist in order to understand her story.

5. Emphasizing the movie tie-in, on the front cover of *Different Seasons*, the title, *Apt Pupil*, appears in larger font. On the spine, the title reads, "*Different Seasons* featuring *Apt Pupil*."

6. Dussander is not surprised; he has total contempt for American teachers and boasts that anyone who has tricked Wiesenthal and Himmler can fool an American teacher. In the film, Todd is not told in advance that Dussander plans to impersonate his grandfather.

7. In the film, the girlfriend is called Becky, not Betty. There is no suggestion that her family is secretly Jewish.

8. The film credits indicate that the man's name is Archie; both times that I have watched the film, I have not heard the name used.

9. In the film, this possible sexual relationship is treated as a joke. When Todd no longer wants to hear atrocity stories, Dussander comments, "you don't seem to be in the mood." Dussander then proceeds to tell a story about a boy, "in a queer way his friend."

10. The four novellas have numerous ironic parallels; plot devices in one reappear slightly differently in another, and, on occasion, so do

characters. Dussander tells Todd he lives on stocks bought for him by a banker who "went to jail for murdering his wife" (127); he identifies the banker as Dufresne, the central character in the first novella, "Rita Hayworth and Shawshank Redemption" (127), which appears under the heading Hope Springs Eternal. While in the first novella there is a safety deposit box that lets Dufresne live happily ever after, there is no hope in the second novella, and no safety deposit box either.

11. Although the change to 1984 suggests George Orwell's *Nineteen Eighty-Four*, another possible reason for changing the time to 1984 is that 1984-85 was Singer's final year of high school.

12. Despite this visual language, the film avoids clearly showing the disturbing photographs that are described in the novella; the photographs that Todd examines in the library tend to be those depicting Nazi figures and thereby function to help him uncover Dussander's identity.

13. Most young adult fiction uses first person homodiegetic narration. Perhaps because the novel is based on a television drama, Strasser uses a heterodiegetic narrative voice, that is, a narrator who is not a character in the story.

14. A heterosexual code of honour also helps. When Laurie's boyfriend, David, is so angry at her criticism of The Wave that he throws her down, his shock at his abusive behaviour makes him realize the danger of the experiment. Their romance restored, they tell Ben Ross that the experiment must stop.

15. In J. Leonard Romm's *The Swastika on the Synagogue Door*, the Jewish protagonist, Terri Lazarus, is discouraged from writing about an antisemitic incident in the school newspaper. Ms. Feingold, the faculty advisor, reminds her that her assignment is reporting on the school prom. When Terri persists, Ms. Feingold cautions her not to make the story "too Jewish" (40). Romm implies that schools fail at Holocaust pedagogy because of their anxiety about appearing too Jewish. In contrast, the young adult novels that I discuss, where the protagonists are either not Jewish or minimally so, imply that the failure is consequent to the nature of teaching history.

16. One of the silences in Jade's narrative is the acknowledgement that for First Nations, Winnipeg has not been a safe place.

17. Bell dedicates the novel to her firstborn son, Eugene Constantine Bell. The biographical note also tells us that, while spending six years as a missionary in Austria, she studied Hebrew at the University of Vienna.

18. On the paperback cover, a dark-haired girl peers over the shoulder of a blond boy.

My Mother's Voice: June 1963

I kept a diary intermittently during my childhood. There is
no entry for the day in September 1962 when I came home
with bloody knees, the result of following the high-school
initiation orders of a grade 12 student. My mother, enraged,
said that the girl was a Nazi. I knew that this wasn't true and
can recall wishing that my mother wouldn't make such a fuss.
Yes, the girl was blonde, but she didn't know that I was
Jewish; I was probably the only Jewish student in my high
school, and I certainly was not going to advertise that fact.

I also kept a diary the following summer. Because my
entries were so sporadic prior to 1963, I cannot point to written comments demonstrating that on a certain date in my
childhood, I started to talk about Nazis. What I do know is
that in June 1963 my diary keeps referring to Nazis, but in a
way that indicates that I was far more willing to watch them
on television than listen to my mother talk about them. I was
still the child who could crow "Mom loves me again"—I still
am—but I was also an adolescent more than willing to
patronize her. In the entry for June 8, 1963, after noting that
"there was a Nazi story" on television, I wrote, "Mom was so
against [the Nazi] that I missed part of a scene when she was
talking." On June 9, I described a program about a society
where people could not laugh. When my mother found the

premise of the show unbelievable, I disagreed: "In 1945 they didn't think that another war could ever beckon. It might." On June 11, I praised President Kennedy's speech, compared segregationists to the Nazis, and wondered whether the segregationist leaders were like Hitler.

Diaries are useful reminders of the difference between the simple stories we tell ourselves about our lives and the more complex reality that we all live. They also remind us of the failure of memory and the silences in our own stories. I can no longer remember why I once wrote "Mom loves me again," but that failure of memory is minor and the words do not trouble me. In writing them here, I challenge the simple stories others tell about me. Does the stereotype of the "survivor's child" adequately convey the more nuanced reality of one who so valued her mother's approval that she carefully recorded her relief when the normal and minor tensions between parent and adolescent were resolved? Why must we conclude that the intensity of a daughter's affection for her mother was produced by her mother's history? Whatever truth resides there, I resist it. No good was produced by Auschwitz.

But one entry in the diary disturbs me because of what it does not say. It is dated June 19, 1963. As usual, watching television, I upset my mother when she told me to clean the farmhouse kitchen and I said that I would do so after my show was over. She began to cry. "I shut the T.V. and sulking cleaned the kitchen." According to my diary, my mother continued to cry intermittently for hours because she saw that "I was mad." When she was still crying after lunch, "I asked her why she was holding it in. So the words came tumbling out but after she was happy again." I have no memory of this incident, and when I tell her of it now, she says that she cannot remember. But why did I not write what she said, and how did I know that "she was happy again"? Was she really crying because of exhaustion and frustration with a teenage daughter who preferred books, television, and movies to dusting? Did I really have the power to make her happy again? I am no longer so confident that the always cheerful voice that I remember hearing is my mother's voice. What I read now is the diary's silence. I know that the adolescent who concluded her entry of June 19, 1963, by reporting the most recent gossip about Elizabeth Taylor and Richard Burton never lost her interest in the representations offered by books, television, and movies. In writing this book, I have tried to bring together that interest in representation and the sound of my mother's voice. But the words that came tumbling out that day are lost. In the end, the voice I create is my own.

Works Cited

Abella, Irving and Harold Troper. *None is Too Many*. Toronto: Lester and Orpen Dennys, 1982.

Abells, Chana Byers. *The Children We Remember*. Photographs from the Archives of Yad Vashem, The Holocaust Martyrs' and Heroes' Remembrance Authority, Jerusalem, Israel. Kar-Ben Copies, Inc. 1983. New York: Greenwillow Books, 1986.

Adelson, Alan, ed. *The Diary of Dawid Sierakowiak: Five Notebooks from the Łódź Ghetto*. Trans. Kamil Turowski. 1996. New York: Oxford University Press, 1998.

Adelson, Alan, and Robert Lapides, eds. *Lodz Ghetto: Inside a Community Under Siege*. Afterword Geoffrey Hartman. Annotations and bibliographical notes Marek Web. Jewish Heritage Writing Project. New York: Viking, 1989.

Adler, David. A. *Child of the Warsaw Ghetto*. Illus. Karen Ritz. New York: Holiday House, 1995.

—. *Hiding from the Nazis*. Illus. Karen Ritz. New York: Holiday House, 1997.

—. *Hilde and Eli: Children of the Holocaust*. Illus. Karen Ritz. New York: Holiday House, 1994.

—. *The Number on My Grandfather's Arm*. Illus. Rose Eichenbaum. New York: UAHC Press, 1987.

—. *A Picture Book of Anne Frank*. Illus. Karen Ritz. Picture Book Biography Series. New York: Holiday House, 1993.

—. *We Remember the Holocaust*. New York: Henry Holt, 1989.

Appelfeld, Aharon. "After the Holocaust." Lang, *Writing and the Holocaust* 83-92.

Apt Pupil. Dir. Bryan Singer. Tristar Pictures/Phoenix Pictures, 1998.

—. Internet Movie Data Base Website. <http://www.imdb.com>.

Aristotle. *On Poetry and Style*. Trans. G.M.A. Grube. The Library of Liberal Arts. Indianapolis: The Liberal Arts Press, 1958.

Arnow, David. "Victors, Not Victims." *Reform Judaism* 27.3 (1999): 20-27.

Arrick, Fran. *Chernowitz!* 1981. New York: Signet-Penguin, 1983.

Auerbach, Nina. "Plaster Saint." Rev. of *Anne Frank, the Biography*, by Melissa Müller. *Women's Review of Books* 16.8 (May 1999): 8.

Baer, Elizabeth R. "A New Algorithm in Evil: Children's Literature in a Post-Holocaust World." *The Lion and the Unicorn* 24.3 (2000): 378-401.

Bauer, Yehuda. *Rethinking the Holocaust.* New Haven: Yale University Press, 2001.

Baumel, Judith Tydor. *Double Jeopardy: Gender and the Holocaust.* London: Vallentine Mitchell, 1998.

Bell, Mary Reeves. *The Secret of the Mezuzah.* 1995. Rev. ed. Minneapolis: Bethany House Publishers, 1999.

Bernstein, Michael André. *Foregone Conclusions: Against Apocalyptic History.* Berkeley: University of California Press, 1994.

Bettelheim, Bruno. "The Ignored Lesson of Anne Frank." *Surviving and Other Essays.* New York: Alfred A. Knopf, 1979. 246-57.

Bialystok, Franklin. *Delayed Impact: The Holocaust and the Canadian Jewish Community.* Montreal: McGill-Queen's University Press, 2000.

Bitton-Jackson, Livia. *Elli: Coming of Age in the Holocaust.* Toronto: Fitzhenry and Whiteside, 1980.

—. *I Have Lived a Thousand Years: Growing Up in the Holocaust.* 1997. New York: Aladdin-Simon and Schuster, 1999.

Bloom, Harold, ed. *A Scholarly Look at "The Diary of Anne Frank."* Modern Critical Interpretations. Philadelphia: Chelsea House Publishers, 1999.

Bosmajian, Hamida. "Memory and Desire in the Landscapes of Sendak's *Dear Mili.*" *The Lion and the Unicorn* 19.2 (1995): 186-210.

Brenner, Rachel Feldhay. *Writing as Resistance: Four Women Confronting the Holocaust: Edith Stein, Simone Weil, Anne Frank, Etty Hillesum.* University Park, PA: Pennsylvania State University Press, 1997.

Brewster, Eva. *Vanished in Darkness: An Auschwitz Memoir.* Edmonton: NeWest Press, 1984.

Bunting, Eve. *Terrible Things: An Allegory of the Holocaust.* Illus. Stephen Gammell. Harper and Row, 1980. Philadelphia: Jewish Publication Society, 1993.

Caruth, Cathy, ed. *Trauma: Explorations in Memory.* Baltimore: Johns Hopkins University Press, 1995.

—. *Unclaimed Experience: Trauma, Narrative, and History.* Baltimore: Johns Hopkins University Press, 1996.

Chapman, Fern Schumer. *Motherland: Beyond the Holocaust: A Daughter's Journey to Reclaim the Past.* New York: Viking, 2000.

Cicioni, Mirna. *Primo Levi: Bridges of Knowledge.* New Directions in European Writing. Oxford: Berg, 1995.

Daniel's Story Videotape Teacher Guide. Washington, DC: United States Holocaust Memorial Museum, November 1993.

Defonseca, Misha. *Misha: A Mémoire of the Holocaust Years.* Boston: Mount Ivy Press, 1997.

Delbo, Charlotte. *Auschwitz and After.* Trans. Rosette C. Lamont. New Haven: Yale University Press, 1995. Trans. of *Auschwitz et après.*

—. "Days and Memory." Rittner and Roth 328-31.

Denby, David. "In the Eye of the Beholder: Another Look at Roberto Benigni's Holocaust Fantasy." *New Yorker* 15 March 1999: 96-99.

Des Pres, Terrence. *The Survivor: An Anatomy of Life in the Death Camps.* 1976. New York: Quokka, 1978.

Doyle, Brian. *Uncle Ronald.* Vancouver: Groundwood Books-Douglas and McIntyre, 1996.

Dwork, Debórah. *Children With a Star: Jewish Youth in Nazi Europe.* New Haven: Yale University Press, 1991.

Eliach, Yaffa, ed. *We Were Children Just Like You.* Brooklyn, NY: Center for Holocaust Studies Documentation and Research, 1990.

Epstein, Eric Joseph, and Philip Rosen. *Dictionary of the Holocaust: Biography, Geography, and Terminology.* Westport, CT: Greenwood Press, 1997.

Epstein, Helen. *Children of the Holocaust: Conversations with Sons and Daughters of Survivors.* New York: G.P. Putnam's Sons, 1979.

Feder, Paula Kurzband. *The Feather-Bed Journey.* Illus. Stacey Schuett. Morton Grove, IL: Albert Whitman, 1995.

Felman, Shoshana. "Education and Crisis, or the Vicissitudes of Teaching." Caruth, *Trauma* 13-60.

—. "The Return of the Voice: Claude Lanzmann's *Shoah.*" Felman and Laub 204-83.

Felman, Shoshana, and Dori Laub, eds. *Testimony: Crises of Witnessing in Literature, Psychoanalysis, and History.* New York: Routledge, 1992.

Filipović, Zlata. *Zlata's Diary: A Child's Life in Sarajevo.* Intro. Janine Di Giovanni. Trans. Christina Pribichevich-Zorić. 1994. New York: Penguin, 1995. Trans. of *Le Journal de Zlata.* Fixot et editions Robert Laffont, 1993.

Fine, Ellen S. "The Absent Memory: The Act of Writing in Post-Holocaust French Literature." Lang *Writing and the Holocaust* 41-57.

Fink, Ida. "*****." *A Scrap of Time and Other Stories* 23-24.

—. "Aryan Papers." *A Scrap of Time and Other Stories* 63-68.

—. "Crazy." *A Scrap of Time and Other Stories* 107-09.

—. "Description of a Morning." *Traces* 81-96.

—. "Henryk's Sister." *Traces* 133-41.

—. *The Journey.* Trans. Joanna Weschler and Francine Prose. New York: Farrar, Straus and Giroux, 1992. Trans. of *Podróz,* 1990.

—. "Julia." *Traces* 183-203.

—. "Night of Surrender." *A Scrap of Time and Other Stories* 93-102.

—. "Sabina Under the Sacks." *Traces* 97-108.

—. *A Scrap of Time and Other Stories.* Trans. Madeline Levine and Francine Prose. New York: Pantheon Books, 1987.

—. "A Second Scrap of Time." *Traces* 53-57.

—. "A Spring Morning." *A Scrap of Time and Other Stories* 39-47.

—. "Traces." *A Scrap of Time and Other Stories* 135-37.

—. *Traces: Stories.* Trans. Philip Boehm and Francine Prose. New York: Henry Holt, 1997.

Flanzbaum, Hilene, ed. *The Americanization of the Holocaust.* Baltimore: Johns Hopkins University Press, 1999.

Frank, Anne. *The Diary of a Young Girl.* Trans. B.M. Mooyaart. Intro. Eleanor Roosevelt. Doubleday, 1952. New York: Bantam, 1993. Trans. of *Het Achterhuis.* Contact, Amsterdam, 1947.

—. *The Diary of a Young Girl: The Definitive Edition.* Ed. Otto H. Frank and Mirjam Pressler. Trans. Susan Massotty. Doubleday, 1995. New York: Bantam, 1997.

Friedländer, Saul. *When Memory Comes*. Trans. Helen R. Lane. New York: Farrar, Straus and Giroux, 1979. Trans. *Quand vient le souvenir...* 1978.

Gable. Cartoon. *The Globe and Mail* 26 April 2000: A14.

Gann, Marjorie. "Holocaust Fact/Holocaust Fiction." Rev. of *Gabi's Dresser*, by Kathy Kacer, *Greater Than Angels*, by Carol Matas, and *Good-bye Marianne*, by Irene N. Watts. *Children of the Shoah: Holocaust Literature and Education*. Special issue of *Canadian Children's Literature* #95, 25:3 (Fall 1999): 167-73.

Gelissen, Rena Kornreich with Heather Dune Macadam. *Rena's Promise: A Story of Sisters in Auschwitz*. Boston: Beacon Press, 1995.

Ginsburg, Mirra. *Three Rolls and One Doughnut: Fables from Russia Retold by Mirra Ginsburg*. Illus. Anita Lobel. New York: Dial Press, 1970.

Goldenberg, Myrna. "Memoirs of Auschwitz Survivors: The Burden of Gender." Ofer and Weitzman 327-39.

Goodrich, Frances and Albert Hackett. *The Diary of Anne Frank: A Play in Two Acts*. Foreword by Brooks Atkinson. Notes and Questions by N.D. MacDonald and J.I. Downie. 1956. Toronto: Irwin Publishing, 1964.

Gourevitch, Philip. "Behold Now Behemoth: The Holocaust Memorial Museum: One more American theme park." *Harper's Magazine* 287:1718 (July 1993): 55-62.

—. "The Memory Thief." *New Yorker* 14 June 1999: 48+.

—. *We Wish to Inform You That Tomorrow We Will be Killed with Our Families: Stories from Rwanda*. New York: Farrar, Straus and Giroux, 1998.

—. "What They Saw at the Holocaust Museum." *New York Times Magazine* 12 February 1995: 44-45.

Greenspan, Henry. "Imagining Survivors: Testimony and the Rise of Holocaust Consciousness." Flanzbaum 45-67.

Grossman, Mendel. *With a Camera in the Ghetto*. Ed. Zvi Szner and Alexander Sened. With text from *The Chronicle of the Lodz Ghetto*. Ed. Lucjan Dobroszycki and Danuta Dombrowska. Trans. Mendel Kohansky. New York: Schocken Books, 1977. Trans. of *Tsalam hilekh ba-geto*. Ghetto Fighters' House and Hakibbutz Hameuchad Publishing House, 1970, 1972.

Hartman, Geoffrey H. *The Longest Shadow: In the Aftermath of the Holocaust*. The Helen and Martin Schwartz Lectures in Jewish Studies. Bloomington: Indiana University Press, 1996.

Hellman, Peter. *The Auschwitz Album: A Book Based Upon an Album Discovered by a Concentration Camp Survivor, Lili Meier*. New York: Random House, 1981.

Hilberg, Raul. *The Destruction of the European Jews*. New York: Harper and Row, 1961.

—. *Perpetrators Victims Bystanders: The Jewish Catastrophe 1933-1945*. 1992. New York: HarperPerennial, 1993.

Hirsch, Marianne. *Family Frames: Photography, Narrative and Postmemory*. Cambridge: Harvard University Press, 1997.

Holm, Anne. *I am David*. Trans. L.W. Kingsland. 1965. Harmondsworth: Puffin, 1969. Trans. *David*. 1963.

Honey, Kim. "The making of a cause célèbre." *Globe and Mail* 25 January 2001: R1+.

Hopkins, Lee Bennett. "Anita and Arnold Lobel." *Books are by People: Interviews with 104 Authors and Illustrators of Books for Young Children*. New York: Citation Press, 1969. 156-59.

Horowitz, Sara R. *Voicing the Void: Muteness and Memory in Holocaust Fiction*. SUNY Series in Modern Jewish Literature and Culture. Albany: State University of New York Press, 1997.

Innocenti, Roberto. *Rose Blanche*. Text by Christophe Gallaz and Roberto Innocenti. Creative Editions 1985. San Diego: Harcourt Brace, 1996.

Into the Arms of Strangers: Stories of the Kindertransport. Dir. Mark Jonathan Harris. Sabine Films/Warner Brothers, 2000.

Karpf, Anne. *The War After: Living with the Holocaust*. London: William Heinemann, 1996. London: Minerva, 1997.

King, Stephen. "Afterword." *Different Seasons* 501-08.

—. "Apt Pupil." *Different Seasons* 111-290.

—. "The Body." *Different Seasons* 293-436.

—. *Different Seasons*. 1982. New York: Signet-Penguin, 1998.

Kopf, Hedda Rosner. *Understanding Anne Frank's The Diary of a Young Girl: A Student Casebook to Issues, Sources, and Historical Documents*. Literature in Context Series. Westport, CT: Greenwood Press, 1997.

LaCapra, Dominick. *Representing the Holocaust: History, Theory, Trauma*. Ithaca: Cornell University Press, 1994.

Laird, Christa. *Beyond the Wall*. 1989. London: Red Fox-Random House, 1999. *But Can the Phoenix Sing?* Julia MacRae, 1993.

Lang, Berel. *Act and Idea in the Nazi Genocide*. Chicago: University of Chicago Press, 1990.

—, ed. *Writing and the Holocaust*. New York: Holmes and Meier, 1988.

Langer, Lawrence L., ed. *Art from the Ashes: A Holocaust Anthology*. New York: Oxford University Press, 1995.

—. "Fiction." Langer, *Art from the Ashes* 235-39.

—. "Foreword." Adelson, *The Diary of Dawid Sierakowiak* vii-x.

—. "Gendered Suffering: *Women in Holocaust Testimonies*." *Preempting the Holocaust*. 43-58.

—. *Holocaust Testimonies: The Ruins of Memory*. New Haven: Yale University Press, 1991.

—. "On Writing and Reading Holocaust Literature." Langer, *Art from the Ashes* 3-9.

—. "Opening Locked Doors: Reflections on Teaching the Holocaust." *Preempting the Holocaust*. 187-98.

—. *Preempting the Holocaust*. New Haven: Yale University Press, 1998.

—. *Versions of Survival: The Holocaust and the Human Spirit*. Albany: State University of New York Press, 1982.

Lanzmann, Claude. "The Obscenity of Understanding: An Evening with Claude Lanzmann." Caruth, *Trauma* 200-20.

—. *Shoah: An Oral History of the Holocaust: The Complete Text of the Acclaimed Film by Claude Lanzmann*. Rev. ed. New York: Da Capo, 1995.

Lappin, Elena. "The Man with Two Heads." *Granta* 66 (Summer 1999): 7-65.

Laub, Dori. "Bearing Witness, or the Vicissitudes of Listening." Felman and Laub 75-92.

—. "Truth and Testimony: The Process and the Struggle." Caruth, *Trauma* 61-75.

Leitner, Isabella. *Fragments of Isabella: A Memoir of Auschwitz*. Ed. and epilogue by Irving A. Leitner. New York: Thomas Y. Crowell, 1978.

—. "Lager Language," *Fragments of Isabella: A Memoir of Auschwitz*. Ed. and epilogue by Irving A. Leitner. New York: Laurel-Dell, 1983. 122-28.

Leitner, Isabella, with Irving A. Leitner. *The Big Lie: A True Story*. Illus. Judy Pedersen. New York: Scholastic, 1992.

—. *Isabella: From Auschwitz to Freedom*. New York: Anchor Books-Doubleday, 1994.

—. *Saving the Fragments: From Auschwitz to New York*. Intro. Howard Fast. New York: New American Library, 1985.

Levi, Primo. *Survival in Auschwitz: The Nazi Assault on Humanity*. Trans. Stuart Woolf. 1958. New York: Collier-Macmillan, 1961. Trans. *Se questo è un uomo*. 1958.

Life Is Beautiful (La Vita è Bella). Dir. Roberto Benigni. Alliance, Miramax. 1997.

Lindwer, Willy. *The Last Seven Months of Anne Frank*. Trans. Alison Meersschaert. New York: Anchor-Doubleday, 1991. Trans. *De Laatste Zeven Maanden: Vrouwen in Het Spoor Van Anne Frank*. 1988.

Linenthal, Edward T., *Preserving Memory: The Struggle to Create America's Holocaust Museum*. 1995. New York: Penguin, 1997.

Lipstadt, Deborah. *Denying the Holocaust: The Growing Assault on Truth and Memory*. 1993. New York: Plume-Penguin, 1994.

Liss, Andrea. *Trespassing Through Shadows: Memory, Photography and the Holocaust*. Visible Evidence. Minneapolis: University of Minnesota Press, 1998.

Lobel, Anita. *Alison's Zinnia*. New York: Greenwillow, 1990.

—. *Away from Home*. New York: Greenwillow, 1994.

—. Letter to the author. 21 March 2001.

—. *No Pretty Pictures: A Child of War*. New York: Greenwillow, 1998.

—. *Potatoes, Potatoes*. New York: Harper and Row, 1967.

—. *Sven's Bridge*. New York: Harper and Row, 1965.

—. *Sven's Bridge*. Rev. New York: Greenwillow, 1992.

Maechler, Stefan. *The Wilkomirski Affair: A Study in Biographical Truth*. Trans. John E. Woods. New York: Schocken Books-Random House, 2001. Trans. *Der Fall Wilkomirski*. Pendo Verlag AG, Zurich, 2000.

Marks, Jane. *The Hidden Children: The Secret Survivors of the Holocaust*. 1993. New York: Ballantine, 1995.

Marrus, Michael R. "'Getting It Right': Some Thoughts on the Role of the Holocaust Historian." *The Holocaust: Memories, Research, Reference.* Ed. Robert Hauptman and Susan Hubbs Motin. Binghamton, NY: Haworth Press, 1998. 147-56.

—. "Good History and Teaching the Holocaust." *Lessons and Legacies II: Teaching the Holocaust in a Changing World.* Ed. Donald G. Schilling. Evanston, IL: Northwestern University Press, 1998. 13-25.

Matas, Carol. *After the War.* Toronto: Scholastic, 1996.

—. *The Burning Time.* 1994. Toronto: HarperCollins, 1996.

—. *Cloning Miranda.* Toronto: Scholastic, 1999.

—. *Daniel's Story.* New York: Scholastic, 1993.

—. E-mail to the author. 19 December 1998.

—. *The Freak.* Toronto: Key Porter, 1997.

—. *The Garden.* Illus. Janet Wilson. Toronto: Scholastic, 1997.

—. *Greater Than Angels.* Toronto: Scholastic, 1998.

—. *In My Enemy's House.* Toronto: Scholastic, 1999.

—. *Jesper.* Lester and Orpen Dennys. Toronto: Scholastic Canada, 1989.

—. *Lisa.* Lester and Orpen Dennys. Toronto: Scholastic Canada, 1987.

—. *Me, Myself, and I.* Time Tracks #3. 1987. Toronto: General, 1991.

—. *The Primrose Path.* Winnipeg: Bain and Cox-Blizzard, 1995.

—. *The Race.* 1991. Toronto: HarperCollins, 1993.

—. *Sworn Enemies.* Toronto: HarperCollins, 1993.

—. *Telling.* Toronto: Key Porter, 1998.

—. *Zanu.* Time Tracks #2. 1986. Toronto: General, 1991.

McDonough, Yona Zeldis. *Anne Frank.* Illus. Malcah Zeldis. New York: Henry Holt, 1997.

McHenry, Eric. Letter. *New Yorker* 29 March 1999: 10.

"Memories … Etched in the Faces of the Past." Flyer. Calgary Jewish Centre Yom Hashoah Holocaust Remembrance Day. Tuesday, 2 May 2000.

Michaels, Anne. *Fugitive Pieces.* Toronto: McClelland and Stewart, 1996.

Miller, Judith. *One, by One, by One: Facing the Holocaust.* 1990. New York: Touchstone-Simon and Schuster, 1991.

Milton, Sybil. "Images of the Holocaust—Part II." *Holocaust and Genocide Studies* 1.2 (1986): 193-216.

Moeller, Susan D. *Compassion Fatigue: How the Media Sell Disease, Famine, War and Death.* New York: Routledge, 1999.

Moger, Susan. *Teaching the Diary of Anne Frank: An In-Depth Resource for Learning about the Holocaust Through the Writings of Anne Frank.* New York: Scholastic Professional Books, 1998.

Napoli, Donna Jo. *Stones in Water.* 1997. New York: Penguin Putnam, 1999.

Nerlove, Miriam. *Flowers on the Wall.* New York: Margaret K. McElderry Books-Simon and Schuster, 1996.

Nikolajeva, Maria. "Sven's Bridge." E-mail to the author. 11 August 1999.

Nir, Yehuda. *The Lost Childhood: A Memoir.* New York: Harcourt, Brace, Jovanovich, 1989.

Nolan, Han. *If I Should Die Before I Wake.* 1994. San Diego: Harcourt Brace, 1996.

Novick, Peter. *The Holocaust in American Life*. Boston: Houghton Mifflin, 1999.

Ofer, Dalia, and Lenore J. Weitzman. eds. *Women in the Holocaust*. New Haven: Yale University Press, 1998.

Orlev, Uri. *The Island on Bird Street*. Trans. Hillel Halkin. Boston: Houghton Mifflin, 1984.

Ozick, Cynthia. "The Rights of History and the Rights of Imagination." *Commentary* 107.3 (March 1999): 22-27.

—. *The Shawl*. 1980. New York: Vintage International-Random House, 1990.

—. "Who Owns Anne Frank?" *New Yorker* 6 October 1997: 76-87.

Paley, Grace. "Faith in a Tree." *Enormous Changes at the Last Minute*. New York: Noonday Press-Farrar, Straus and Giroux, 1974. 75-100.

Paterson, Katherine. "Hope and Happy Endings." *The Spying Heart: More Thoughts on Reading and Writing Books for Children*. New York: E.P. Dutton, 1989. 172-91.

Pausewang, Gudrun. *The Final Journey*. Trans. Patricia Compton. New York: Viking, 1996.

Raphael, Linda Schermer, and Marc Lee Raphael, eds. *When Night Fell: An Anthology of Holocaust Short Stories*. New Brunswick: Rutgers University Press, 1999.

Reichel, Sabine. *What Did You Do in the War, Daddy? Growing Up German*. New York: Hill and Wang, 1989.

Rev. of *Fragments: Memories of a Wartime Childhood* by Binjamin Wilkomirski. <http://amazon.com>. April 22, 1998; April 24, 1998; March 29, 1999.

Rev. of *Saving the Fragments* by Isabella Leitner. *Kirkus Reviews* 53.14 (15 July 1985): 702.

Richter, Hans Peter. *Friedrich*. Trans. Edite Kroll. New York: Holt, Rinehart and Winston, 1970.

Ringelheim, Joan. "The Split between Gender and the Holocaust." Ofer and Weitzman 340-50.

—. "Women and the Holocaust: A Reconsideration of Research." Rittner and Roth 373-418.

Rittner, Carol, and John K. Roth, eds. *Different Voices: Women and the Holocaust*. New York: Paragon House, 1993.

Rochman, Hazel. Rev. of *The Big Lie* by Isabella Leitner. *Booklist* 89.11 (1 February 1993): 982.

—. "Should You Teach *Anne Frank: The Diary of a Young Girl?*" *Book Links* 7.5 (May 1998): 45-49.

Rochman, Hazel, and Darlene Z. McCampbell, eds. *Bearing Witness: Stories of the Holocaust*. 1995. New York: Orchard Books-Grolier, 1999.

Romm, J. Leonard. *The Swastika on the Synagogue Door*. Illus. Spark. 1984. Los Angeles: Alef Design Group, 1994.

Roseman, Kenneth. *Escape from the Holocaust*. Do-It-Yourself Jewish Adventure Series. New York: Union of American Hebrew Congregations, 1985.

Rosenberg, Maxine B. *Hiding to Survive: Stories of Jewish Children Rescued from the Holocaust*. New York: Clarion, 1994.

Rosenfeld, Alvin H. "Popularization and Memory: The Case of Anne Frank." *Lessons and Legacies: The Meaning of the Holocaust in a Changing World.* Ed Peter Hayes. Evanston, IL: Northwestern University Press, 1991. 243-78.

Roskies, David G. *Against the Apocalypse: Responses to Catastrophe in Modern Jewish Culture.* Cambridge: Harvard University Press, 1984.

Roth, Philip. *The Ghost Writer.* 1979. New York: Fawcett Crest, 1980.

Rothberg, Michael. *Traumatic Realism: The Demands of Holocaust Representation.* Minneapolis: University of Minnesota Press, 2000.

Russell, David L. "Reading the Shards and Fragments: Holocaust Literature for Young Readers." *The Lion and the Unicorn* 21.2 (1997): 267-80.

Sallot, Jeff. "CanLit lions defend boy writer." *Globe and Mail* 29 January 2001: A1+.

Schoenberner, Gerhard. *The Holocaust: The Nazi Destruction of Europe's Jews.* Trans. Susan Sweet. Intro. Allan Gould. *Der Gelbe Stern* 1960. Edmonton: Hurtig Publishers, 1985.

Shandler, Jefffrey. *While America Watches: Televising the Holocaust.* New York: Oxford University Press, 1999.

Shavit, Zohar. "The Untold Story: What German Writers Tell Their Children about the Third Reich and the Holocaust." *Children of the Shoah: Holocaust Literature and Education.* Special issue of *Canadian Children's Literature* #95, 25:3 (Fall 1999): 90-119.

Shawcross, Nancy M. *Roland Barthes on Photography: The Critical Tradition in Perspective.* Crosscurrents: Comparative Studies in European Literature and Philosophy. Gainesville: University Press of Florida, 1997.

Shawn, Karen. *The End of Innocence: Anne Frank and the Holocaust.* International Center for Holocaust Studies. New York: Anti-Defamation League of B'nai Brith, 1989.

Sherman, Jason. *Reading Hebron.* Toronto: Playwrights Canada, 1997.

Sherman, Ursula F. "Why Would a Child Want to Read about That? The Holocaust Period in Children's Literature." *How Much Truth Do We Tell the Children? The Politics of Children's Literature.* Ed. Betty Bacon. Marxist Dimensions. Minneapolis, MN: Marxist Educational Press, 1988. 173-84.

Siegal, Aranka. *Grace in the Wilderness: After the Liberation 1945-1948.* 1985. New York: Puffin, 1994.

—. *Upon the Head of the Goat: A Childhood in Hungary 1939-1944.* 1981. New York: Puffin, 1994.

Siegel, Bruce H. *Champion and Jewboy: Two Novellas.* Illus. Spark. Los Angeles: Aleph Design Group, 1996.

Sims, C. "USHMM Worksheet 39010." E-mail to the author. 17 August 2000.

Smith, Frank Dabba. *My Secret Camera: Life in the Lodz Ghetto.* Photographs by Mendel Grossman. Pre-publication copy. San Diego: Gulliver Books-Harcourt, 2000.

Sokoloff, Naomi. "Childhood Lost: Children's Voices in Holocaust Literature." *Infant Tongues: The Voice of the Child in Literature.* Ed. Elizabeth Goodenough, Mark A. Heberle, and Naomi Sokoloff. Detroit: Wayne State University Press, 1994. 259-74.

Sokoloff, Naomi B. *Imagining the Child in Modern Jewish Fiction.* Johns Hopkins Jewish Studies. Baltimore, MD: Johns Hopkins University Press, 1992.

Sontag, Susan. *On Photography.* New York: Farrar, Straus and Giroux, 1977.

Spencer, Pam. Rev. of *Saving the Fragments* by Isabella Leitner. *School Library Journal* (August 1986): 114.

Spiegelman, Art. *Maus: A Survivor's Tale, I: My Father Bleeds History.* New York: Pantheon, 1986.

—. *Maus: A Survivor's Tale, II: And Here My Troubles Began.* New York: Pantheon, 1991.

Stein, André. *Hidden Children: Forgotten Survivors of the Holocaust.* Toronto: Viking Penguin, 1993.

Stephens, Elaine C., Jean E. Brown, and Janet E. Rubin. *Learning About the Holocaust: Literature and Other Resources for Young People.* North Haven CT: Library Professional Publications-Shoe String Press, 1995.

Stephens, John. *Language and Ideology in Children's Fiction.* Language in Social Life Series. London: Longman, 1992.

Strasser, Todd. *The Wave.* New York: Bantam Doubleday Dell, 1981.

Stratford Festival of Canada Visitors' Guide 2000.

Sullivan, Edward T. *The Holocaust in Literature for Youth: A Guide and Resource Book.* Lanham, MD: Scarecrow Press, 1999.

Tal, Kalí. *Worlds of Hurt: Reading the Literatures of Trauma.* Cambridge Studies in American Literature and Culture. Cambridge: Cambridge University Press, 1996.

Teacher Guide: Remember the Children, Daniel's Story. United States Holocaust Memorial Museum, Division of Education, 1999.

Tec, Nechama. *Dry Tears: The Story of a Lost Childhood.* Wildcat Publishing, 1982. New York: Oxford University Press, 1984.

Telushkin, Rabbi Joseph. *Jewish Literacy: The Most Important Things to Know About the Jewish Religion, Its People, and Its History.* New York: William Morrow, 1991.

Todorov, Tzvetan. *Facing the Extreme: Moral Life in the Concentration Camps.* Trans. Arthur Denner and Abigail Pollak. New York: Henry Holt, 1996. Trans. *Face à l'extrême.* 1991.

Trites, Roberta. *Waking Sleeping Beauty: Feminist Voices in Children's Novels.* Iowa City: University of Iowa Press, 1997.

Van der Kolk, Bessel, and Onno van der Hart, "The Intrusive Past: The Flexibility of Memory and the Engraving of Trauma." Caruth, *Trauma* 158-82.

Van der Rol, Ruud, and Rian Verhoeven. *Anne Frank Beyond the Diary: A Photographic Remembrance.* Intro. Anna Quindlen. Trans. Tony Langham and Plym Peters. New York: Viking Penguin, 1993.

Viano, Maurizio. "*Life Is Beautiful*: Reception, Allegory, and Holocaust Laughter." *Jewish Social Studies* 5.3 (1999): 47-66.

Vice, Sue. *Holocaust Fiction*. London: Routledge, 2000.

Vishniac, Roman. *A Vanished World*. Foreword by Elie Wiesel. New York: Farrar, Straus and Giroux, 1983.

Voigt, Cynthia. *David and Jonathan*. New York: Scholastic, 1992.

Vos, Ida. *Anna is Still Here*. Trans. Terese Edelstein and Inez Smidt. Boston: Houghton Mifflin, 1993. Trans. *Anna is er nog*. 1986.

—. *Hide and Seek*. Trans. Terese Edelstein and Inez Smidt. Boston: Houghton Mifflin, 1991. Trans. *Wie nieht weg is wordt gezien*. 1981.

"Were You Forced To Work For the Nazis?" *Jewish Free Press* 8 March 2001: 5.

Wiesel, Elie. Interview. *Art out of Agony: The Holocaust Theme in Literature, Sculpture and Film*. With Stephen Lewis. Toronto: CBC Enterprises, 1984. 151-69.

—. *Night*. Trans. Stella Rodway. MacGibbon and Kee, 1960. New York: Discus-Avon, 1969. Trans. *La Nuit*. 1958.

—. "A Plea for the Dead." Langer, *Art from the Ashes* 138-52.

Wild, Margaret. *Let the Celebrations Begin!* Illus. Julie Vivas. 1991. Sydney: Omnibus Books, 1992.

Wilkomirski, Binjamin. *Fragments: Memories of a Wartime Childhood*. Trans. Carol Brown Janeway. New York: Schocken, 1996. Trans. *Bruchstücke*. Judischer Verlag im Suhrkamp Verlag, 1995.

Yolen, Jane. *Briar Rose*. The Fairy Tale Series. New York: Tom Doherty, 1992.

—. *The Devil's Arithmetic*. New York: Viking Kestrel, 1988.

—. Website. <http://www.janeyolen.com>.

Young, James E. "Holocaust Documentary Fiction: The Novelist as Eyewitness." Lang, *Writing and the Holocaust* 200-15.

—. *Writing and Rewriting the Holocaust: Narrative and the Consequences of Interpretation*. Bloomington: Indiana University Press, 1988.

Zelizer, Barbie. *Remembering to Forget: Holocaust Memory Through the Camera's Eye*. Chicago: University of Chicago Press, 1998.

Zuccotti, Susan. *The Italians and the Holocaust: Persecution, Rescue, and Survival*. Lincoln: University of Nebraska Press, 1987.

Index